Chasing the Blues

Chasing the Blues

A TRAVELER'S GUIDE
TO AMERICA'S MUSIC

JOSEPHINE MATYAS
AND CRAIG JONES

Backbeat
Books

Guilford, Connecticut

Backbeat
Books

An imprint of Globe Pequot, the trade division of
The Rowman & Littlefield Publishing Group, Inc.
4501 Forbes Blvd., Ste. 200
Lanham, MD 20706
www.rowman.com

Distributed by NATIONAL BOOK NETWORK

British Library Cataloguing in Publication Information available

Library of Congress Cataloging-in-Publication Data available

ISBN 978-1-4930-6060-3 (paperback)
ISBN 978-1-4930-6061-0 (e-book)

∞™ The paper used in this publication meets the minimum requirements of
American National Standard for Information Sciences—Permanence of Paper
for Printed Library Materials, ANSI/NISO Z39.48-1992.

We humbly and respectfully dedicate this book to the millions of enslaved Africans who were captured and transported to the New World against their will and whose suffering and spirit for survival gave birth to the music we have come to know and love as the blues.

We cannot begin to comprehend the lived experience of the originators of this marvelous artistic and cultural form. The best we can do is absorb it, celebrate it, and encourage others to learn from it. That's the purpose of this book.

This book is also lovingly dedicated to Athena, who—every day—shows us everything that is good about this world.

Finally, we dedicate this book to the people of the Delta who treated us with the utmost respect and kindness. We look forward to our return.

CONTENTS

PREFACE: HOW TO USE THIS BOOK

We want you to visit the Mississippi Delta, soon, and to take this book with you. That is our primary purpose in writing it, to inspire you to visit the birthplace of the Delta blues. There is no place like it in the world, and the more you learn about it, the more this will reveal itself to you.

And we want you to visit soon because history is slowly but inexorably leaving the Delta behind, as it does to all creation. The men—mostly men—who defined the original Delta blues styles have long ago left the stage, but the second and third generations of those innovators are still playing, still singing, and still carrying the torch of this magisterial music and cultural form. So the sooner you get there, the better your chance of experiencing what remains of it.

This book is not an authoritative history of or a guidebook to the Delta blues. But it does cover an exhaustive number of stops and experiences that will help you understand and appreciate the blues. That authoritative book may never be written because the very definition of the Delta blues is fluid, contested, and contingent. That said, this book will—if nothing else—inspire you to ask the kinds of questions we didn't think of. And that will make our whole exercise worthwhile.

Our bottom-line claim is that you can much better understand the nature of twentieth-century popular music if you try to understand the blues and the Delta blues in particular. This book will help you do that.

GETTING THE MOST OUT OF *CHASING THE BLUES*

We want you to "dip in" and "dip out" of this book—not necessarily to read it as you would a narrative novel. Write in the margins, make notes, and use highlighter pens. It's designed to be read in snapshots as you explore this part of the world (or perhaps from an armchair at home). Each section can stand alone, and—for those who crave details about history and politics—chapter 2 is a deeper dive into those topics. Our overall goal is that by understanding more of what you see and hear, you will come away with a richer appreciation and a more satisfying enjoyment of the experience.

In addition to the in-depth look at history and politics, chapters are divided into geographic regions. There are also chapters on the founding fathers of the blues, the instruments most closely associated with the blues, and how a handful of British bands and musicians were said to have saved the blues by sending it back to America.

Some of what's here you will already know if you know anything about the blues at all. But if you take this book and follow our recommendations and travel the Delta roadways, enjoy barbecue or fried chicken along the way, visit the places we write about, and follow up with the suggested readings and YouTube viewings, the book will have achieved our purpose. You'll be happy, and we'll be satisfied.

The Delta is a place of constant change, which means that some of the places we want you to visit may not exist when you roll up in front of them. But there may be new establishments in their place, and, in any event, there will always be live blues and great barbecue across Mississippi.

A WORD ABOUT US

We are not blues scholars, but we are lovers of the blues who have traveled widely in the Delta—and across much of North America—and returned home with the conviction that the Delta is a unique and extraordinary place, the story of which deserves to be told more widely. One of us is an award-winning travel writer specializing in the United States, Europe, Canada, and the Caribbean. The other is a PhD political economist, writer, and lifer professional musician. Both of us came to be deeply interested in the Delta, and the more time we spent there—and the more we learned about it—the more enthralled we came to be. The Delta does that to you.

And it will do it to you too. Do yourself a lifetime favor. Take this book with you and travel the Mississippi Delta. (visitmississippi.org)

ACKNOWLEDGMENTS

We happily thank the wonderful people of the Delta whose time and good nature we abused in hours of interviews—people like Roger Stolle, Webster Franklin, Robert Terrell, Bill Lester, Bubba O'Keefe, Mike Bostic, Sylvester Hoover, Dr. Jim Brewer, Tommy Couch Jr., Hartley Peavey, Ronnie Eldridge, Greg Johnson, David Hood, and the numerous curators of museums and cultural centers and university staff and docents who gave of their time and insight to further our research. We also sat down with talented musicians of the blues wherever we could find them to learn from their direct experience of life and music.

Our editorial team at Backbeat Books answered every request promptly and with good cheer. We have enjoyed working with them and appreciate their skill and guidance through this process.

Thanks as well to Brand USA and, specifically, Sana Keller, who provided help and support to make our travels possible.

Finally, we say a great big thank-you for the patience of all those people—and projects—we have had to put aside to complete this book.

1

THE ROOTS OF AMERICAN POPULAR MUSIC

The front door to our house is sapphire blue. It's a regular door on an ordinary street, but if you look closely, you can see dings and scratches left by a steady flow of guitar cases, unwieldy keyboards, and music stands. When you play, create, and teach music, the gig comes with a stream of musicians and their gear. There are times when a wide barn door on a sliding track would be more suitable—more elbow room, fewer chips in the paint.

The dings and marks tell just one part of our story. To us—a writer and a writer-musician—our blue front door is the portal to a lifestyle that blends our passions of music, writing, and travel. It's the color of the sky and the sea; it's often part of a song title; it's the cover of our Canadian passports; and in the pecking order of American-born song, blues is the root from which much twentieth-century popular music grew.

OUR STORY

The first thing people want to know is how we ended up "living the dream": two pre-retirement adults, with our dog, in a tricked-out camper van, no schedule (so they think), bags of cash (imaginary), stoked with wanderlust and going with the wind.

It begins with a deeply ingrained curiosity. We both read voraciously and are obsessed with current events as well as how the arc of history sculpts the land and people we encounter. One of us—Jo—is a full-time travel writer with the kind of gig you wish you had if you really wanted to work for pennies an hour and be traveling one-third of the year, following a schedule to all points of the compass, from the high desert of Arizona to the savanna of Kenya to the Arctic tundra and all destinations in between. Craig writes public policy as part of the growing gig economy and is a lifer musician who paid his dues in the 1970s and 1980s, learning his chops on bandstands from Newfoundland to Vancouver Island. Picture the kind of guy who could spend every waking hour happily playing and singing jazz, folk, blues, and rock and roll or reading politics, philosophy, and history.

In our household, the overlapping lifestyles of writing and music produce a creative synergy, and when we looked, we saw a field of possibilities. As a writer and a musician (two get-poor-quick careers), we almost always travel on a shoestring budget with writing assignments in hand, an overarching mission, and a grueling timetable. We wanted that "dream" lifestyle, but with only imaginary bags of cash in hand, we needed to find a realistic way to make it happen. Conjuring up a plan to explore the roots of American music seemed a natural fit: music, travel, culture with some history, and a lot of local foods on the menu. We decided a long road trip was in order to search for the headwaters of the music on which we were raised. The southeastern part of the United States is a hothouse of roots American song—the musical forms that grew from this region changed the world.

That was the easy part. We combined our passions, stocked the van, loaded the dog, locked our blue front door, rolled down the driveway, and pointed ourselves south. Along the way, we learned everything we possibly could about the music, gathering material and experiences to write about those song-infused destinations.

So when we hit on the idea of following that music to its source, we knew we were in for an intense learning experience. What we didn't know was that we were going to have so much fun and be eyewitnesses to the lives of so many fascinating people.

A JOURNEY OF A THOUSAND MILES

We knew we needed to be mobile: to go to communities large and small, talk with people, play music on their front porches and stages, eat their foods, swap stories, and laugh with them. Step one was to purchase a used Class B recreational vehicle (RV)—also known as a camper van conversion—and learn the road-tripping lifestyle. This turned out to be the ideal device for our purposes: spacious enough to live and sleep in but nimble enough to navigate remote twisty back roads and small enough to park in a standard downtown space but large enough to create a compact, on-the-road office (well, *almost* an office space, as it does take some juggling and a certain commitment to compromise).

We are also dog lovers, so we needed enough room to take Eleanor Rigby—our personable English Shepherd—who turned out to be more popular than either of us. We quickly learned that to instantly break the ice with total strangers, get a smart, well-trained, good-looking dog and take it everywhere.

Over the past eight years, we've nurtured this nomadic work/life combo of itchy feet, planning, and a good measure of luck into a series

The authors' rolling office and home
JOSEPHINE MATYAS

of long road trips, each with a specific theme that always includes the music of the region. Our first trip in 2013—exploring the roots of American music—was 5,600 miles over six weeks from Ontario, Canada, to the southeastern states. We followed one drawn-out, serpentine trail, studying the styles of music that took root and flourished in America. We visited several times more, once spending more than a month delving as intensely as possible along the back roads and into the small communities of Mississippi. We had the time of our lives meeting people, listening to their written and musical stories, walking through their neighborhoods, and learning how music forms the sonic backdrop of their experience.

WHAT ARE THE ROOTS OF AMERICAN MUSIC?

Music comes from a place and time. It's a living, evolving creation, and the styles that formed were outgrowths of people, their specific geography and history, and their technology, culture, and circumstances. When they migrate to other parts of the world—as both the Europeans and the Africans did to North America—they carry those influences with them. Mixed together with the geography and culture of their new homelands, the old music changes, evolves, and grows, often bringing people together. Music that is not passed on dies because it's the reproduction of that music that infuses new life energy into it from one generation to the next. No transmission across generations, no legacy to endure. New forms emerge and are born as different people strum, pick, beat, and sing their stories.

It helped us to imagine three different wellsprings that supplied the foundations for American popular song: European classical forms, traditional British country and folk (the music of ordinary people), and the music celebrating African spiritual roots. In rough terms, this provided us with a simple, workable structure. Look through any music collection, and you will see how these wellsprings are the seed stock that germinated in the North American soil, growing into homegrown forms, including the Delta blues, rockabilly, mountain bluegrass, jazz, Cajun, and zydeco.

In the early years, long predating the American Revolutionary War, folk and traditional music arrived with the early colonists from England, Wales, Ireland, and Scotland. Many of these immigrants settled in the hills and valleys—the gullies and hollows—of Appalachia. It's that southern tier of New York State to northern Mississippi where immigrants from the United Kingdom put down roots and unpacked their Old World music traditions. In many cases, this very early mass migration to the New World were castoffs from the mother country—many of them overflow from England's prisons. Something about the rural poverty of Appalachia, the intense religiosity, and the ancient ethnic hatreds (or the comparative isolation), married to a do-it-yourself ethic, produced an abundance of instrument making and storytelling through song. Music was a form of communication, diversion, and entertainment and an outlet for creativity and pleasure.

Before the advent of commercial radio in the 1920s, song cultures were regionalized, traveling as they had for thousands of years from mouth to ear and from hand to eye. Isolation played a role in the development of localized sounds and styles. At its heart, American traditional music is rooted in the Scots-Irish customs of Appalachia, mainly passed down through families. As this music was written and recorded, it came to be known as country music. These same Scots-Irish frontier folk eventually moved west from the coastal communities of North and South Carolina by way of the Appalachian Trail and into the wilderness of northern Mississippi.

Then, in the early 1900s, along came radio, followed by musical recordings on hard, brittle shellac discs. The proliferation and popularity of radio and the Victrola home phonograph blurred and obliterated geography, place, and style. These were the great democratizers, forever changing the way listeners experienced music. For the first time in human history, anyone could hear a voice or instrument that was not in their immediate presence.

At the forefront, the Grand Ole Opry in Nashville—the longest-running radio broadcast in U.S. history—disseminated country music throughout the continent as far as its 50,000 watts could blast. Across most of the continental United States, musical giants-to-be like Elvis Presley and Johnny Cash were glued to the family radio every Saturday night to catch the Grand Ole Opry broadcast. Many thousands of people came to know names like Hank Williams, Patsy Cline, Marty Robbins, the Carter Family, Bill Monroe, Ernest Tubb, Kitty Wells, and Minnie Pearl through the Grand Ole Opry.

A second musical wellspring arrived on American shores via European high culture, specifically classical and church music. Church or sacred music held a special role. It contributed to training musicians and supplying themes for lyrics, infusing and informing everything it touched.

The original transplants to the New World were fleeing religious persecution, but they were also deeply religious themselves. They brought with them a large canon of spiritual and sacred music to which they added in their new homeland. This sacred music blended the tonalities of high Protestant culture with the prayers of the common people. As gospel rang out from the small rural churches, it worked its way into the blues and then to soul, rhythm and blues, and rock and roll.

A final musical wellspring was imported from Africa and filtered through the sensibilities and experience of Africans in the Caribbean and in the slave states of the Deep South. The blues emerged from these slave communities stretching from Virginia through the Carolinas, Georgia, Alabama, Mississippi, Louisiana, looping west to include Arkansas and Texas. It was concentrated in the Mississippi Delta, an agriculturally rich area of massive cotton plantations with tens of thousands of enslaved Africans toiling in fields as far as the eye could see. Crucial to controlling this slave population was their indoctrination into the religious beliefs of the slaveholders, who used their interpretation of biblical texts—backed by ample use of violence—to convince their workforce that Whites were their natural betters and entitled by God to hold them in bondage.

Every part of this region produced a culture distinct to its setting, but the sheer concentration of enslaved persons in the Mississippi Delta—and the appalling conditions of their captivity—inspired what came to be called the blues. Cotton was big business, and that's why so many slaves were brought to the Delta. Creating music was a powerful way for them to shape their own lives. And the Delta was an isolated place, enabling slaves to develop their own forms of music, drawing on ancient African rituals and rhythms. The result was a style of blues deeply rooted in the earliest culture of the Black experience in America.

And it was from the Delta, through mass migrations from those inhumane conditions, that the Delta blues found its way to the rest of the world. This does not mean the blues originated solely in the Delta—but what we name the "blues" is largely a product of Mississippi Delta plantation life.

As these imported music traditions evolved and rubbed against each other, they changed, cross-pollinating, absorbing ideas, and creating new audiences to bring us, in the fullness of time, soul, jazz, Motown, and rhythm and blues. Music still comes from a place and time, but it increasingly comes from the collision with other forms of music—from the ceaseless conversation that is the consequence of its reproduction across generations and peoples. Our aim was to trace the blues back to its geographical and cultural origins in the Delta.

WHY THE BLUES?

How does it come about that two middle-class people from white-bread Canada think they have what it takes to follow the blues to its roots in the Mississippi Delta? *Who do we think we are?* We asked ourselves that too. At its heart, we see value in building bridges and in learning about a history not our own.

We went looking for a framework, a context in which to better understand the music flowing from our turntable, CD player, and MP3. It wasn't enough for us to know there is a museum in this town or a juke joint down that country road—we needed to understand how the blues were formed and under what conditions in people's lives, what drove the music to the surface, and how—and why—it spread. How did the history and the geography of the South and the Mississippi Delta help shape the birth of this style of music? Why is Mississippi so often called the "cradle of American music"?

Call it our quest to uncover the deep story of what brought the blues into being, what pushed it out of its home territory, and what propelled it into the rest of the world. We wanted to get our arms around these forces and factors and to deepen our understanding of this incredibly rich and tragic region.

As products of twentieth-century popular culture, we had been marinated in the sounds and stories of its songs; the blues provided—directly and indirectly—the soundscape of our own lives. We were born at the dawn of rock and roll, the musical and cultural earthquake our parents saw as a society endangering scourge that threatened to undermine all that was good and moral about Western civilization. And rock was definitely born of the blues. By the time we were old enough to listen to and choose our own music, the blues had moved beyond rock and roll and infected virtually every form of popular music (soul, rhythm and blues, country and western, and gospel). Some blues players were able to cross over into the mainstream. For blues great B. B. King, a 1968 gig at San Francisco's historic Fillmore West was a commercial game changer. He played his show to a sold-out house of White music fans. The establishment had embraced the blues.

In every real sense, the blues permeated our own musical sound tracks, even if not directly from the founders themselves.

There's another reason the blues was central to our musical quest: it's the source from which other genres flow, the bedrock of American popular music. Legendary Chicago bluesman Willie Dixon said it best: "Blues are the roots, the rest are the fruits."

Think of jazz as the little brother of the blues and soul and rhythm and blues as first cousins (or closer). Even country and western—White man's blues—became infected with the blues from its earliest days.

THE "DEVIL'S MUSIC"

When the blues emerged in the early twentieth century, to the first listeners—especially if they were sufficiently "churched"—it was the "devil's music" straight up. It was associated with a low class of itinerant, no-account, hard-drinking musicians who were willing to go home with any woman who offered them the opportunity, married or not, and who often maintained a girlfriend or two in every little town they happened to play in.

Early blues performers often moved from town to plantation to city— from juke joint to party house to street corner—sometimes leaving a trail of unfathered "yard" children in their wake. In the ironic juxtaposition of Saturday night/Sunday morning, they sometimes alternated between street corners busking for nickels and Sunday morning fire-and-brimstone sermons preaching the gospel. Blues and gospel are intertwined— the vocal characteristics of gospel songs are a fixture in the blues; the rhythms and twelve-bar structure were imprinted into the gospel sway found in Black churches. They share an emotional intensity, although the subject matter is different. Take "Jesus" out of a rollicking gospel song and replace it with "baby," and you've got a blues tune.

Blues musicians stayed up all hours playing Saturday night music that made otherwise God-fearing people shimmy, shake, and frolic with each other in ways that they would repent hours later. They may have been charismatic and some even profoundly talented, but they were classic "bad boys" who few fathers wanted their daughters to bring home. Many a bluesman suffered the lifelong disapproval of family members for his choice of music.

At Dockery Farms—the Mississippi plantation that B. B. King identified as the home of the blues—historian Bill Lester told us, "When the bluesmen showed up, everyone got drunk, swapped girlfriends, and stabbed each other." They weren't welcome everywhere.

The tunes these hard-bitten guys—mostly men but some notable women—sang on those street corners and in those brothels, juke joints, house parties, and town squares were adapted from what they heard on the plantations, behind the prison walls (like Mississippi's infamous Parchman Farm), in the churches of their childhood, behind the mules they steered through the fields, and from the work gangs chained together that laid railroad track or constructed levees and drainage ditches.

THE BLUES IS A FEELING

"Feeling" is the word that recurs in almost every definition or attempt to embrace this music. Since time immemorial, people have grappled with various descriptions for melancholy. Today, we call it depression or anxiety, but this very human experience has gone by many names, and the one closest to the history of life in the Delta is the "blue devils" or simply the "blues." The blues spoke to the real-world circumstances of those at the bottom of the social order about the state of their ordinary lives: love, sex, betrayal, and pain.

In Indianola, Mississippi, at the B. B. King Museum and Delta Interpretive Center, Robert Terrell (the director of operations and a musician himself) was quick to tell us, "It's real. Once you feel it, you know it's there. It's a music everyone can relate to—doesn't matter your race or situation. It resonates with everyone. It's something that comes from the inside."

The influential gospel bluesman Blind Willie Johnson sang a traditional spiritual all too familiar to an era when thousands of young women died in childbirth. It was simple in structure but emotionally powerful:

> Motherless children have a hard time when the mother is gone.
> Motherless children have a hard time when the mother is gone.
> There's all that weeping and all that crying . . .
> Motherless children have a hard time when the mother is gone.

"Blues in the Delta," observed historian Robert Palmer, "was created not just by Black people but by the poorest, most marginal Black people."

Frederick Douglass, a former slave and nineteenth-century abolitionist, remembered how the old slaves of his childhood would "make the dense old woods, for miles around, reverberate with their wild notes . . . they were mostly of a plaintive cast, and told a tale of grief and sorrow. In the most boisterous outbursts of rapturous sentiment, there was ever a tinge of deep melancholy."

"When you lie down at night, turning from side to side, and you can't be satisfied no way you do, Old Man Blues got you," the late blues guitarist Huddie William "Lead Belly" Ledbetter told music archivist Alan Lomax, whose early twentieth-century field recordings form one of the rich collections at the Library of Congress. Lomax observed "feelings of anomie and alienation, of orphaning and rootlessness—the sense of being a commodity rather than a person; the loss of love and of family and of place—this modern syndrome was the norm for the cotton farmers and transient laborers of the Deep South."

"Blues is a feeling," we were told by bandleader King Edward in Jackson, Mississippi, where he hosts a regular Monday night house gig. King Edward is a fixture on the traditional Mississippi blues scene, and his simple words explain its universality to all people at all times. The blues is the music of real people living with trials, setbacks, and joys. Everyone has the blues at some point. And some live it their whole lives. It's primal to the human experience.

BLUES: ONE OF AMERICA'S GREATEST EXPORTS

When two music genres come face-to-face, they produce a frisson that ultimately transforms both, often creating a new sound and spirit. That's certainly true of the early origins of twentieth-century music. By the mid-1950s, blues was dying as an art form in America, eclipsed by the craze of rock and roll (which was, ironically, born of the blues).

In major harbors, like New Orleans, merchant marine sailors bought blues records and took them to be "discovered" by English port-city youth in places like Liverpool. The compelling energy of the blues infected skiffle, jug band, traditional jazz, and other rhythms. The artists of the British Invasion—the Rolling Stones, the Animals, the Beatles, the Yardbirds, pre-Hollywood Fleetwood Mac, and John Mayall's Blues Breakers (with Eric Clapton)—were captivated by the stories and rhythms of the Mississippi Delta blues.

"Europe threw a lifeline to the blues," is how Ronnie Eldridge, a Mississippi amateur blues historian, explained it to us. Before those merchant marine sailors shuttled records across the Atlantic, even American blues giants like Muddy Waters struggled to get regular gigs. But when the music hit the English port cities, it was taken up with gusto, and the result was shot back across the Atlantic, breathing new life into a homegrown American art form.

Reflecting on the era in his autobiography *Life*, Keith Richards, guitarist and cofounder of the Rolling Stones, wrote, "The most bizarre part of the whole story is that having done what we intended to do in our narrow, purist teenage brains at the time, was to turn people on to the blues, what actually happened was we turned American people back on to their own music. And that's probably our greatest contribution to music."

SO WHAT?

It's hard to overstate the impact of the blues on popular music, particularly rock and roll, which was its direct descendant. "The blues got pregnant," sang Muddy Waters, "and they named the baby rock and roll." Imagine: no blues, no Elvis, no Beatles, no Animals, no Motown, no Rolling Stones, no British Invasion, no thousands and thousands of other artists. Why is this? Because of the simplicity of its form, the compelling nature of its story, its shimmy-and-shake danceability, and its gut-level connection to everyday experience.

Equally important, the parents of the rock and roll generation hated it. Start with the name: "rock and roll" is slang for sex. Worse, it was associated, in the minds of White people, with the spiritual energy and verve of Blacks. Put these two meanings together, and the threat to White audiences was immediate and unmistakable.

Memphis record producer Sam Phillips—the visionary who launched the careers of Elvis Presley, Carl Perkins, Roy Orbison, Johnny Cash, and Jerry Lee Lewis—put it best: "Without the cooperation of total resentment on the part of the parents, rock n' roll would have had a rougher time makin' it." We had those parents ourselves, schooled in the traditions of European high classical music culture. Our parents argued that rock and roll was a fad that would never last, that it was loud, chaotic noise. Bands like the Beatles were dismissed by our grandparents, who insisted, "They're just making up those words." But our parents were solidly in the mainstream for their generation, and—like the record company executive who told Beatles manager Brian Epstein that "guitar groups are on the way out"—they were wrong.

The beautiful and evergreen part of our musical journey is the story of how we are all ultimately drawn into each other's heritage and a part of each other's biography. Music came to North America from many points on the compass, but however pure it was on arrival, it was soon contaminated—which is to say enriched—by contact with what was already here.

Those dings and marks in the sapphire blue paint are like the keys to our insatiable curiosity. They opened our minds to the journey ahead and piqued our interest in the music that was born and grew in North America. All we had to do was be open to following the trail laid out before us.

IN THE WORDS OF THE BLUES GREATS:

- Mississippi-born Willie Dixon, late poet laureate of the blues: "The blues are the true facts of life expressed in words and song, inspiration, feeling, and understanding."
- Eric Clapton: Blues is "the music of hope and triumph over adversity."
- B. B. King: "The blues are the Three L's—living, loving and, hopefully, laughing."

The twelve-bar blues is the most common musical form of the blues. The blues is generally played in a 4/4 time signature—this means four beats to every bar and that every quarter note counts as one beat. The basic blues is a simple progression of three chords based on the first, fourth, and fifth degrees of an eight-note scale. In musician-speak, it unfolds over a three-line stanza supported by a conventional twelve-bar harmonic structure.

2

LAND, RIVER, COTTON, AND PEOPLE: THE HISTORY AND CENTRALITY OF THE BLUES

Music lovers know the Delta blues only as a musical genre but little about its geographic, sociocultural, and political origins. In order to truly understand this most American form of song, you have to know something about the place and circumstances in which it was born. There's a human and physical geography that gave rise to the sad and soulful strains of the music. Much of it begins in the Mississippi Delta, in the heart of America's Deep South.

There are those who like to take what we call a closer look into historical events, political goings-on, and the like. The more detail, the better. But not everyone wants their history and politics served up in this manner—they prefer the Coles Notes version, with just enough detail to create context. This chapter is intended for readers who lean toward the "deep dive." The slave-based economy, the development of plantations, the social and physical realities of living conditions, and events like the Great Flood of 1927, the effects of mechanization, and the Great Migration are covered in more detail here.

For those readers looking for a more concise version of events, the introductions to each of the following regional chapters (chapters 3 through 5) begin with that Coles Notes version. There is just enough information to cover the basics about the land and the people across Mississippi. And for more detail, just flip back into chapter 2.

All art is a product of its circumstances—not just individuals but their surroundings and the conditions of their lives—and the better we understand these, the better we appreciate the blues. Some readers will, with justification, complain that we have left out important elements, and to that we plead "guilty" and reply that one has to select and that any selection is necessarily imperfect. For those who want a more in-depth look, there are suggestions for additional reading at the end and throughout the book.

In order to grasp its appeal, we have to review the circumstances—geographic, political, cultural, racial, and sociological—from which the blues emerged. No travel guide to the Delta can do justice to every aspect, but we can summarize some of the more important elements in this chapter.

WHY LAND AND RIVER MATTER

A delta is usually the geographic meeting of a river with an ocean—the point at which rich river sediment fans out to form a large triangle as the Nile does when it meets the Mediterranean. But that does not describe the Mississippi Delta, which is several hundred miles north of the Gulf of Mexico.

The Mississippi Delta is a vast, leaf-shaped, mostly flat, alluvial floodplain comprising some 7,000 square miles in the northwest corner of the state and bordered by the Mississippi River on the west and the smaller Yazoo River to the east: 200 miles long and eighty-seven miles across at its widest point, or roughly 4.4 million acres encompassing all or part of twenty different counties. It's an expanse of rich, dark black, agricultural soil, regarded as one of the most fertile crop-growing regions in the nation. The Mississippi's watershed drains thirty-two states and two Canadian provinces, and the river has long been an important navigational and communication link between the Gulf of Mexico and numerous ports of call to the north.

There's incredible power in that waterway. As the second-longest river in North America, the Mississippi flows generally south for 2,350 miles from its source in northern Minnesota and is divided into the upper Mississippi, from its headwaters to the Missouri River; the middle Mississippi, which is downstream from the Missouri to the Ohio River; and the lower Mississippi, which flows from the Ohio River to the Gulf of Mexico. It's the lower third of the majestic, storied river that runs through the Delta.

The state of Mississippi is part of the Gulf Coastal Plain comprising mostly lowlands and low rolling hills, featuring a subtropical climate that is humid most of the year. The high rainfall and long growing season combine to make for prime conditions for agriculture on a mass scale. In high summer—cotton and vegetable season—the long days of heat and humidity can be unforgiving, hot and sticky enough to drop you to your knees.

When the first European settlers arrived from Spain, France, and the United Kingdom, they encountered a territory of incredible agricultural potential. But it was not a simple matter of planting and harvesting. Much of what became vast plantations was low-lying swamp dotted with groves of cypress trees, thick with mosquitos and overrun by alligators, venomous snakes, and various threats to life, including malaria and other insect-borne diseases. The land had to be cleared and drained, a huge, extremely labor-intensive and years-long undertaking. The first settlers

Much of what was drained and became plantations was swamp with thick groves of cypress trees
JOSEPHINE MATYAS

tried but failed to enslave the Native American peoples who had lived in the region for thousands of years. They then turned to imported African slaves to work the land, a brutal job that took years and, because of frequent flooding from the mighty river, had to be repeated regularly. Controlling the recurring floods has been a major challenge since the first settlers arrived. Sugarcane, tobacco, rice, and indigo were among the first crops grown in the Delta, but market pressures pushed toward cotton as global demand increased beginning around 1800.

Today, while driving across the Delta, it's hard to fathom how much human labor must have been required to clear this land for cultivation and to imagine the violence and oppression inflicted on the enslaved persons who worked it. The remaining cypress groves look majestic from the highway, but their heavy trunks required many hours of ax swinging to fell and remove. And there would have been hundreds of thousands of them across this territory before it was suitable for the production of export crops.

THE GLOBAL DEMAND FOR COTTON

Cotton was once as important to the global economy as oil is today; indeed, it was one of the very first commodities driving the early rise of global capitalism. The climate and soil of a wide swath of the American South met the conditions under which the plant thrived: the right amount of rain, the right patterns of rainfall, and the right number of days without frost. Much of the history of the Delta is the story of rising and falling demand for this commodity, which, well into the twentieth century, necessitated massive quantities of labor to plant, cultivate, and harvest. Although the labor itself did not require advanced skills—children were pressed into work as soon as they could be made useful—the sheer number of workers necessary to produce a profitable quantity of cotton required not only large estates, essentially plantations comprising thousands of tilled acres, but also huge numbers of cultivators. By necessity, this meant long hours in sweltering sunlight on sunny days and long hours draining fields following torrential downpours or recurring floods. There's an old saying in the South that "cotton don't like to get its feet wet," so extensive irrigation and drainage of standing water was an important time-consuming and labor-intensive reality of industrial-scale cotton cultivation.

The plant itself compels the cultivator to bend over, which is why we use the term "high cotton" to denote good times: when the cotton grows tall, it literally means you don't have to break your back to pick the fluffy, white bolls. Although brutal, cruel, and unjust, slavery was an efficient system of labor organization, and the southern landowners and planters—in alliance with their northern bankers, brokers, merchants, and European buyers—had every incentive to preserve this mode of exploitation as long as possible.

Cotton was produced all over the world, from China to Turkey to the Middle East. But various factors, including local customs and patterns of land ownership, limited the scale of production, keeping its price high and availability low. Furthermore, not all varieties were suitable to its largest European market. The short-staple cotton variety, grown on most American plantations, had to be painstakingly cleaned by hand, one plant at a time. What made the important difference was Eli Whitney's invention of the cotton gin, a machine that quickly and efficiently separated cotton fibers from seeds, increasing productivity by a huge factor, overcoming a significant processing bottleneck, and setting off a "cotton rush" through the global economy.

Demand rose sharply in the early 1790s as Europe's most important source—Saint-Domingue, now Haiti—succumbed to revolution. Cotton producers sought new territory and moved westward from South Carolina and Georgia toward Alabama, Mississippi, Louisiana, and Texas, a migration propelled by the movement of cotton prices. The growing demand motivated expansionist thrusts into new territories.

"So rapid was this move westward that by the end of the 1830s," wrote Sven Beckert, Harvard University historian and the author of *Empire of Cotton*, "Mississippi already produced more cotton than any other southern state." This put the American slave states in a unique position. They were tightly connected to the growing market in Europe without the constraints of family subsistence, mutual obligation, and political arrangements characteristic of other cotton-producing regions in North Africa, China, and India. Slaves were a self-renewing labor supply that could—with the application of sufficient violence and terror—be worked to death, or at least prevented from rebelling or running away.

That's why, between 1500 and 1800, more than 8 million central and West Africans were captured and transported to the Americas by Spanish and Portuguese traders, later to be joined by British, French, Dutch, and Danish slavers. As global demand for cotton increased, so

By the end of the 1830s, Mississippi already produced more cotton than any other southern state

TUNICA CONVENTION & VISITORS BUREAU

did the demand for slaves. No one really knows how many slaves survived the Middle Passage from Africa to the New World or how many died in transit. But by its peak, Black slaves outnumbered White planters and their straw bosses by a considerable margin across the Delta— in some places the ratio ran as high as ten to one. By 1850, a decade before the start of the American Civil War, each family in Washington County owned, on average, more than eighty slaves. Stephen Duncan, the largest planter in the Delta, claimed ownership of 1,036 slaves by the late 1850s. By 1859, some 60,000 Delta slaves harvested an astounding 66 million pounds of cotton.

Slavery, then, was the moral and physical engine powering both the revolutionary industrial prosperity of England and the astonishing material advances of the United States and Europe during the first half of the 1800s. Slavery benefited the southern states enormously, making them incredibly prosperous, but it also had benefits for the northern states, whose merchants, bankers, and traders brokered and processed the product for export. And it also benefited the traders, brokers, and merchants in the United Kingdom and across Europe who purchased and processed the raw material exported from the slave states. In 1858, James Henry Hammond, a plantation owner and U.S. senator, warned that "England would topple headlong and carry the whole civilized world with her" if production by slave labor were endangered. Profitable cotton required slave labor. "No power on earth dares to make war upon it. Cotton *is* king."

Senator Hammond's support of slavery was hardly a minority view. Slavery was defended by numerous articulate and powerful figures in American politics on practical, economic, social, moral, and even religious grounds. Many of the first Anglo-Saxon migrants to the Delta practiced Presbyterianism, which they brought from their ancestral Scots, English, and Irish homes. While some later became Baptists or Methodists, the Calvinism of their homeland left its residue wherever they put down roots. One element of this Calvinist strain was the belief that human nature is so corrupted by original sin that we are unable to exercise faith in Christ by our own will. God predetermines some to be saved and others to be damned eternally—even before birth—a doctrine that religious landowners employed to argue that slaves needed to accept their place in God's plan.

A literalist reading of scripture endorsed, for plantation owners, biblical sanction for slavery. Church and religious authorities held that slavery was outside their ecclesiastical authority—a civic issue—even invoking the Old Testament to remind their congregants that the ancient Israelites kept slaves and that, were there any residue of doubt, Jesus offered no specific objection to slavery in the New Testament. That religious doctrine and teaching could be turned to the defense of the South's "peculiar institution"—through the curse of Cain, God had decreed slavery even before it had come into existence, and hence slavery was a concept of divine decree—should hardly surprise us. Religion can be made to justify anything.

By the 1830s, when the cotton boom was well under way, any lingering doubt about the justice or injustice of slavery had been adjourned, and religious instruction turned to the business of creating and reproducing a compliant and obedient Black underclass who would not challenge the sociopolitical or racial hierarchy that so benefited the White overclass. This was the sociocultural and political philosophy that took root in the soil—and in the minds of White landowners—throughout the Delta.

That their wealth was sustained by intolerable injustice and violence was well understood by everyone—not least the planters, whose vast prosperity depended on their capacity to secure the political future of slavery and, to the greatest extent possible, extend it into the new territories of the American West. That, of course, was a cause of the coming war.

By the time the first shots of the American Civil War were fired in April 1861, cotton was the most important commodity in the world's most important industry, making the Mississippi Delta in the early nineteenth century the rough equivalent of Saudi Arabia in the twentieth century. By one estimate, in 1862, one of every sixty-five people living on the planet—approximately 20 million souls—was involved in the cultivation of cotton or the production of cotton cloth. "The industry that brought great wealth to European manufactures and merchants, and bleak employment to hundreds of thousands of mill workers," wrote Beckert, "also catapulted the United States onto center stage of the world economy." By the end of the American Civil War, however, the cotton-fueled economies of the slave South lay in ruins.

DEBT BONDAGE: THE RISE OF SHARECROPPING

But that was far from the end of the story because the global demand for cotton actually exploded just as slavery formally—if not actually—ended, creating powerful incentives for landowners and merchants to aggressively increase crop yields through the spread of alternative forms of production. These new forms became the means to commercially viable cotton production until the introduction of mechanical harvesting in the 1940s.

Immediately following the death of President Lincoln on April 15, 1865, southern power holders and their legislative representatives began looking for ways to reestablish their battered economic system to, in effect, restore the political, social, cultural, and economic supremacy of the White establishment. Landowners sought to re-create a world as close as possible to the antebellum status quo but on the basis of wage labor. The challenge they faced was stark: left to their own devices, freed slaves would produce primarily for their own needs and perhaps a small local market. Once freed, former slaves could choose to migrate out of the South and force up wages, which would drive down profits. The landowners had to find a way to limit the mobility rights of their former slaves—that is, bind them to the land—while extracting more product out of them without paying them more for it. In this struggle, they were politically supported by elites in the northern United States and across Europe—whose primary concern was getting more cotton for their spindles, mills, and merchants. But the former slaves had other ideas and pressed these through political channels. By 1867, a political stalemate took hold between freed slaves and landowners. Ultimately, the halfhearted commitment toward Reconstruction of President Andrew Johnson's administration (1865 through 1869) tilted the playing field toward former slave owners, reinstating much of their local and regional power to restrict the rights and liberties of freed slaves.

Out of this deadlock arose a labor regime called sharecropping: former slaves and their families worked specific plots of land with credit from landowners (for seed, tools, housing, and so on)—but without the brutal straw boss supervision of prewar slavery—and received a share of the crop at harvest. By 1900, more than three in four Black sharecroppers in the Delta kept back a share of their crop or paid a fixed sum to the landowner while retaining the crop. In theory, the system seemed fairer than slavery, but in practice, it worked better for landowners than sharecroppers. The global market for cotton was volatile; prices bounced around from year to year. At the end of a good year, a hardworking sharecropping family might make enough to buy new clothes and even a car.

But most years were not good. The debts from one year were rolled over into the next year so that families who stayed on the same plantation found themselves falling steadily behind year after year regardless of how hard they worked or how good prices might seem to be. Some plantations printed their own currency and sold their sharecroppers everything they needed from a commissary—a company store—further tying the sharecropper's family to the landowner. Over time, an informal system of mutual dependency emerged in which former slaves who felt they were being mistreated vanished in the nighttime—or moved to another plantation—which put harshly exploitative landowners in danger of not having enough labor to harvest their crops.

As if the human-designed system was not misery enough, along came the boll weevil—what we today call an "invasive species"—from Mexico that moved into the southern United States in the late nineteenth century, infesting all cotton-growing areas by the 1920s. The most destructive cotton pest to take up residence in North America, it traveled up to 160 miles per year and destroyed, by 1913, more than 30 percent of the

An abandoned sharecropper's home
JOSEPHINE MATYAS

cotton crop. Over the following decade, the weevil caused an average
crop loss of up to 26 percent, a substantial hit to the ability for sharecroppers and landowners to scrape out a living.

The combination of vast prosperity for a small minority of landowners generated by brutal slavery requiring egregious violations of human
dignity, followed by defeat in war and the humiliation and chaos that
attended Reconstruction plus the social upheaval provoked by emancipation and the injustice of sharecropping—all these elements and more
combined to create a particular sociology across the South whose specific
qualities were examined and described in insightful detail by author and
Mississippi native David Cohn.

Born in Greenville in the lower Delta and educated at Yale University
in Connecticut, his books and articles wrestled with his home state and
its cultural contradictions. Cohn was Jewish in a sea of Protestants, and
this fact, perhaps, gave him an outsider's perspective to complement his
insider's point of view. In his evocative writings, like *Where I Was Born
and Raised* (1948), he draws an arresting portrait detailing the complex-
ity of Delta civilization: simple, almost naive on the surface but seething

with subterranean contradictions and disharmonies. Embracing both fanaticism and tolerance, the Delta welcomes all faiths, including the depravities of the Ku Klux Klan. Although spending heavily on education, its students strive for little more than the ability to read and write. The stern circumstances of life, as Delta civilization understood it, made little room for the pursuit of culture for its own sake. The mostly Protestant Irish, English, and Scots settlers brought with them an Old World skepticism for book learning and distrust of the higher arts. The indulgence of poetry, for example, could damage a man's reputation—even worse if he was discovered to be writing it. The Delta's prosperity, controlled by a small minority, engendered a feudal cast of mind among its elite, making them distrustful of political innovation and openly hostile to change. A whole system of codes and norms had evolved to preserve White domination of the numerically Black majority.

Cohn loved his Delta home, but he did not pull his critical punches. From Cohn's perspective, the White overclass civilization of the Delta had—through the imposition and justification of brutal slavery—sustained a form of what we would today call "moral injury," and this self-inflicted trauma was aggravated by the brooding apprehension that such oppression could not last forever and that, in the fullness of time, the Black underclass might, with justice, rise up to destroy them. For that reason, among others, the White overclass went to great pains to ensure that Black blood not be mixed with White but—here a contradiction—were somewhat less exercised if White blood was poured into the veins of Blacks. Indeed, the greatest violence was reserved for Black offenses against White women.

Although slavery in the United States was officially abolished in 1865 with the adoption of the Thirteenth Amendment, the slave states of the South ignored it and even continued it, but the prohibition had the unintended consequence of increasing the value of slaves. Breeding was intensified; able-bodied men and women were essentially turned into stud producers of salable children. Slaves were considered chattel, property, commodities, and rentable laborers, a practice that caused considerable friction with poor White workers who saw their average wages being driven downward. Slaves built the infrastructure of the South: their labor created the roads, houses, public buildings, docks, and railroads.

For its part, the Black underclass was compelled to chart its course within a context created and reproduced for them by the needs and prejudices of White landowner society. Every signal in the social environment reminded Blacks that they lived within the constraints and expectations of a predominantly White social power structure—while the White overclass was likewise imprisoned within a set of codes that existed under the awe of noblesse oblige, which governed and controlled the limits of racial relations as much for the White overclass as for the Black underclass.

One can only imagine the cognitive dissonance and moral disorientation that this cluster of contradictions, class, and racial resentments created and sustained for the White landowners and their lower-class White hired hands. One cannot begin to imagine the outrage it must have provoked among generations of former slaves and their children.

THE BLACK CODES: THE OVERCLASS STRIKES BACK

Former slave owners understood their postwar dilemma only too well. They hardly needed the analysis of David Cohn: former slaves could no longer be compelled through direct violence, yet their labor was still needed en masse to meet the global demand for cotton. The challenge confronting landowners and their political allies was to craft a legal regime that acknowledged that freedmen could no longer be treated as property yet constrained the civil and political rights of former slaves sufficient to ensure their availability as low-wage agricultural workers. Accordingly, Mississippi was the first state, in 1865, to enact "Black Codes." The Black Codes legislatively limited the freedom of former slaves by compelling them with the force of law to work in the White-dominated agricultural economy and to prohibit them from voting, owning guns, and learning to read and write. This was, in practice, a legal device for turning free labor into "voluntary" contractual employment backed by the threat of the criminal justice system. The laws functioned to transform former slaves—that is, African American persons who were not currently "under contract" to a landowner—into agricultural workers or else face prison.

These laws amounted to the first official response of the former Confederate states to emancipation of their Black citizens after rejoining the Union. The Black Codes encompassed three areas of state law—civil rights, apprenticeship, and vagrancy—which worked, in concert, to limit rights of mobility, labor, and autonomy. Blacks were granted access to the courts but denied the right to serve as witnesses against

White people—effectively affirming that they were not equal to Whites under the law. Former slaves could not rent or lease land where they chose, and city dwellers were required to carry written evidence—like an internal passport—of their employment and residence. If they worked for an employer longer than one month, they were required to sign labor contracts that limited their freedom of movement and compelled them to commit to long-term employment.

A key legal instrument of the Black Codes was the use of so-called vagrancy laws by which homeless, unattached, or unemployed former slaves could be arrested and fined and—if they could not pay—incarcerated in convict leasing camps to work off their fines. Vagrancy served as a flexible pretext permitting the legal oppression of former slaves across Mississippi. These laws proved so flexible in their application that they survived in many states well into the 1960s (and were ultimately used against different groups, including civil rights activists, Vietnam war protesters, hippies, and so on, that challenged the post–World War II socioeconomic and cultural establishment). Vagrancy laws were key to filling and sustaining the population of Parchman Farm, the fearsome Mississippi State Penitentiary, with former slaves and lower-class Whites. Once incarcerated, of course, inmates were at the mercy of the prison administration and, for all intents and purposes, invisible to the rest of the society. They were, in actuality if not law, re-enslaved.

PARCHMAN FARM: SLAVERY REINVENTED

The maximum-security Parchman Farm is just a few miles south of Tutwiler, about a half-hour drive south of Clarksdale, right in the center of what would have been miles and miles of cotton plantations stretching out in every direction. Countless thousands of men and women cycled through Parchman, including Bukka White, Son House, Sonny Boy Williamson II, and Elvis Presley's father, Vernon, for assorted contrived, serious, and trivial offenses.

Founded in 1901 and now the state's oldest prison facility, it was built on the model of penal farming on public lands birthed in the Carolinas. Located on 20,000 acres of lush Delta soil in Sunflower County, the prison encompasses lands once owned by a prominent family of whom J. M. Parchman was the patriarch and first warden. Even now, at the start of the twenty-first century, the shadow cast by the troubled past of Parchman stretches into the present. "The history of Parchman is a prime example of how dehumanization and neglect are intrinsic to separating people from their freedom," wrote opinion columnist Jamelle Bouie in a January 2020 issue of the *New York Times*.

According to William Banks Taylor, professor of criminal justice at the University of Southern Mississippi, lawmakers of the post–American Civil War era "considered the existence of a large and rapidly growing African American convict population and the unrealized public revenues of a brutal policy that since the Civil War had delivered the captive labor of Black convicts to private business interests." In other words, state lawmakers sought to reclaim some of the revenue captured by the private sector through the leasing of prison labor to private businesses, a system of cruel, gratuitous penology that, Taylor writes, "might well have been worse than slavery."

Parchman Farm was—in the mind of Governor James K. Vardaman (aka Mississippi's "White Chief" between 1904 and 1908)—a solution to his "Negro crime" problem: a surplus of former slaves and their families seeking exit from the hardship and persistent poverty of sharecropping and migrating into towns and cities seeking alternative employment or simply escape from the hardship of rural life. Vardaman viewed these people as a threat to the homes and livelihood of urban Whites. Contriving a way to secure their labor served two purposes: it got them out of the urban environment of the White establishment—thereby ensuring, in the mind of Vardaman and his supporters, the safety of the White man's home and women—and it made their labor available for the state's purposes. Vardaman was not averse to exploiting racial fears to accomplish this objective. By the outbreak of World War I in 1914, Parchman consisted of five penal farms and two lime plants, making up the hub of a massive self-sufficient plantation system spread across thousands of acres of prime agricultural land. The massive operation was intended to be self-sufficient and profitable for the state.

"The state penitentiary system at Parchman," observed a 1957 report from the *New York Post*, "is simply a cotton plantation using convicts as labor. The warden is not a penologist, but an experienced plantation manager. His annual report to the legislature is not of salvaged lives; it is a profit and loss statement, with the accent on profit." In his writings, ethnomusicologist Alan Lomax calls their zeal for work "Southern Protestant Colonial," amounting to a "passion for forcing others to labor hard in the hot fields and woods . . . the Southern penologists joyously and self-righteously humiliated, bullied, beat, often tortured, and some-times murdered their charges." Lomax compared state prisons in the South—from which he and his father collected many work, field, and prison songs—to "Nazi concentration camps" for their torture and in-timidation of the Black community in Mississippi and across the South. "The horrid shadow of this remorseless system, in which so many men disappeared, lay over the whole South, carrying a threat that has not entirely vanished."

Penology was not evidence-based policy during the early years of the twentieth century when Parchman earned its notorious status. There was little consideration of who the prisoner might become as a result of brutal incarceration at the hands of the state. When he visited Parchman Farm to collect recordings of song, Alan Lomax observed that the pris-oners were forced to rise in the dark and run to their work in the fields, prodded on at gunpoint by guards riding alongside on horseback. In this environment—to which a person could be condemned for life—singing, especially group singing, was a powerful force that soothed the soul, built a communal experience, and kept emotions from overwhelming. Wherever Lomax traveled, he heard stories of self-injury or mutilation as one form of escape from the brutality of prison labor. Out of this furnace of inhumanity, multiple field hollers, laments, and songs emerged that told about and expanded the vocabulary of what evolved into the Delta blues. The prison functioned as an incubator—with the church and the juke joint—of what would come to be known as the Delta blues, creat-ing and reproducing a language and shared experience for incorporation into the Delta's distinctive culture and music in which what became the blues could be transmitted across regional populations and from older to younger prisoners.

Parchman, sharecropping, and Black Codes were all human contriv-ances for oppressing other humans. Many thousands of former slaves and sharecroppers exited the Delta as soon as they could following the American Civil War, but many thousands stayed behind too, bound to the only life they knew, the ties of family, and fear of the unknown.

One enemy common to Black and White, rich and poor, planter and sharecropper—a power greater and less tractable than even the most powerful landowners—was the great river. The Mississippi demanded a role in the unfolding drama of life in the Delta. For thousands of years before the arrival of Europeans, it had distributed prime fertile soil across the Delta on a recurring basis—ensuring its spectacular agricultural productivity—yet in a matter of hours, it could also displace man and beast without mercy or afterthought. The management of the mighty river had occupied the best minds of the region for as long as Europeans had occupied the Delta.

"THE PEOPLE OF THE DELTA FEAR GOD AND THE MISSISSIPPI"

And so begins a chapter in David Cohn's iconic 1948 look at his home state, *Where I Was Born and Raised.*

Wherever in history humans and waterways have coexisted, the humans have had to accommodate themselves to—or find ways to protect themselves from—the water. Floods were a regular part of existence across the Delta, but it took the flood of a century to shine a light on the culmination of a succession of political decisions and engineering errors. Those decisions had outsized consequences on the people and fortunes of the Delta. In *Rising Tide: The Great Mississippi Flood of 1927 and How It Changed America,* John Barry details how decades of political deadlock and magical thinking embodied in the "levees only" policy underestimated the power of a river to move what attempted to constrain it.

There are, of course, multiple ways to manage the regular flooding of a major waterway like the Mississippi, including creating spillways to divert water from the main current to lessen the pressure on the existing riverbed. Although expensive, dredging silt off the bottom can create more space for water to pass through shallows or narrow channels. Then there's the practice of building up the shoreline through elongated artificially constructed walls—called levees—that act as enhanced riverbanks by directing and containing the current flow. Prior to 1882, Delta landowners and planters took matters into their own hands to build and maintain levees, but these efforts were of limited effectiveness because levees were expensive and it was hard to agree on consistent construction standards.

Levees are labor intensive but cheaper if built with slave labor as they were before the American Civil War. They tend to increase the value of land adjacent to the river, which can then be farmed, giving landowners a stake in the levee system of flood control. In response to a long-standing dispute between a civilian engineer and the chief of the U.S. Army Corps of Engineers, Congress created the Mississippi River Commission in 1879 to oversee federal funding for flood control. Congress also authorized the Army Corps of Engineers to participate in levee construction if and where matters of navigation (a federal matter) were concerned. Although the Commission envisioned both civilian and military engineering input, the Army Corps of Engineers came to monopolize all aspects of the river's flood control management.

By 1885, the Mississippi River Commission had come to adopt a "levees only" policy that was premised on the belief that the force of moving water—contained by levees—would move silt along the river bottom and carry it to the Gulf of Mexico in sufficient volume to ensure that no other water management strategies would be necessary. Over several decades, then, the Army Corps of Engineers built levees, some as high as four stories, on both banks of the river running the 1,100-mile distance from Cairo, Illinois, to New Orleans while closing off the natural floodways and outlets on which the river had relied for thousands of years.

The "levees only" policy became a kind of dogma to which both the Army Corps of Engineers and the Mississippi River Commission were committed. It also had the (perhaps unintended) consequence of increasing the value of land adjacent to the mighty river, which in turn enhanced the influence of the landowners who benefited from the increased land value. What few people understood was that the stronger current—created by constraining the Mississippi within levees—did not, in practice, move as much silt along the bottom of the river as was theorized by the "levees only" advocates. Floods that carried less water—in the early part of the twentieth century—rose higher than earlier floods that had carried more. And the 1912 flood devastated the lower Mississippi, smashing height records on seventeen of the eighteen river gauges between Illinois and the Gulf. But it was not until 1927 that the bill for the "levees only" policy would come due, and when it did, the structure of Delta society would face its most severe test.

THE BILL COMES DUE: THE GREAT FLOOD OF 1927

Nature, lest we need reminding, has a tendency to violently upend human affairs. The winter of 1926 and early 1927 saw unprecedented extreme weather events, including tornados and snowstorms, across the Mississippi floodplain, causing thousands of little tributaries, rivers, and creeks across roughly one-third of the United States to swell to bursting. The rain fell in such volume that the Arkansas River at one point

Map of the Mississippi River Flood of 1927
NATIONAL ARCHIVES AND RECORDS

flowed backward from the pressure of the Mississippi. Numerous levee breaches and floods had already occurred well upstream from the Delta in Arkansas and Missouri but nothing on the scale of what was to come.

Easter weekend brought storms to the Delta, which meant more rain. The *Chicago Daily Tribune* predicted "the most disastrous flood this country has ever had," while the *New Iberia Enterprise* of New Orleans predicted "the greatest of all floods since the days of Noah." On Good Friday, April 15, 1927, the *Memphis Commercial Appeal* warned that "the roaring Mississippi River, bank and levee full from St. Louis to New Orleans, is believed to be on its mightiest rampage . . . considerable fear is felt over the prospects for the greatest flood in history." And so it proved to be.

Rivers run to the sea. If something—a dam or a levee or an obstacle—prevents it from flowing where gravity dictates, then the river's mass and kinetic energy simply accumulate. Both the energy to stop, contain, or divert the river and the energy of the river itself grow in tandem, and one must eventually yield to the other. This is not theory. This is reality. An important determinant of how dangerous a flood will be is the height of its crest, which is not a wave but the highest point to which a river rises. The height, in turn, is a factor of the volume of water but also the speed at which the crest moves downstream. Faster is better because slower means more pressure exerted for a longer period of time on a levee system—if levees are the sole means of controlling water as it was on the Mississippi.

Additionally, slower floods, carrying the same volume, push the water level higher. In some places, the river flows in a straight line and moves faster. In others, it collides frequently with bends or rapids or slows for other reasons. The friction created by wind, riverbank, riverbed, and sediment can vary the velocity with which the river pushes toward the sea. The Mississippi River features whirlpools as large as 800 feet long and 200 feet across, big enough to swallow trees and even boats. It meanders for miles, turning and twisting around corners as it has for millennia. The most dangerous floods tend to include several flood crests—the first of which may force later crests to rise higher than they otherwise would. In the spring of 1927, according to John Barry, "the United States Weather Bureau at Cairo, Illinois, noted ten distinct flood crests moving down the Mississippi."

There is no way to do justice in these pages to the human cost that accompanied the Great Flood of 1927. Everyone in the Delta understood that a massive failure of the levee system meant destruction on an unimaginable scale. Everyone understood that their only salvation was reinforcing the levees, building them higher than those on the opposite bank, and that the burden of that backbreaking, soul-destroying work of filling and carrying sandbags would fall to the more than 30,000 Blacks, poor Whites, and convicts of both colors who did not possess the social status to supervise others or the money to escape. According to Barry's history, only ten earthmoving levee machines were available for 800 miles of levees. There were mules, of course, but never enough. What was abundant were poor sharecroppers filling sandbags at sixty to eighty pounds each, carrying them up the slope, and returning for the next. The river pressed on unrelentingly, and the humans had no choice but to do the same. The crisis brought out the worst in the higher-status Whites, particularly those with guns and social authority. Of course, the American Legion ran kitchens and cooked thousands of meals every day, but as the water rose, men were simply washed away by the torrent, their bodies never recovered, as they worked to reinforce the levees. The reckoning was coming.

Levees can fail for any number of reasons. A piece of wood left during construction can rot and leave a cavity that the river finds and enlarges. Animals burrowing into the levee, even crawfish, can weaken it. The levee is made of soil, but not all soil is suited to the construction of a levee, plus it's expensive to transport soil from elsewhere where it might be needed just as badly. High winds or passing boats can pound the levee with waves ripping out or gouging holes and saturating sandbags. And the biggest of all dangers, of course, is the unrelenting pressure of the water; the longer the river rises against the levee, the greater the pressure and the more saturated the levee becomes. Sooner or later, the force of the water against the levee produces sand boils, little volcanoes of water that burst through the levee and may surface 200 yards or more behind it. The people of the Mississippi learned that when a sand boil shoots up clear water, it is not dangerous, but when that water is muddy, it signals that the river is eroding the core of the levee. The unyielding pressure on the levees creates a dilemma on both sides of the river because everyone knows that they're going to get washed away if the levee breaches on their side first. So both sides want the levee to breach on the opposite bank, and neither side wants to relieve the pressure and risk flooding themselves. Both sides, then, have an incentive to reinforce the levee on their side and pray for a breach on the other.

Nature, unlike we mortals, makes no mistakes, and that puts tremendous pressure on the people of the Delta to get everything right—a tall order under the best of circumstances. And these were not the best of circumstances. It just kept raining and raining. Early April delivered record downpours. By the middle of the month, the first government-built levee crumbled in Dorena, Missouri, more than 250 miles north of the Delta. A surge of water pushed south, bursting more levees, flooding more than a million acres of land, and leaving 50,000 people homeless. And that was not even the opening act. There had been numerous smaller breaches for weeks prior; the river was just getting started.

When the levee system began to fail in the spring of 1927, it was similar to how a Hemingway character describes going bankrupt: "at first gradually, then suddenly." Levees had been breaching all up and down the river system, crevices opening and water pouring over the top where men could not keep sandbags in place. On Good Friday, some fifteen inches of rain fell in the space of eighteen hours across sections of the Delta. The main event arrived on the morning of April 21 at Mounds Landing, twenty-seven miles north of Greenville, a vulnerable spot where the river turns a corner. Sometime around eight o'clock in the morning, 100 feet of levee was simply pushed out by the river, carrying scores of men with it. The Delta experienced a deluge of biblical proportions. It was the most epic natural disaster America had seen in the extent of the devastation, the duration of the event, and the impact on individuals, families, and communities. The Great Flood submerged almost 17 million acres to a depth of thirty feet in some places, destroyed or washed away hundreds of thousands of buildings, killed livestock in uncountable numbers, and made more than 600,000 people homeless.

When all was said and done, according to a report in *National Geographic*, "twenty-seven-thousand square miles were inundated . . . about equal to the combined size of Massachusetts, Connecticut, New Hampshire, and Vermont. By July 1, even as the flood began to recede, 1.5-million acres were under water. The river was seventy miles wide."

There are estimates the crevasse at Mounds Landing poured out so much water that in a space of ten days, it would cover 1 million acres of Delta to a depth of ten feet—and the river would continue to flow through that crevasse for months. No one knows how many human lives were lost because, tragically, most were Black and poor, and keeping records of missing or dead Black and poor people was no one's priority.

Those who could afford to exit the Delta on the first train they could catch had already done so, but for months following the Mounds Landing breach, the only dry land available to the vast majority of flooded sharecroppers was along the tops of the still-standing levees, the very earthworks that had been built to hold back the river. Two days after the breach, more than 10,000 refugees were crammed onto the eight-foot-wide crown of the levee in Greenville in a line that stretched for more than five miles. The desperate evacuees were crowded into tent cities—which became concentration camps—surrounded by the destroyed detritus of their lives and property: remnants of their homes, the dead and bloated carcasses of their livestock, and those too slow to get out of the water's raging path. It was rainy and cold, the water supply was contaminated, and everyone was at risk for typhoid and cholera. What followed in the subsequent months surely stands as one of the darkest chapters in this region's tortured history. To summarize it too briefly, the flood and its aftermath pitted humans against nature, humans against each other—including racial and sexual violence—and individual landowners against their honor and pride.

The planters understood that if they evacuated their field hands and sharecroppers to safety, they would flee the Delta. They knew that their economic prospects and their harvest depended on subjugated labor, lots of it, if they were to salvage their cotton empire. They also knew that their submerged crop was mostly lost for the season, a huge economic blow to the region. So they did what was, from their standpoint, economically rational: they employed their disproportionate political power to prevent their labor force from fleeing. They stranded them on the levees and prevented their evacuation.

By the time the waters receded in August 1927, forcing the relocation of hundreds of thousands of people, the composition of the Delta's labor force would never be the same. The flood accelerated the trickle of migration that had started in the early years of the twentieth century, and racial tensions, exacerbated by efforts to combat and recover from the flood, incentivized many more Blacks to quit the Delta and restart their lives elsewhere.

THE DECLINE OF EMPIRE

Empires rise and decline, and there are usually numerous reasons for both. The roaring demand for cotton could not have lasted forever without provoking alternative sources around the globe, and that's exactly what happened. The American Civil War—and the resulting cotton famine, called "the biggest commercial catastrophe in the world"— compelled merchants in Europe to push for the expansion of production in India, Egypt, and Brazil, and these producers soon became major players, reshaping the global empire of cotton. But that did not happen overnight, and the cotton producers of the Delta did not surrender their supremacy peacefully. The decline of cotton's hold on the region was driven by a couple of factors that are central to our story. Of these, the most important were the out-migration of the Delta's mostly Black workforce combined with labor-saving technology.

Between roughly 1915 and the beginning of the 1960s, an estimated 5 million people left the rural South for jobs and opportunities in the industrial North and western states. The demand for industrial workers to feed the World War I effort acted like a magnet drawing people into factories and off the plantations and farms of the Delta. The Great Depression (1929 through 1939) slowed somewhat the tide of people migrating out of Mississippi, but it resumed again with the onset of World War II as war industries ramped up production and the demand for labor—and accelerated in tempo again after 1941 when the United States declared war on Japan and Germany.

Yet another factor that drove Black workers out of their southern homes was the persistence of racial violence, particularly in the states of the former Confederacy. By one estimate, nearly 3,500 African Americans were lynched between 1882 and 1968, 539 in Mississippi alone. This fervor of extrajudicial executions was only the public face of a far larger and more pernicious regime of exclusion and oppression known as the era of Jim Crow, which expressed itself in numerous laws and statutes intended to institutionalize the supremacy of Whites. Whatever the purpose of Jim Crow laws, those Blacks who could move on did so. In 1910, Blacks comprised one of every three persons across the South, falling to one in five a century later. Add to this the allure of better-paying jobs in the industrial hubs to the north and east of the Delta—and a marginally less punitive political climate—and you have a prescription for mass migration from the sharecropper economy into the congested, densely populated, highly industrial, urban economies of Chicago, St. Louis, Detroit, and Kansas City.

A third factor was the introduction and widespread deployment of harvesting and processing machinery to drive down the cost of production. As early as 1944, the writing was on the wall when the International Harvester Company introduced a production-ready machine capable of eliminating the labor of fifty people. At a stroke, the cost of producing a bale of cotton plummeted from $39.41 (handpicked) to $5.26 (machine picked)—a savings of roughly 85 percent. As Ted Gioia explained in *Delta Blues*, "The sociological implications of this innovation would prove to be far more profound than any economic or agricultural impact" because it upended the incentives of the White-planter class who had, up to that point, used coercion and violence to prevent their labor force from migrating to higher-wage regions and jobs. Suddenly, these same producers had every incentive to drive their labor force out of their shacks and off the land so that they could plant even more cotton. Today, one of the most striking features of the Delta are the digitally straight furrows cut into the rich topsoil by GPS-guided plowing machines—lines so straight that a human could not make them. The same computer-controlled technology manages the harvest, and the outcome is that many fewer humans are needed for a task that once consumed thousands of lives and most of the calendar year.

A MELTING POT OF MUSICAL TRADITIONS

Throughout its history as the cotton engine of the world economy, the Delta was a mélange of different musical and cultural traditions. What we today call the blues emerged out of a cauldron of brutal oppression of Blacks by Whites and the influence of various genres and styles of music as they were available in and around the Delta's many plantations, lumber and turpentine camps, levee and railroad chain gangs, prisons, house parties, street corners, and juke joints. Few musicians of this era and place would have been exposed to just one or two styles. A lot of music in the Delta was handmade by ordinary people singing to distract themselves from the burden of their work and lives or as a way to share with others their sense of helplessness and hopefulness. Anywhere that slaves or sharecroppers or convicts were found working together, there arose rhythms and melodies derived from African roots that functioned to share the grief and hardship of their experience, to console each other in misery, and to bring hopefulness for better prospects.

Some took a liking to European classical music, even dancing minuets in high-culture European style. Tin Pan Alley—the name given to a collection of New York City songwriters and publishers who dominated popular music in the late nineteenth and early twentieth centuries—and its sounds and rhythms fused with local variations of country music, gospel, ragtime, minstrel, and whatever else was going around.

After the end of the American Civil War and before Reconstruction stalled, these vagabond musicians journeyed from town to plantation to railroad station to lumber camp to street corner to juke joint to house party, picking up new songs, styles, and ways of playing, with imitation being the highest form of flattery. These itinerants were called songsters, musicianers, or musical physicianers, and their repertoire consisted of ballads and story songs over simple chordal accompaniment. Some called them "jump-up songs," but they were not known, at this stage anyway, as "blues." That came later.

One can be persnickety and insist that only twelve-bar musical forms of the AAB variety are "blues" in the true sense, but the original songsters of the era would not have been so discriminating. Early bluesman Charley Patton recorded lots of songs in an AAB form, but we can legitimately regard his shorter eight-bar ballads with an AAB form as blues too.

The AAB form features two identical lines—typically over a twelve-bar progression—followed by a third different line. For example:

> A: My baby's ramblin' and her ramblin' brings me down,
> A: Lord, my baby's ramblin' and her ramblin' brings me down,
> B: Seems like I always get the blues when my baby's outta town

Everywhere music was played, this "blues" sensibility inflected itself into local sounds and styles just as it was in turn inflected by local sounds and styles. That's the nature of music: cross-pollination is the norm. And, like any art form, it lives and dies on audience reaction. What we today know as the "blues" would not have survived on those street corners, house parties, juke joints, and chain gangs if it didn't resonate within the souls, lived experience, and spirits of a lot of people.

OUT OF TREMENDOUS SUFFERING

What we call the blues emerged from the shared experience of slaves and sharecroppers across the cotton-producing regions of the Deep South as they sought forms of expression to make sense of the injustice of their situation—a situation forced on them and over which they were largely powerless.

When the first Blacks were brought from Africa, they were forbidden from engaging in their ritualistic dances and ceremonies. Even drumming was forbidden because slave owners suspected that the drummers could encode messages that Whites could not understand, perhaps planning rebellion. The slave owners, traders, and brokers regarded their property as subhuman and treated them appallingly, routinely breaking up families, separating mothers from children, and murdering noncompliant individuals. Torture and brutality were wide-spread. There was no conception of human rights because slaves were not considered human. The Old Testament scriptures that slavehold-ers employed to justify their oppression of Blacks became the basis of the faith that the Blacks picked up and made their own—though they drew different lessons from it—and so we see what becomes the blues emerge organically from the blending of work songs, prison songs, gos-pel, church music, and the ancient rhythms and vocalizations imported from Africa. Each one of these traditions drew on and influenced the others, morphing and evolving from region to region and era to era.

The issue of how the blues became known as the devil's music—the songs of immorality, eroticism, corruption, and low-life whisky-drinking n'er-do-wells in juke joints—arises from its association with the people who created it, from their experience of suffering and disempowerment generation after generation, and from the fact that the money spent on whisky and moonshine in juke joints on Saturday nights did not find its way into the collection plates of entrepreneurial preachers on Sunday morning. This put Saturday night house party musicians into direct

The blues have often been maligned as "the devil's music"
JOSEPHINE MATYAS

economic competition for the very limited resources of sharecroppers and their families. Preachers, then, however sincere their faith and desire to save the souls of their parishioners, had every reason to stigmatize those with whom they were in direct economic competition. So it ought not surprise us that many blues musicians moonlighted as preachers when gigs were scarce or when they had an attack of conscience: performance is, after all, performance, and only the venues change. The blues also turned out to be the perfect vehicle for oppressed people—pushed to the very margins of dignified life—to address the most profound philosophical questions that belabor every human being: to find hope and relief from the circumstances of their daily existence.

THE BLUES WERE BORN

It's easy to romanticize the roots of the blues and those early players or to assume that what we today call the blues means roughly the same thing to everyone. The songs we identify as traditional blues were the popular music of its time and place—and the label came along later as a marketing device or to distinguish specific artists from others. The melancholy song style was born sometime around 1900, but exactly when the term "blues" was coined is a date that is hotly contested. But the bedrock of the blues was in place long before the nomenclature stuck, from the field hollers and work songs to the hymns and ragtime melodies.

It's helpful to understand that the blues did not emerge from one place or region at one time. What we have come to call the blues emerged in many places over a long period of time, but we're going to concentrate on that portion of Mississippi that produced the great wealth of what came to be known as the "Delta blues" because it is what found its way to cities like Chicago and became justifiably famous. Had the Delta blues not migrated north, it could have died and never made it to the United Kingdom, where it found faithful players and ardent fans.

As the saying goes, Europe, meaning primarily England, threw a lifeline to the blues, saving an American form of music that was beginning to struggle. (There's much more on that interesting development in chapter 8.) The titans of the blues—Muddy Waters, Howlin' Wolf, Willie Dixon, Little Walter, Robert Johnson, and so on—may not have understood *themselves* to be inventors or innovators of a precious form of country, traditional, or folk music. Like most entertainers of their day and ours, they wanted commercial success, nice clothes, fast cars, lots of liquor, and beautiful women on their arms. More than anything, they wanted coin—as much as they could pocket—and that necessitated gigs and audiences, also known as bums in seats or bodies happily jiggling across a dance floor. 'Twas ever thus where live music is concerned.

Nor should we fall for the misapprehension that people like Robert Johnson were somehow emblematic of the blues—for the truth is that he was, in his lifetime, a comparatively minor character who made a few recordings (twenty-nine in all) and was not particularly outstanding among the people with whom he consorted during his short years. Many other artists were much better known in the Delta—and outside—in the late nineteenth and early twentieth centuries when what became known as the "blues" was the popular music of its day. But, decades later, players like Johnson loom larger than life.

As we proceed through this book, we'll meet many iconic blues musicians who transitioned seamlessly between the Saturday night juke joint "devil's music" and the Sunday morning sacred music of the southern church. In the human (perhaps all too human) pursuit of a living, many blues musicians and performers started in the church—that's where they learned their first music—and carried it into the juke joints, speakeasies, and private parties that dotted the Delta and populated the larger urban centers all the way north to Chicago. The blues—or what we have come to call the blues—was the music of this underclass of poor, hardworking, but desperately oppressed class of Blacks who migrated out of the Delta and brought with them their distinctive take on their experience and their place in the world.

3

THE UPPER MISSISSIPPI DELTA

The late Hugh Sidey, best known as a *Time* magazine journalist, wrote, "The Mississippi Delta is God's laboratory for this old republic. Its wealth and poverty, arrogance and humility, passion and reason, black and white in a raw mix found no other place in the nation. How it comes out there may foretell the future of this country." Tantalizing words to those with an appetite to learn, a respect for history, a road map, and a tank full of gas.

We may not have known it, but we were destined to make it to the Delta. Looking back now, that is obvious. This part of the continent, the nation, and the state is the ideal intersection of land, history, culture, and music. As a destination, it's the catnip of a lyrical journey.

Are there words for this? If it were larger, that blue sign—"Welcome to Mississippi, Birthplace of America's Music"—should be populated with footnotes. Writers have called it *The Most Southern Place on Earth* (a book by James Cobb) and suggested that its importance punches above its weight—"To understand the world, you must first understand a place like Mississippi" (asserted Nobel Prize–winning novelist William Faulkner).

As we traveled across Mississippi, our immediate challenge was holding our minds in two places simultaneously: one that no longer exists and one that exists in the here and now. Mississippi's past casts a long shadow over its present. The decline of King Cotton devastated the economic life of the

Delta, yet Mississippi persists in the people and values as well as the norms and manners just below the surface. History weighs heavily here.

One-on-one, Mississippians are so darn pleasant to spend time with. But in many spots around them, the economy has largely moved on, leaving communities that once throbbed with vigorous commerce in the detritus of a long-gone age. Yet in other spots, a revitalized marketplace is breathing new life and energy into downtown main streets, shops, and neighborhoods.

This land, so beautiful and complex, spawned an art form that was both beloved and reviled. "For large portions of the community, the blues was still the devil's music," wrote unabashed fan and British Broadcasting Corporation journalist Giles Oakley, "the music of immorality, licentiousness, eroticism, whisky-drinking, juke-joints, low life, violence, a source of corruption, the harbinger of social disruption."

We began—as many visitors in search of the blues do—in the upper part of the Delta. On our maps, we drew an imaginary line east to west just below Cleveland, so this upper part included the communities northward. A crash course about land and water, people and struggles, and food and drink goes a long way toward understanding and appreciating this more northerly part of the Delta. This is the mythical home of Robert Johnson's Crossroads, King Biscuit Time, and the plantations where blues greats like Charley Patton and Muddy Waters honed their chops. It's where we found Dockery Farms, an 1895 cotton plantation and the singular spot that B. B. King declared as the true "home of the blues."

The sections below on the land, water, and people touch on the main points to appreciate when understanding how the blues began, flourished, and spread. Chapter 2 provides a closer look into the geography and the history of the Delta. It's the spot to turn to for a much more detailed examination.

LAND AND WATER

What Is the Delta?

The Mississippi Delta is a wide, flat floodplain in the northwest corner of the state, several hundred miles north from where the river spills into the Gulf of Mexico.

For thousands of years, the Mississippi went where it wanted, regularly overflowing its banks and depositing what some have called the thickest, most fertile topsoil in the world. It was both a blessing and a curse to the people and the economy of the Delta.

The Land Was Carved into Plantations

In the 1700s, the crescent-shaped hinterland of the Delta was carved into great tracts that were cleared of forests and tilled to plant sugarcane, rice, indigo, and tobacco. When the plantation owners bought up this land, it was swampy and filled with deep-rooted cypress trees. Clearing, burning, tilling, planting, and harvesting was achieved through the grueling work of tens of thousands of slaves. Today, while driving across the Delta, it's hard to fathom the millions of man-hours that would have been needed to clear and prepare the land for the cultivation of cotton and other crops.

Seasonal Flooding

Regular flooding destroyed crops and communities but also renewed the soil. The power of the great river and the destructive nature of its flooding became a staple of blues lore. It came to define the culture of the Delta. And to survive it all, White and Black cultures collided, and out of it came songs telling the stories and struggles of ordinary people.

THE PEOPLE AND THE STRUGGLES

The Mississippi Delta Cotton Kingdom

This part of the South was known as the Mississippi Delta Cotton Kingdom. It was a strictly segregated society, made up largely of Black field hands working the region's massive plantations. Slaves were human chattel, a self-renewing resource that could—with the application of sufficient violence—be worked continuously or at least prevented from rebelling or disappearing into the night.

The Black Codes

Immediately after the American Civil War, Mississippi enacted the Black Codes, a set of laws to legislate a segregated society in which Blacks were denied the full spectrum of political and civil rights afforded to

Whites. The goal was to restrict the movement and rights of Black Missis-sippians, ensuring their availability as a cheap source of agricultural labor.

Among the Black Codes were "vagrancy laws" targeting African Amer-icans and poor Whites by routinely picking up those not contractually attached to plantations and sending them to prisons where they provided a free workforce for the state. The laws sought to transform freed slaves into agricultural workers or else face prison.

The Rise of Sharecropping

By 1867, a political deadlock spawned an arrangement known as sharecropping: former slaves and their families worked specific plots of land with an advance through the landowner's company store for seeds and equipment and received a share of the crop at harvest.

By 1900, more than three-quarters of freedmen in the Delta were sharecropping. But if prices dropped, weather was bad, or the harvest was poor, many sharecroppers ended the season deeper in debt to the landowner.

People Voted with Their Feet

Sharecroppers—both Black and White—who found themselves sink-ing deeper and deeper into debt, year after year, simply packed up and hit the road.

Another factor that drove Black workers out of their southern homes was the persistence of racial violence. By one estimate, between 1882 and 1968, more than 500 African American persons were lynched in Mississippi alone.

Industry in the north needed workers to feed the military production demands of World War I and World War II, becoming a magnet drawing people into factories and off the plantations and farms.

The Impact of Technology

In the late 1700s, harvest time would have seen thousands of pickers lining rows, hunched over, dragging long white cotton sacks and work-ing from sunup to sundown. The catchphrase used was "can to can't"—a description of the length of the workday in the fields.

All that changed with the mass introduction of technology. According to the National Cotton Council of America, hand labor is no longer used in the United States to harvest cotton.

In modern-day Mississippi, GPS-equipped planters capable of working two dozen rows at a time and equally enormous cotton-picking machines harvest the fibrous white cotton bolls. Many fewer humans are needed for a task that once consumed entire lives and most of the calendar year.

ROAD-TRIPPING THE UPPER DELTA

At the dawn of the twentieth century, the musicians of the Mississippi Delta enjoyed small followings but were largely unknown outside the region. The music of players like Booker "Bukka" White, Charley Patton, and Willie Brown succinctly captured the labor, love, and frustrations of poor sharecropping families trying to exist in hardscrabble conditions.

The flat plantations and the front porches of the tenant cabins across the upper Delta were home to players like Muddy Waters, Robert Johnson, Howlin' Wolf, and Eddie "Son" House. They grew up as the children of slaves and sharecroppers, immersed in the wild music of Saturday night and the redemptive songs of gospel the next morning.

Many of the pioneer blues musicians and singers came from an era when they picked cotton and plowed behind a mule. Spirituals and gospel were nurtured in churches across the state, and the blues were built on the songs of fieldworkers plucking cotton and building levees to hold back the floodwaters of the river. Call-and-response, field hollers, front porch jams, juke joints, and frolicking houses became the birthplaces of what would become the blues.

Now and again as we drove, we asked ourselves, Why are we doing this? We debated it, pondered the question, developed theories (some quickly discarded), and in the end decided it was driven by that intersection of music and writing in our own lives, coupled to our off-the-leash curiosity. We wanted to meander from one small Mississippi town to the next, to see for ourselves what lies outside the major blues mecca of Clarksdale. We needed to know more about the blues, to drill deeper than the cockamamie yarn of Robert Johnson's pact with the devil sealed at midnight on a country road.

There was a danger in gazing through the van window as we whizzed by countless tumbledown structures, rows of empty storefronts, and dilapidated houses. These *are* hard times across the Delta; there is no denying that fact. We stopped, got out, scratched the surface, and discovered it's the people, not just the abandoned buildings, who carry the flame for a rich albeit battered culture. You come to the Delta for what it is now and how it has been shaped by history, and you also come for what it used to be. To push down the door locks, roll up the windows, and zoom along would be to turn away from a soulful music history and some of America's deepest, most powerful cultural contributions.

"Much of what is profoundly American, what people love about America," observes the National Park Service, "has come from the Delta, which is often called the cradle of American culture."

"The Mississippi Delta begins," wrote native son and author David Cohn, "in the lobby of the Peabody Hotel in Memphis and ends on Catfish Row in Vicksburg." It's a perfect descriptor that captures not just the geography of the river but also the history, politics, and culture of the area anointed by that meandering flow of water. To non-Mississippians, it can be confusing: no, this Delta is *not* the mouth of the majestic, muddy river where it empties into the Gulf of Mexico. The Mississippi Delta sits in the northwest corner of the state—a good 200 miles from the Gulf. It's the wide floodplain between the Yazoo River on the east and the Mississippi River on the west.

On one of our trips, we entered from the north after exploring Memphis (look for details on the blues in Memphis in chapter 6), zigzagging back and forth from one blues-rich site to another. Most travelers associate the city of Clarksdale with the blues—home to the Crossroads landmark, how could you not?—but there are many other blues sites scattered all across the upper Delta. Some are marked by the distinctive plaques of the Mississippi Blues Trail, a museum without walls (msbluestrail.org), while others are not yet part of the official trail. It would be nearly impossible to stop at them all; we were aiming for a primer, the highlights from which we could get a sense of what forces impacted, shaped, and forged this most American of music styles.

Our first stops were along the rural side roads and small communities surrounding Robinsonville and Tunica in the upper corner of the Delta and a short drive south from Memphis. From there, we detoured away from Mississippi and crossed the river to explore Helena on the Arkansas side, a town that was the dynamic center of live blues and radio in the

1930s and 1940s. We drove back over the river and on to Clarksdale, often an epicenter for blues pilgrims, then south toward Cleveland with stops at Tutwiler, Parchman, Merigold, and Dockery Farms.

TUNICA

Before the gaming industry came to town in 1992, Tunica and neighboring Robinsonville were surrounded by Delta plantations of black alluvial soil stretching out to the horizon, cotton fields, and broken-down sharecropping shacks. For years, Tunica County was the most poverty-stricken region in the nation's poorest state. Then came the gaming industry, and garish casinos sprouted up along the riverbanks. Casinos in Mississippi must be on riverboats in the water (with the exception of the Gulf Coast), which explains the waterside clustering in Tunica County. Whatever you think of casinos and gaming with their free drinks and cheap buffets, the blackjack tables and one-armed bandits brought jobs and opportunities outside the plantation economy. It's been a careful-what-you-wish-for scenario—more places to make money, more places to lose it.

There are two main routes to explore this corner of the state: the new, divided roadway along Highway 61 and the Old Highway 61 just a stone's throw to the west. The older blacktop—widely revered as the "original blues highway"—overlaps the newer highway, as some stretches were lost in the construction. The older stretch plays like an unhurried blues riff, richer in musical lore and deeply authentic, hopscotching through historic communities like Robinsonville, Hollywood, Clack, and Maud. (tunicatravel.com/blues)

Son House Mississippi Blues Trail Marker

Just south of the county line, along Old Highway 61, we drove on past seemingly endless tilled fields, the landscape smooth as an ironing board. A Mississippi Blues Trail marker recognizes the home community of Eddie "Son" House, an early blues master who led a life of startling contradictions, with one foot solidly planted in gospel and the other in a lifestyle of excess. He was known for his strong performance style and his passion for the church—a sometime preacher who also did time at the notorious state prison at Parchman Farm. He was as powerful a preacher as he was a blues performer—performance is performance, and only the venues change. Recorded in the early 1940s by Alan Lomax for the Library of Congress/Fisk University archives, House's musical career fell into a lull until he was discovered by a new audience during the 1960s folk-blues revival. His charismatic performance style, singing, and emotive expressions were a strong influence on both Robert Johnson and Muddy Waters.

Gateway to the Blues Museum

Whether you know nothing about the blues or live and breathe the music, it's worth a stop at the outstanding Gateway to the Blues Museum, under the same roof as the Tunica Visitor Center.

The two have found a home in an old wooden train station, relocated from nearby Maud. The moving experts sliced off the roof, hoisted the historic building onto a contraption of steel beams and dollies, and shuttled it up the road to its current location along Highway 61 just north of Tunica. Local and state coffers invested several million dollars—helped

A renovated wooden train station houses the Tunica Visitor Center and Gateway to the Blues Museum
JOSEPHINE MATYAS

along the way by a 100-year loan of priceless instruments and memorabilia from a local casino—and created a multimedia, archive-rich, and information-packed introduction to the Mississippi music experience. Efforts were made to save as much of the structure as possible, right down to the original *No Smoking* signs hand painted onto the wooden walls. Using an old train station has special meaning, as the blues extended out from the Mississippi Delta from a depot just like this one. The railroad was omnipresent. By 1906, 90 percent of cultivated Delta acreage was within five miles of railroad tracks.

From start to finish, this museum is a wide-ranging exhibit on the development of the blues in the Delta. In addition to video, audio clips, shadow boxes, and links to the official Mississippi Blues Trail markers, more than 700 items are rotated through the galleries. Dozens of instruments (old and new, some signed by famous blues artists like Eric Clapton and B. B. King), sheet music, a vest worn by Jimi Hendrix, and even the simple wooden grave marker from the final resting place of Lizzie Douglas (aka "Memphis Minnie") are samples of the impressive collection.

The first gallery answers the question, What Is the Blues? The music of hard times and hard living rose out of the tunes found in the Black spirituals, field hollers, call-and-response work chants, and prison songs that fused into what became the blues of the early twentieth century. It is filled with emotion and tells the stories and struggles of ordinary people.

The structure of a blues tune is laid out in a way that even music newbies can understand: from the fingerpicking style favored by bluesmen (chords with the left hand, melody with the right) to the AAB lyric structure, where a first line is sung, repeated, and then followed by a final line that resolves the issue or answers the question. There's a step-by-step display of uniquely blues sounds created on a slide guitar with a piece of bottleneck, pocket knife, or round of pipe.

The second gallery—Why Here?—explains the unique geography of the Delta. For thousands of years, the Mississippi River (the fourth-longest river in the world) routinely flooded its riverbanks, creating expansive sedimentary bottomlands thick with layer after layer of fertile silt. The power of the river and the impact of its flooding became a staple of blues lore (listen to an old classic like Charley Patton's "High Water Everywhere"). The grind of daily plantation work spilled over into the music of front porch jams and juke joint Saturday nights where workers would socialize and blow off steam. Boat and dockworkers often sang, spreading popular music and sharing their songs up and down the river.

W. C. Handy's cornet is on display at the Gateway to the Blues Museum
JOSEPHINE MATYAS

The railways that moved the harvested cotton, tobacco, and indigo to market also carried traveling musicians seeking a wider world, spreading the seeds of the Delta blues to points beyond Mississippi.

At the center of the third gallery—Changing Times—is the cornet of William Christopher "W. C." Handy, the African American musician, composer, and bandleader who called himself the "Father of the Blues." In 1903, while sitting on a rail station platform in Tutwiler, Handy was caught up in the strange sounds of "a lean, loose-jointed Negro" playing slide guitar with a knife blade, singing a plaintive tune, and accompanying himself "with the weirdest music I ever heard."

Handy did not invent the blues, but he certainly knew how to capitalize on the business opportunity of writing and marketing sheet music. His mark of fame really arises from his composition and publishing of music. He founded Handy Brothers—a family-owned music publishing house still in operation today—and built a catalog of wildly popular music that became the foundation that drew heavily on the blues.

The gallery documents the spread of the blues through the transformative technologies of radio and recorded music in the 1920s, the electrification of the blues with the invention by Les Paul and Leo Fender of the electric guitar, and the Great Migration, which pushed the blues out of the Delta to the taverns and bars of the northern cities. In times of racial segregation, a collection of southern, eastern, and midwestern nightclubs along the Chitlin' Circuit featured African American singers, bands, and entertainers, including blues notables like Muddy Waters, Billie Holiday, John Lee Hooker, and B. B. King. The Chitlin' Circuit included performance venues where it was safe and acceptable for African American musicians and entertainers to perform during the era of racial segregation. The name comes from a popular soul food dish "chitterlings," which are stewed pig intestines.

The fourth gallery—the Mississippi Blues Trail—is a vibrant experience. It begins with a room of colorful paintings by Memphis artist George Hunt, immortalizing eight seminal blues artists: Son House, Jimmy Reed, Charley Patton, Robert Johnson, Muddy Waters, Howlin' Wolf, Sonny Boy Williamson II, and B. B. King. The large paintings are set against black walls depicting nighttime on a Delta plantation, complete

Key seminal blues artists are honored in colorful displays at the Gateway to the Blues Museum

JOSEPHINE MATYAS

The shiny National Style O Resonator guitar is one of many guitars on display at the Gateway to the Blues Museum
JOSEPHINE MATYAS

with twinkling stars and the chirping of crickets. Each artist is honored with a biography and archival treasures, including a circa-1930s National Duolian Acoustic guitar played by Charley Patton, Sonny Boy Williamson II's harmonicas, and a copy of Robert Johnson's death certificate.

This gallery of the blues founders flows into an extensive display of "guitar porn," as it is called in our house. If you want to understand the history, role, and evolution of the guitar, this is your corner. Glass display cases are filled with one guitar after another, including a shiny National Style O Resonator, a customized Gretsch G6138 "Cigar Box" signed by Bo Diddley, a Fender Eric Clapton Stratocaster autographed by "Slowhand" himself, and a cherry red Gibson ES-335 signed by Chuck Berry (who internalized blues, country, and rhythm and blues to help birth rock and roll).

The final gallery of the museum—Blues and Beyond—traces the folk music revival of the 1960s that rediscovered the sounds and styles of the Delta blues. Acclaimed folklorists, the father-and-son team of John and Alan Lomax, documented the blues of the Delta, and as fans dug into this archived material, they uncovered the music of the early bluesmen. These artists—players like Son House and "Mississippi" John Hurt— enjoyed a rebirth of interest in their music as White audiences turned on through the resurgence of folk music.

Across the Atlantic and at home, White rock and roll artists repackaged blues standards, breathing life into a struggling art form. During the British Invasion of the early 1960s, bands like the Rolling Stones channeled Muddy Waters and Howlin' Wolf, and the Yardbirds (eventually morphing into Led Zeppelin) drank heavily from the well that was the Delta blues. (There is much more detail about U.S.–U.K. blues history in chapter 8.)

The last display in the museum is a glass-enclosed recording booth where inspired visitors can belt out a blues tune and e-mail it home. On the way out, look up—the ceiling is festooned with a multicolored medley of suspended guitars.

The Hollywood Café

Just three stoplights south of the Gateway Museum and a jog west to Old Highway 61, we pulled into the wonderfully atmospheric Hollywood Café. The boxy, white building was once the commissary on the old Frank Harbert plantation and is now a Delta dining institution ("home of the fried dill pickle," its signature dish) with a menu heavy into barbecue, ribs, and catfish served with traditional sides like baked beans, hushpuppies, slaw, and cornbread. Mississippi author John Grisham was a regular at the café, making mention of it several times in his bestseller *A Time to Kill*.

This is the "newer" location of the Hollywood. In 1983, the original diner—also a plantation commissary building six miles down the road in the village of Hollywood—burned to the ground. A year later, the business reopened in the current digs at the intersection of Casino Strip Resort Boulevard and Old Highway 61.

At both locations, the Hollywood boasts a long and honorable music connection. Back in the day, the legendary Eddie Son House (one-time preacher turned blues singer and guitarist) lived on the nearby plantation and often gigged at the diner. Rumor has it that it was in the 1930s that he observed the dramatic change in Robert Johnson's skills as a guitarist, making the best known of all blues quotes, that Johnson must have "sold his soul to the devil." The back wall of the small, raised stage

The Hollywood Café has a long connection to Delta music
JOSEPHINE MATYAS

is decorated with black-and-white photos of bands and a quirky, home-made six-string guitar fashioned from a shiny aluminum bedpan.

In 1991, the diner was immortalized in the last verse of the song "Walking in Memphis" by singer-songwriter Marc Cohn. The lyrics narrate Cohn's spiritual pilgrimage through southern gospel music and his inspirational encounter at the Hollywood Café with retired Arkansas schoolteacher-pianist Muriel Davis Wilkins, with whom he performed "Amazing Grace." His song's noteworthy lyric "Tell me are you a Christian, child? and I said, 'Ma'am, I am tonight!'" was a hit on Billboard's charts in America and on charts in the United Kingdom, Ireland, Germany, and France and was later covered by a host of artists, including Cher, Lonestar, and Paul Anka. (thehollywoodcafe.com)

Abbay & Leatherman Plantation

We rolled down the windows for the short drive west along Casino Strip Resort Boulevard to the Abbay & Leatherman Plantation, significant as a boyhood home of myth-shrouded blues icon Robert Johnson.

The Abbay & Leatherman Plantation was where Robert Johnson spent his childhood
JOSEPHINE MATYAS

Abbay & Leatherman was established in 1832 when Richard Abbay purchased the flat tracts of land from the local Chickasaw Indian tribe, creating one of the oldest and largest plantations in the Delta. At peak production, more than 450 families lived on and worked the plantation, including young Robert Johnson, who made a home in a tenant shack in the 1920s with his mother and stepfather.

According to the Mississippi Blues Trail marker outside the still-operational plantation office, the young Johnson was "recalled only as a good harmonica player who had limited skills as a guitarist during his adolescent years here on the Abbay & Leatherman Plantation." He picked up some basic playing skills while living on the plantation and took his blues inspiration from neighboring Delta players like Son House, Charley Patton, and Willie Brown.

Those primitive playing skills all changed when Johnson moved away in the early 1930s, returning more than a year later with formidable prowess over the instrument, prompting Son House to famously kick around the idea about an alleged deal with the devil in return for guitar chops: "When Robert Johnson got through playing, all our mouths was open. He sold his soul to the devil to get to play like that."

HELENA, ARKANSAS

Delta Cultural Center

It's a short drive past fields of white cotton, up and over the Mississippi River, to the Arkansas town of Helena, where then-governor Bill Clinton (no slouch with a saxophone) helped establish a state museum dedicated to the history and heritage of the Arkansas Delta. The Delta Cultural Center houses two permanent exhibits key to the blues of the region—Delta Sounds and the King Biscuit Time Radio Studio. The river may separate the states, but from a musical perspective, it made sense to include the Arkansas side in our exploration of the music. (deltaculturalcenter.com)

During the steamboat era, Helena was a wild hot spot of sin—bootlegging, gambling, nightlife, and live music pulled deckhands from the docks and field hands from the nearby plantations, and the street corners and clubs were filled with hungry musicians who devoured the business. The streets were awash with rough saloons, juke joints, and houses of ill repute. At one time or another, bluesmen Robert Johnson, Sonny Boy Williamson II, Willie "Pinetop" Perkins, David "Honeyboy" Edwards, and Muddy Waters all found themselves gigging and living in and around Helena.

The Delta Sounds Gallery presents the music that grew from the field hollers of the late 1800s, the woeful expressions of the earliest blues that were born of the struggle to survive in settings of the day-to-day grind. As the songs evolved, they gave artistic voice to hopes for a better future, expressed political convictions (sometimes in layers of meaning that plantation overseers did not detect), and worked in highly personal ways to rid the listener of the "blues."

In the wake of the American Civil War, former African American slaves found some new freedoms in travel, work, and religion—in theory. However, come the turn of the twentieth century, oppressive Jim Crow laws ("separate but equal") rolled back the supposed political equality of the new Black citizenry, condemning them to inferior circumstances and opportunities. At the same time, wealthy Delta plantation owners faced a potential labor shortage and introduced an unjust system of sharecropping, tilted heavily in favor of the rich landowner. Some African Americans chose to chase new careers as musicians rather than the hard, manual labor in the fields, many moving away from the Delta and carrying the message of the blues.

The gallery follows threads of a historical time line, beginning with the early songs from the field, songs of independence, and finally spirituals and songs of hope. There's a long, white canvas sack, used when picking cotton (each adult could harvest 400 pounds of fiber from a "sunup to sundown" workday); an original autographed copy of W. C. Handy's sheet music for "St. Louis Blues"; and the satchel belonging to Sonny Boy Williamson II, including guitar strings, cowbells, harmonica, and an amplifying cone.

But it's in the second gallery, the King Biscuit Time Radio Studio, where the groundbreaking importance of Helena's blues scene is told. The town was home to King Biscuit Time, the longest-running blues radio show in the United States—"Monday to Friday since 1941. 17,000 shows and counting"—on the Radio KFFA broadcast responsible for blanketing live, local blues across the airwaves on both sides of the river. Sponsored by King Biscuit Flour, the weekday radio program was an instant sensation, launching the careers of several musicians, including harmonica player Sonny Boy Williamson II and guitarist Robert Lockwood, who became the Delta's first blues radio stars. Muddy Waters and B. B. King were devotees, breaking from work in the fields to listen to the King Biscuit hour. Dominating the center of the room is the radio booth for KFFA 1360, where, until his passing in 2018, legendary deejay "Sunshine" Sonny Payne broadcast just after noontime each weekday. Past shows are available online as podcasts.

Across the street, the long wall by the levee has been painted with a music-themed mural of local blues artists and a nod to King Biscuit Time.

An important part of Helena's claim to blues fame happens every October with the King Biscuit Blues Festival, billed as the largest blues festival in the South. Blues of all styles and from all regions of America are showcased on multiple stages of "Da Biscuit," drawing tens of thousands of hard-core fans from around the globe to the multiday event, which has run since 1986. The event goes well beyond music with a sanctioned barbecue contest, food booths, and arts and crafts vendors. (kingbiscuitfestival.com)

In Helena, Arkansas, the long wall by the levee has a music-themed mural of local blues artists
JOSEPHINE MATYAS

CLARKSDALE

Clarksdale gets good mileage from its claim as the Crossroads, where Robert Johnson allegedly sold his soul in a Faustian pact to master the guitar. It's a well-worn blues legend that not only is unlikely (unless you believe in that sort of hocus-pocus) but also causes serious scholars of the blues to roll their eyes in bemusement. The imaginative speculation does, however, make for effective marketing, hence its prominence in the lore of Clarksdale.

The towering Crossroads guitar sculpture is at the intersection of U.S. 49 and U.S. 61, right across the street from Abe's Bar-B-Q, an atmospheric diner where the Formica booths are often filled with locals. The promise of "swine dining" on the sign outside seduced us: pork sandwiches, ribs, ham plates, hot tamales, and all the sides to go with genuine pit barbecue, including Abe's signature comeback sauce. The third-generation, family-run restaurant opened in 1924 and can probably count bluesman Robert Johnson as an early customer. (abesbbq.com)

The Crossroads guitar sculpture is at the intersection of US 49 and US 61 in Clarksdale
JOSEPHINE MATYAS

Deal with the devil or not, Clarksdale has more than enough solid blues cred to make it a major stop on any music pilgrimage, just as it was for the earliest bluesmen and blueswomen who either came from or passed through this musical hub.

"Historically, this was the golden buckle on the cotton belt, surrounded by all these cotton plantations that had all these workers," explained Roger Stolle, proprietor of Cat Head Delta Blues & Folk Art, a blues enthusiast who is a cofounder of the annual Juke Joint Festival and author of books on the Mississippi blues. "Now we'll never know where that first blues note was played or the first song that we call a blues song, but we know they were playing them here by 1900 because by 1902 we started having written accounts about them."

Founded in 1865—after the American Civil War—the Clarksdale region was frontier wilderness where cheap, fertile land was cleared for large-scale cotton production. With the plantations came a massive number of workers, warehouses, rail lines, barges, and steamboats up and down the Sunflower and Mississippi rivers, providing easy access to a ready market. With cotton, there was a crazy amount of money in town.

In 1920, the *Wall Street Journal* called Clarksdale "The Magic City" because of all its millionaires.

The early 1900s was Clarksdale's commercial high-water mark, but with an economy based on cotton, cotton, and cotton, there was no other manufacturing to provide stability and much-needed growth as twentieth-century automation slashed farm-based jobs. More and more low-wage workers abandoned agriculture and moved north, drawn by the promise of industrial opportunities in the big cities. As recently as the 1980s, large-scale, computer-operated farm tillers, planters, and harvesters slashed even deeper into the local job market. The result is a struggling downtown marked by some vacant storefronts, but there are many local musicians and business owners committed to preserving blues culture and traditions. The past few years have seen a revival of sorts under way with more upscale eateries, entertainment, and lodging. (visitclarksdale.com)

Downtown Clarksdale Walking Tour

And what a downtown it is! Walkable, history-drenched, peppered with official Mississippi Blues Trail markers, beautiful architecture (sadly, too much of it still boarded up), and a growing number of shops, music venues, and restaurants often run by blues devotees marinating in the authentic vibe.

"We want to help keep businesses alive here," explained mover and shaker Bubba O'Keefe, who represents the tourism bureau and is cofounder of the popular Juke Joint Festival and the local developer behind Yazoo Pass, one of the city's more hip bistros offering home-baked goods, a creative menu, and a captivating sound track. (yazoopass.com)

Others are relatively new arrivals, like harmonica expert and shop owner Deak Harp—"Chicago blues meets Mississippi Hill Country"—who has built custom harps for blues heavy hitters like James "Superharp" Cotton and Charlie Musselwhite. At one time, Harp lived the road life, touring with Cotton, but when they crossed through Clarksdale, he jumped off the bus. "This is the melting pot. This is where all those cats worked," he explained. "The blues were developed here." (deakharp.com)

In many Mississippi towns, one doesn't need to make an extra effort to meet people. Southern hospitality is all over creation. In Clarksdale, locals must see more than their share of awestruck blues tourists, but that doesn't stop them from helping with directions or kicking off a conversation.

Deak Harp lived the touring road life, but when he got to Clarksdale he jumped off the bus and set up a harmonica specialty shop
JOSEPHINE MATYAS

We ended up leaning on the hood of our camper jawboning with Josh "Razorblade" Stewart, a local legend who passed away after our visit but had lived a lifetime of the blues. In an interview with *Living Blues* magazine, the septuagenarian recalled the cotton plantation era of his youth. "I started chopping and picking cotton, age of six. We worked five, six days a week, ten hours a day in the hot sun, as long as it didn't rain. We had to pick 200 pounds of cotton. If I didn't pick 200 pounds, I'd get a whooping. Mama, sho'd pull the cotton stalk up with all the cotton bolls on it and go to whooping me. So I'd come up with 200 pounds. They'd be out there picking cotton, and I'd put six sacks on top of the mules, balance them, and get them to the trailer where they could weigh them."

Clarksdale born and raised, Razorblade's nickname came from his sharp style of dress. "I had a band called the Deep Cuts," he told us. "We had a Razorblade, Switchblade, Pocketknife, Butcher Knife, Nail File, and a Butter Knife. They had to be sharp to play with me."

A half hour later, we left with one of his homemade CDs.

The next day, we crossed paths with Razorblade again, this time in performance mode. He was dressed to the nines in a classic pinstripe suit and tie, onstage at the downtown Bluesberry Café, a family-run diner known for its weekend blues breakfasts, visits by music celebrities, and the honor of being the only local club to be inducted into the San Diego–based Blues Hall of Fame.

We had multiple experiences of southern graciousness and hospitality, just one of them with Razorblade. In the thirty seconds it took Jo to return to the camper van to retrieve her camera, Craig was called onstage and handed a bass guitar. Razorblade needed a groove, and it didn't matter that the only bassist available was a cracker from Canada. As long as he could "lay it down," it was all good. Craig grooved for the next half hour with the Sunday morning pickup band.

In Clarksdale, the rail tracks separated White and Black business districts. The iron line bisects the community, reproducing the trope about the "right side" and the "wrong side" of the tracks. Just over the south side of the Yazoo and Mississippi Valley Railroad tracks, there's a Mississippi Blues Trail marker to identify the New World neighborhood, "a breeding ground for ragtime, blues, and jazz music in Clarksdale's early days as a prosperous and adventurous new cotton town, when brothels here attracted both White and Black clientele." In its glory days, storefronts were full, sidewalks were jammed, and on Saturday night, plantation workers poured into town until curfew, after which revelers packed up the party and moved the carousing back to the plantations.

According to Roger Stolle, "The New World was the African American business district. On a Saturday afternoon, if you were in a hurry over there, you couldn't walk on the sidewalks, it was just packed, you couldn't move, you'd have to walk on the street. Now you could fire a cannon and not hit a soul over there. That's just how massive it was in terms of all the workers."

One New World business that has survived the falloff in foot traffic is Messengers, the oldest, continuously running business in Clarksdale, a combination pool hall, domino den, juke joint, and café, operated by the same African American family since 1907.

A short stroll down Sunflower Avenue, there is a blues marker at the historic Riverside Hotel, a tired-looking, red brick building that was home through the 1940s to traveling musicians like John Lee Hooker, Ike Turner, and Robert Nighthawk. Before becoming a hotel, the building was the G. T. Thomas Hospital, the Clarksdale medical facility for

Blacks that was infamous as the place where sultry diva Bessie Smith died in 1937 following a highway accident. At the time, the "Empress of the Blues" had a sizable following and was one of the most highly paid African American performing artists. The story of her passing was misreported as the great singer being refused treatment at a Whites-only hospital, creating a controversy that has since been corrected.

Although it's no longer open for business, a Mississippi Blues Trail marker at Wade's Barber Shop recognizes the contribution to Clarksdale's blues scene of the late Wade Walton. Walton chose a career with a striped pole and scissors over his love as a blues performer. Or, rather, he often combined the two, performing for customers and tourists during the 1990s.

In the same neighborhood are markers acknowledging other Clarksdale musical luminaries: soul pioneer Sam Cooke ("You Send Me," "Twistin' the Night Away," "Another Saturday Night"), who lived there as an infant; the dedication of lifelong townie and formidable blues guitarist "Big" Jack Johnson; and the site of the W. C. Handy family home for the two years he was hired as orchestra leader for a brass band and came under the spell of the Delta's bluesy sounds. Local boy and rock and roll pioneer Ike Turner launched his career playing blues and boogie-woogie piano in the bars and joints of the city. Ike Turner and the Kings of Rhythm are often credited with the first rock and roll song, "Rocket 88," recorded at Memphis Recording Service in 1951 (later renamed Sun Studio).

The Mississippi Blues Trail plaque at 257 Delta Avenue marks the radio studio of WROX, known for its historic blues and gospel broadcasts by African American deejays, including Early Wright and Ike Turner with his "Jive Till Five" show. Ike Turner, the King Biscuit Entertainers, Robert Nighthawk, and others performed live from the studio at this location.

Delta Blues Museum

The historic Clarksdale freight depot, built in 1918 for the Yazoo and Mississippi Valley Railroad, has been repurposed as home to the state's oldest music museum and the world's first museum dedicated to the blues. The mission of the museum is to tell the story of the Delta blues through the voices of the artists. There is also an arts and education program to teach children to sing and play the blues.

The long, narrow space is divided into three sections: a history gallery of photos, posters, stage wear, instruments, and memorabilia tracing the heyday of the blues in the Delta and the key players who traveled through the region, leaving their imprint on the music and the communities; a large, bright space dedicated to the man everyone knew as Muddy Waters, one of the world's most magnetic, best-loved, and most influential bluesmen; and a rich trove of books, music, and takeaway souvenirs in the gift shop.

The displays describe the Delta as isolated from the social and artistic trends happening across the rest of America. As a result, Blacks in the Delta developed their own styles of music, largely free of outside influences, often drawing on their own internal music traditions. This gave rise to a constantly evolving style of blues, deeply ingrained in the earliest experiences of Africans, transported as slaves to the land of the Cotton Kingdom.

The history gallery's glass cases are filled with clues to the lives and music of some of the Delta's earliest bluesmen and blueswomen, with

The Delta Blues Museum display illustrates the recording equipment carried around by Alan Lomax
DELTA BLUES MUSEUM

An old juke box is one of the many displays at the
Delta Blues Museum
DELTA BLUES MUSEUM

many original and sometimes rare artifacts. There's a pair of shiny black
shoes belonging to blues singer Bobby Rush, a Patriot electric guitar
played by local guitar sensation "Big" Jack Johnson, copies of two of the
three known photos of Robert Johnson, the microphone used by WROX
rhythm and blues deejay Early Wright on his show *The Soul Man*, guitars
belonging to John Lee Hooker, an original vinyl record of Charley Patton's "Pony Blues," the barbershop chair from Wade's Barber Shop, and
the enormous tin sign from Three Forks, the Mississippi juke joint where
Robert Johnson allegedly drank poison in August 1938.

There are exhibits dedicated to the fertile land formed by the regular
flooding of the river and the attempts to control the water. Other displays
illuminate the lives of pivotal bluesmen like Robert Johnson and Charley Patton. In Johnson's case, his fame has only grown after his death,
especially with the reissue of his Columbia Records tracks that caught
the attention of musicians like Bob Dylan, the Rolling Stones, and Eric
Clapton, who raised Johnson to godlike status. His modern-day appeal
may sit in his passionate delivery of dark themes in songs like "Me and

the Devil" and "Hellhound on My Trail." Charley Patton was a celebrity in his own time with a colorful history that included eight marriages, lots of drink, and several stints in jail. Often a true showman in performance, Patton penned the classics "Pony Blues," "A Spoonful Blues," and "High Water Everywhere." His rhythmic playing and performance mojo influenced Son House, Muddy Waters, Howlin' Wolf, and Robert Johnson.

We were immediately drawn to the museum's centerpiece—the weathered cabin inside this museum that shows the humble beginnings of one of the greatest blues artists. In the large, sun-filled addition to the original freight depot sits the reconstruction of McKinley "Muddy Waters" Morganfield's childhood home relocated from the grounds of nearby Stovall Plantation.

Made from rough-hewn cypress logs, the one-room cabin served as slave quarters before the Emancipation and as a dwelling for Stovall cotton field laborers after the end of the American Civil War. Around 1918, Muddy moved with his grandmother to the plantation as a young child and lived in this cabin until he left the Delta for Chicago in the early 1940s.

Reconstruction of Muddy Waters's childhood cabin at Stovall Plantation is a highlight at the Delta Blues Museum

DELTA BLUES MUSEUM

The Muddywood Guitar was made from a few boards
salvaged from Muddy Waters's childhood home
DELTA BLUES MUSEUM

The cabin fell into a shambles until it was pummeled by a tornado in 1987. Just one day after the storm, Billy Gibbons of the Texas blues-rock trio ZZ Top visited the homesite on Oakhurst Stovall Road, picked up a few boards that had blown loose, and had a guitar made from the wood. The Muddywood Guitar is often out on loan to spread the message from its permanent home in the Delta Blues Museum: the instrument fashioned from those boards symbolizes rock and roll's indebtedness to the blues. (deltabluesmuseum.org)

Cat Head Delta Blues & Folk Art

Clarksdale's go-to shop for blues posters, music, books, folk art, and updates on blues events across the Delta is Cat Head. Proprietor Roger Stolle, a transplant from Dayton, Ohio, was briefly waylaid by a career in marketing before he came to his senses and followed his passion to the Delta. Stolle likes nothing better than to play the blues, research the blues, write about the blues, film the blues, promote the blues, and talk the blues. He is a man on a mission, and that mission is preserving the Delta blues. Stolle is also a cofounder of the wildly popular Juke Joint Festival held every April in downtown Clarksdale.

"The blues is the truth, the basis of everything in life, so everyone can relate to it," explained Stolle as he tweaked the volume of the ever-present blues sound track in the store. "It's also the foundation of almost all popular music—certainly American popular music—so everyone's been touched by it whether they know it or not.

"The blues will never go away, that's an absolute fact. It just permeates everything, whether you realize it or not, recognize it or not. But what *is* going away and *will* go away are the culturally connected guys who actually were there and lived to tell about it. That's what the door is closing on. It's generational, but we're really reaching the last generations that actually grew up in the exact same environment as Charley Patton, Robert Johnson, Muddy Waters. Right now you can still catch guys that grew up in juke houses and juke joints, brew house parties, and worked on cot-

Cat Head Delta Blues & Folk Art is Clarksdale's go-to shop for all thing blues plus info on events
JOSEPHINE MATYAS

Cat Head proprietor Roger Stolle was drawn to Clarksdale by his love of the blues
JOSEPHINE MATYAS

ton plantations. The guys of that era, they are going away. The message of Mississippi today is you have to come *now* to experience it. You'll see it firsthand instead of reading about it." (cathead.biz)

Red's Lounge

One of the last-standing, truly original Clarksdale juke joints, Red's Lounge is *the* institution locals steered us to for authentic blues. With a haphazard interior that looks like it was halted mid-construction (bales of pink ceiling insulation sag into plastic vapor barrier, lights and cooling fans are more shabby decoration than function), what Red's doesn't deliver in chic and polish it makes up for in the genuine article. If you're looking to eat, the cardboard boxes of pork rinds stacked in the corner provide clues to the menu. Proprietor Red Paden rings up snacks and cheap beer at a vintage cash register that is basically a drawer attached to a machine missing all the crucial parts, like the number keys. The word "firetrap" gets whispered around—and thank god there is no smoking allowed—but the music is great, and the ambience is like nothing back home. Red is also the engine behind the fairly new Red's Old-Timers

Red's Lounge is one of the last-standing, truly original Clarksdale juke joints
JOSEPHINE MATYAS

Blues Festival, featuring Mississippi/southern blues acts by performers sixty years old and up.

On the sidewalk in front of Red's, a Mississippi Blues Trail marker pays homage to "Big" Jack Johnson, the late, great, monster guitarist and song master who was dedicated to keeping the Delta blues tradition alive in his community. When not touring, Red's was Johnson's home base.

Ground Zero Blues Club

Although it may not have original juke joint shtick on its side, Ground Zero (opened in 2001) replicates the Delta blues experience on a larger scale in an unbeatable location right beside the railroad tracks in downtown Clarksdale and a stone's throw from the Delta Blues Museum. The blues venue has captured a lot of media attention because of its commitment to the live music experience as well as the big-name power of its owners, among them Academy Award–winning actor and Delta resident Morgan Freeman and Clarksdale mayor Bill Luckett.

The popular Ground Zero Blues Club in Clarksdale is known for great music
JOSEPHINE MATYAS

It seems that every fan of the blues who makes the pilgrimage to Clarksdale stops for an evening at Ground Zero. The club has boosted the local music scene with live bands Wednesday through Saturday. The massive brick building creates a big footprint to match—a large sound system, an amazing collection of graffiti-scribbled walls inside and out, authentic decor of shabby couches lined up along the front porch, and a flow of good tunes. (groundzerobluesclub.com)

Hambone Art & Music

Located right in the historic downtown, the popular Hambone venue is open daily and showcases local and touring musicians who play blues, roots, Americana, folk, and jazz. (stanstreet.com)

Stovall Plantation

A short drive from downtown Clarksdale, the Stovall Mississippi Blues Trail marker sits in the middle of nothing—just a gentle rise of grass

Stovall Plantation was the site of a one-room log cabin, home for almost three decades to Muddy Waters
JOSEPHINE MATYAS

lined by trees beyond which there are more acres of cotton. At the edge of the ditch were a few stray cotton plants, looking like they made a break for it to escape the razor-straight furrows. These days, there is no building at the marker spot, but through most of the 1900s, this was the site of a one-room log cabin, home for almost three decades to McKinley Morganfield, the blues great nicknamed Muddy Waters by his grandmother, who watched him gravitate toward mud-filled puddles as a child.

Born in the community of Rolling Fork in the southern part of the Delta, Muddy was one of ten children. His parents separated when he was an infant, and as a toddler, he moved to Stovall Plantation with his grandmother. As a youngster, he taught himself to play the harmonica and as a teenager picked up his first guitar, a Stella ordered by mail from Sears, Roebuck and Company. He sang in juke joints on Saturday nights and church choirs on Sunday mornings, feeling the pull of both. The influence of the church was strong, as were his not-so-clean living idols, blues masters like Charley Patton and Son House.

"Back then there was just three things I wanted to be," he is quoted in Robert Palmer's history of the Delta, *Deep Blues*, "a heck of a preacher, a heck of a ball player, or a heck of a musician. I *always* felt like I could beat plowin' mules, choppin' cotton, and drawin' water."

But before music money found his pockets, Muddy—the man B. B. King dubbed "Godfather of the Blues"—sold moonshine and share-cropped on the large Stovall Plantation, picking cotton and driving tractors. In the ramshackle cabin once on this spot, Muddy Waters was first captured on primitive equipment by Alan Lomax for his 1941 Library of Congress field recordings. Two years later, Muddy left the Delta to pioneer a popular, electrified style of blues in Chicago and was recorded by the Chess Records label. He'd spent close to the first half of his life being shaped by rural Mississippi and the last half in the big cities of the North, creating blues classics like "I Just Want to Make Love to You" and "Rollin' Stone," which later was taken up as the name of one of history's greatest blues-saturated rock and roll bands.

In 1987, a tornado demolished the family cabin. The remains are on loan from Stovall Plantation to the Delta Blues Museum in Clarksdale, where it has been partially rebuilt to show the great singer's humble beginnings.

There's a shrine-like magnetism that tugs blues fans to the flat-as-a-tabletop fields along Oakhurst Stovall Road. This is a spot where musical history was made. As Muddy once said in plain words, "That's my religion—the blues is my religion."

Juke Joint Festival

Every April, Clarksdale celebrates the family-friendly Juke Joint Festival—half music festival, half small-town fair, and "all about the Delta." The festival features racing pigs, artisan crafts, and authentic blues in every club, on storefronts, and on almost every downtown street corner. It's a golden opportunity to hear and see some of the last original bluesmen who are still remaining on the stage. Festival co-organizer Roger Stolle enthused, "If this event doesn't make you smile, then your lips must be broken. Blues music, juke joints, monkeys riding dogs. I mean, what else do you need to know? It's absolutely ridiculous in the best of ways!" Thousands of visitors agree. They come from dozens of foreign countries and at least forty-seven U.S. states. (jukejointfestival.com)

Racing pigs and live blues are part of the Juke Joint Festival in Clarksdale
JOSEPHINE MATYAS

Every instrument imaginable is being played at the Clarksdale Juke Joint Festival
JOSEPHINE MATYAS

Blues players come from far and wide to play the street corners of the popular Juke Joint Festival

Homemade suitcase guitar and suitcase amplifier show up on the streetcorners in Clarksdale
JOSEPHINE MATYAS

Deep Blues Festival

More music has come to Clarksdale: the Deep Blues Festival has been held at two local venues—the Juke Joint Chapel at the Shack Up Inn (four miles outside town) and the New Roxy, a former cinema in the heart of downtown's historic district that has found new purpose as a vibrant art, music, and theater venue. (deepbluesfest.com)

Sunflower River and Blues & Gospel Festival

Organized in 1988 by *Living Blues* magazine cofounder Jim O'Neal and Dr. Patricia Johnson, the long-running festival has been honored as one of America's Top 10 Places to hear authentic music. The festival is recognized with its own Mississippi Blues Trail marker. (sunflowerfest.org)

TUTWILER

As the calendar flipped into the early 1900s, Alabama-born musician W. C. Handy found himself in Clarksdale as the leader of a popular

Black dance orchestra, the Knights of Pythias. The band was steeped in the music of Handy's classical training—ragtime, light classical, music from written scores—but a serendipitous nighttime encounter on a train platform in neighboring Tutwiler was the stuff that changed the course of musical history.

According to Handy's telling, he was waiting on the platform bench when he was taken aback by "the weirdest music I had ever heard" as a "lean, loose-jointed Negro had commenced plunking a guitar beside me while I slept. . . . As he played he pressed a knife on the strings of a guitar in a manner popularized by Hawaiian guitarists who used steel bars. The effect was unforgettable. His song, too, struck me instantly. 'Goin' where the Southern cross' the Dog.' The singer repeated the line three times." The refrain referred to the intersection of two rail lines at nearby Moorhead, where the Yazoo Delta Railroad (nicknamed the Yellow Dog) and the Southern Railroad crossed at right angles. A decade later, Handy would recall the crossing in his own blues composition, "The Yellow Dog Rag," later renamed "Yellow Dog Blues."

Handy knew business opportunity when he saw it. He took this primitive music and incorporated the style into his own compositions,

The mural in Tutwiler tells the story of W. C. Handy meeting an early blues musician
JOSEPHINE MATYAS

creating and publishing sheet music for songs that had previously been heard only on street corners, on front porches, and in rural juke joints. Through this shrewd business move, Handy popularized the blues, helped create a blues craze, and, along the way, assumed the handle "Father of the Blues."

Tutwiler is also close to the birthplace of the late John Lee Hooker, who played a distinctive electric guitar–style adaptation of the Delta blues after he migrated north to Detroit. Two of Hooker's songs, "Boogie Chillun" and "Boom Boom," made the Rock & Roll Hall of Fame's original list of the 500 Songs That Shaped Rock and Roll.

The rail depot is long gone, and Tutwiler is now a small scattering of shops and homes, several boarded up with weathered sheets of plywood. Adjacent to the abandoned rail line, there is a long mural with panels showing the region's cotton history, its abundant fishing, the presence of a steam engine, and two men sitting on the station bench. One man in a suit sits with his hat in his lap. The other, in ragged clothes, is playing a guitar across his lap. It was, in fact, a happy accident that helped launch the blues from its rural roots and onto the stages and into dance clubs in cities across the South.

PARCHMAN FARM

On the smooth gray tarmac of Highway 49 West, we passed the front gates of the infamous Parchman Mississippi State Penitentiary, where there's a Mississippi Blues Trail marker across from the road, although prison officials aren't keen about gawkers hanging around.

It's not intuitive to think about music and prisons, but Parchman played an important role in the Delta blues because it acted as a hothouse where the music was reproduced and transmitted across generations. Spread over 16,000 acres of prime cotton-growing land, inmate laborers broke the monotony and the wearisome grind of the fieldwork with songs, hollers, and spirituals—women more gospel, men more blues.

In the fields and in the cells, the prison experience produced an abundance of music. As men and women cycled through Parchman, they shared life stories and experiences—as they do in any culture—and a prison ethos developed, including work songs. With the constant churn of inmates through the prison, the blues culture was an ever-renewing force. For many years, there was a Parchman blues band, and several of the old-timers still perform at the annual Clarksdale Juke Joint Festival.

Parchman was an enormous work farm, and in many cases, its prisoners weren't necessarily guilty of anything other than being a vagrant who was locked up and made to work for nothing. Until mid-century, the for-profit cotton plantation generated dollars for the state that was second only to tax revenues. The walls of the state's oldest prison house hundreds of stories with musical ties. When Elvis Presley was three years old, his father, Vernon, was sent to Parchman for eight months for forging a four-dollar check. B. B. King's cousin, blues singer Bukka White, did time for assault, and celebrated guitarist Son House was locked away for allegedly murdering a man at a Saturday night frolic gone off the rails.

The concentration of African American prisoners created a highly enriched environment for the sharing and the cultivation of a culture, forever infusing blues music, lyrics, and themes. It was this incubator effect that drew the attention of father-and-son folklorists John and Alan Lomax when they made repeated visits in the 1930s to observe and record the wellspring of music inside the confines of the prison setting.

In *Jail House Bound: John Lomax's First Southern Prison Recordings*, the elder Lomax explained the draw of the notorious prison: "My son and I conceived the idea this summer that the best way to get real Negro singing in the Negro idiom and the music also in Negro idiom was to find the Negro who had had the least contact with the whites. And so we loaded up a recording instrument in our Ford car and visited remote lumber camps; great cotton plantations where the Negroes were in proportion to the whites in twenty-five or 100 to one; and certain prison camps in four of the southern states. We were right in our theory I think because—especially in the prison camps—we found the Negroes completely isolated from the whites."

The Lomaxes were able to capture the tuneful riches of inmates like Bukka White, whose powerful chops were so admired that guards and inmates pooled their money to buy him a guitar. Across the decades, the notorious Parchman Farm prison was at the heart of many blues laments by artists like Charley Patton, Mose Allison, Terry "Big T" Williams, and John Mayall & the Blues Breakers, some of whom had done time, others who used the setting in their songs.

MERIGOLD

It was on the wide, flat floodplains that lie on both sides of the famed Blues Highway 61 that planter barons from South Carolina and Georgia sought new territory in a westward migration fueled by the accelerating upward movement of cotton prices. According to commodity historian Sven Beckert, "So rapid was this move westward that by the end of the 1830s, Mississippi already produced more cotton than any other southern state."

To meet the growing demand, tens of thousands of enslaved Blacks were brought in to work the fields, in the process losing their freedom, their way of life, their families, and, in many cases, their lives. The rural juke joints were spots to socialize, dance, and forget everyday troubles, playing an integral part in the development of the blues. Since the early 1900s, with the depopulation of the Delta—as many workers moved away to escape racial strife and look for employment—the remnants of the plantation culture fell into disrepair, were bulldozed, or were boarded up.

One of the last standing and operating authentic juke joints in a cotton plantation setting was Po' Monkey's, two miles west of Highway 61 near Merigold. Po' Monkey's was open for live music weekly, but with

Although now closed, Po' Monkey's was one of the very few rural plantation juke joints to survive into this century

JOSEPHINE MATYAS

the passing of its longtime owner, Willie "Po' Monkey" Seaberry, the contents of the historic juke joint (including the infamous collection of pornographic toy monkeys) were sold at auction to settle the estate. Seaberry had kept the juke joint tradition alive from 1963 until his death in 2016. Open or shut, the atmospheric, one-room Po' Monkey's shack is worth a drive-by. As one of the very few rural plantation juke joints to survive into the twenty-first century, it's a must-see blast from the past for travelers seeking the authentic sights and sounds of the Delta. It's easy to get to and hard to miss—the location has a Mississippi Blues Trail marker and a National Register of Historic Places plaque.

CLEVELAND

Dockery Farms

The late B. B. King, who knew a thing or two about the blues (being one of the greatest blues guitarists ever), once named Dockery Farms the birthplace of the blues: "You might say it all started right here." Several of the original plantation buildings have been designated a National

Historic Dockery Farms was the spot where B. B. King said "you might say it all started right here"
JOSEPHINE MATYAS

Historic Site and were restored under a National Park Service Save America's Treasures Grant. Dockery is a short drive east of Cleveland along Mississippi Highway 8.

In the early 1930s, at the height of its production, the landmark property covered forty square miles and had its own doctor, churches, schools, blacksmith, post office, commissary, currency, and railroad spur (along the Peavine branch of the Yazoo and Mississippi Valley Railroad, which blues players rode from one plantation to another).

Delta State University professor emeritus of art and executive director of Dockery Farms Foundation, Bill Lester—whose great-grandfather came to the area in 1880, became the largest landowner in Mississippi, promptly lost it all gambling, and then won it back again days later—has a theory: "We're pretty sure the blues started here at Dockery. Now, nobody is trying to say the first blues note was written here. Nobody has any idea where the first blues note was written but so much of the blues got played here at Dockery, got taught here at Dockery, that's why B. B. King says it's the birthplace of the blues."

Dockery had its own railroad spur along the Peavine branch, which blues players rode from one plantation to another
JOSEPHINE MATYAS

Dockery Farms plantation even had its own commissary coins
JOSEPHINE MATYAS

The bluesmen of the time had a gig circuit across the Delta. "It's another misnomer for you to think they were welcome everywhere they went," Lester explained to us as we wandered the historic site. "Most of the small towns would run 'em off. So they looked for these isolated plantations where they could play out in the country."

With the hint of a southern drawl, Lester ticked off the list of influential blues players who cycled through Dockery Farms. "Charley Patton was one of the very first people to play the blues or get recorded, and he taught so many people how to play here. Howlin' Wolf grew up here when he was a child. He got here when he was about six, left here when he was about twenty-one. Pop Staples of the famous Staple Singers came here as a very young child and left as a teenager. Both of them professed that Charley taught them everything they needed to know to become who they were. Henry Sloan came here, Willie Brown came here, Son House came here, Robert Johnson came here. All of the blues performers came here because of the situation right here."

That "situation" was an eager audience with money in their pockets, free time, and a bridge over the Sunflower River to sharecroppers' shacks, known as frolicking houses.

"Everyone got paid on Saturday afternoon. Mr. Dockery had three to four thousand people working for him, and they'd all have a pocket full of money—Dockery commissary coins. The one that was most important was the twenty-five cent piece 'cause that's what the blues singers charged the people. On any given Saturday afternoon there would be close to maybe a thousand grown men or women standing out here, and they would have just gotten paid. So the blues singers would come on the train and play for free right here for a few minutes. After they'd played for about twenty minutes, they'd walk across the one lane bridge over the river to what they called Big Lou's frolicking house."

Big Lou and the bluesmen colluded. In 1920, there was no electricity, no radios, no fans, no indoor potties, no phones, and no televisions. Big Lou would strip his house of furniture on Saturday afternoon, hang big mirrors on the walls, and put a coal oil lantern in front of each mirror so that the house would explode with light.

"They'd raise all the windows so they'd be the only house with light. Everything else would be pitch black dark. So when you walked across that one lane bridge, there were takers there to take your money. You couldn't cross the bridge unless you paid."

Do the math: on any given Saturday afternoon, Charley Patton would play to a thousand grown men who happily paid twenty-five cents each for a night of music and frolicking. At a time when a brand-new car cost about $210, a bluesman like Patton could make that—and more—in one night. It's said that Charley Patton was the only Black man to wear White man's Sunday school clothes and drive a brand-new car.

"All that wild music would start," smiled Lester. "When I first moved here forty years ago, I was foolish and asked Tom Cannon—Charley Patton's nephew—why couldn't the children go to the frolicking house? That eighty-year-old man squinted and grinned and said to me, 'Because Mr. Bill, they *frolic* there.' With all that alcohol and frolicking, this was seen as the devil's music."

Pondering life for people on the plantation, Lester said, "I always think in my mind what it must have been like to work and burn somewhere between twelve and eighteen thousand calories—that's the exact same number of calories that an Olympic athlete burns when they practice swimming—every single day and listening to nothing but what? Wind, hummingbirds, and lightning, and each other all week long. And all of a sudden—whaaaaow—on a Saturday afternoon! What that must have done to them. I think about that feeling that they must have had.

We can debate whether that was a good feeling or a bad feeling or something they should have been feeling or not been feeling. But I know the feeling—and so I felt it before, and probably all of us have. To think that they went through all that tough, tough, tough, tough—and here was one thing that they could really let loose on and enjoy. And so, it must have been something. Saturday nights must have been something."

The farm is still in the Dockery family, the fields are rented out for crops, and several of the beautifully restored buildings are open to visitors. "And thousands come each year," said Lester. What remains is original, including the seed house, cotton gin, commissary storage building, and front porch of the commissary. The best introduction to the property begins on an audio box at the front of the old service station bordering the highway. After that, wander the property, poke around the buildings, gaze over the Sunflower River where the one-lane bridge used to hit land, and just try to imagine all that frolicking. (dockeryfarms.org)

W. C. Handy's Enlightenment

In his book *Father of the Blues*, W. C. Handy wrote about two encounters that opened his eyes to the blues. One was on the train platform at Tutwiler, and the other was what he called his "enlightenment" in Cleveland.

Handy's professional orchestra had been playing a gig in Cleveland and was finding it a challenge to keep the dance floor full (every dance band's nightmare). When asked if his band could play some "native music," Handy complied as best he could, but the audience response was lukewarm. The next request was a little more specific: Would Handy mind if some local fellows played a few dance songs? A ragtag trio— bass, guitar, and mandolin—took to the stage and started to play, and the crowd went wild, showering the band with a "rain of silver dollars." Handy immediately "saw the beauty of primitive music" and its commercial potential. He took pen to paper and created written arrangements, a few years later taking the blues with him to Beale Street in Memphis and eventually on to New York, where he established Handy Brothers Music Co., a successful family-owned publishing company.

Martin & Sue King Railroad Heritage Museum

To really understand how music moved across and beyond the Delta, we needed to grasp how the spread of the "new" music called the blues and the railroad were inseparable. In large part, it was the network of rail lines that spread the blues, the story that is told at this small museum in downtown Cleveland.

In 1884, a single rail line through the Delta connected Memphis to New Orleans. The terrain was no-man's-land—heavily wooded wilderness with acres of cypress and snake-filled swamps. Construction was difficult. Before the tracks were built, there were only remote settlements, mostly on high ground, and only the small plantations close to the riverside had easy access to markets. Flooding of the Mississippi River was an annual occurrence, building up small, natural levees (after the catastrophic Great Flood of 1927, the U.S. Army Corps of Engineers built the larger concrete levees in place today). Once the railroad was completed, acreage inland was cleared, the lowland muck was drained, and larger plantations were developed. The original Highway 61 ran beside the railroad, creating more direct access to territory that had once been wilderness.

Plantation life was closely bound to the railroad; its shining rails were a way in and out of the harsh realities of Delta life. They came to symbolize escape and freedom from oppression and poverty. The clackety-clack of riding the rails had a certain steady rhythm, songs were played on railway station platforms (think of W. C. Handy's early blues encounter in Tutwiler), and many blues songs featured train travel—"This Train" by Sister Rosetta Tharpe, "Midnight Special" by Huddie "Lead Belly" Ledbetter, and "Southbound Train" by Muddy Waters, who boarded a Chicago-bound train from Clarksdale in 1943 and never returned to live in the Delta. As Alan Lomax observed, "Black railroad gangs laid the track . . . it is their spirit that infuses the Delta railroad songs."

The Railroad Heritage Museum has many artifacts, including tools, old schedules, and maps, to illustrate the growth of rail lines and the era of the railroad blues across the Delta. At the center of the room is the largest O-gauge model train layout in Mississippi, complete with the details of mid-twentieth-century small-town life. (mississippimuseums.org)

Delta State University

At the Cleveland campus of Delta State University, there are two ways to experience the blues. For a leisurely stay, it's possible to sign up for an experiential learning tour that covers the story of the Delta and its importance to the rest of the world.

For a hit-and-run stop, the Cast of Blues masks exhibit in the foyer of Ewing Hall is a striking display of fifty-five face casts by blind artist Sharon McConnell-Dickerson, who began the project to create life casts of the faces behind the music she loved. A life cast captures the bone, muscles, pores, scars, and lines of life that cannot be seen in any other way.

McConnell-Dickerson shaped the masks from damp gauze and plaster, creating three-dimensional, exact replicas of the performers' faces, including Willie "Pinetop" Perkins, David "Honeyboy" Edwards, and Willie "Po' Monkey" Seaberry. (deltastate.edu)

Mississippi Grammy Museum

When the Recording Academy began its search for a sister location to the Grammy Museum in Los Angeles, Mississippi was the place that made sense. So many forms of music could be traced back to the region—from country to blues to soul to rock and roll. The 28,000-square-foot facility was opened in early 2016 and has hosted special events and music fans from around the world.

The museum's main purpose is the music, history, and civil rights education of youth, building on field trips with blues, drumming, songwriting, and deejay workshops to create deeper experiences than just walking through the doors and gawking at slinky dresses and televised speeches from the red carpet.

We're not really drawn to the celebrity trimmings, so we beelined straight for the Mississippi Gallery, a large section of the museum designed to celebrate the musicians and songs that make the state the "birthplace of America's music."

The flat, luminous Mississippi Music Table holds court in the center of the room, with an enormous touchscreen surface to satiate the twitchy fingers of even the most profoundly desperate smartphone addict. Half the museum's exhibits are interactive, and this million-dollar table is the granddaddy of the collection, creating what the curators claim is one of the most technologically advanced museums in the world. Everything on the glowing screen connects back to Mississippi: either is a Mississippian, has been influenced by a Mississippian, or has influenced a Mississippian.

The Music Table experience is a rabbit hole linking the connections between generations of Mississippi musicians and one to get happily lost in very easily. Tap the screen picture of B. B. King, and up pops the details of his life, his music, and his many awards. Click deeper to see how King was influenced by groundbreaking bluesmen like Charley Patton and Muddy Waters but also how he influenced contemporary players like Eric Clapton and Keith Richards. Follow those threads to learn about who played when and where, whom they learned from, and whom they inspired. Before you know it, an enjoyable hour will have vanished (although you'll have a much deeper appreciation for Mississippi's homegrown musical talent), and it will be time to head a few steps away to the Mississippi Music Bar. Slip on a set of headphones and dial up a menu of Grammy-winning songs, either written or sung by a Mississippian.

The tall glass cases in the Mississippi Legends section are like rummaging around in the closets of the state's best-known music stars. There's Willie Dixon's passport, a harmonica that belonged to Sonny Boy Williamson II, Roebuck "Pop" Staples's (patriarch of the Staple Singers) Fender Jazzmaster guitar, and a white jumpsuit with snazzy blue trim that once took Elvis's female fans to the brink of crazy. (grammymuseumms.org)

FINDING FOOD AND DRINK

A Plate of Mississippi Barbecue

Barbecue pit masters work their magic with a combination of wood chips, delicious sauces, and great cuts of meat.

- Abe's Bar-B-Q, Clarksdale
- The Hollywood Café, Robinsonville
- Airport Grocery, Cleveland
- Hicks Tamales & Barbecue, Clarksdale

Blue Plate Special

Scan the menu for "a meat and three"—pick your meat and add several sides. Popular ones are potatoes, macaroni, creamed corn, collard greens, lima beans, and corn bread.

- The Senator's Place, Cleveland
- The Blue & White Restaurant, Tunica

Southern Fried Chicken

Everyone has a favorite way to prepare fried chicken—coated, seasoned, and then deep fried until crispy and golden.

- The Blue & White Restaurant, Tunica
- The Senator's Place, Cleveland
- Gus's World Famous Fried Chicken, Southaven

Pond-Raised Catfish

Mississippi-farmed catfish is a Delta favorite.

- The Hollywood Café, Robinsonville
- Fat Baby's Catfish House, Cleveland
- Ground Zero Blues Club, Clarksdale

Hot Delta Tamales

A Mississippi-born treat of spicy meat encased in cornmeal, wrapped in a corn husk, and simmered.

- Abe's Bar-B-Q, Clarksdale
- Airport Grocery, Cleveland
- Hicks' Tamales, Clarksdale

Pimento Cheese

Beloved as the "caviar of the South."

- Yazoo Pass, Clarksdale
- The Dutch Oven, Clarksdale
- Hooker Grocer + Eatery, Clarksdale

Fried Green Tomatoes

A classic southern side dish of sliced green tomatoes, breaded, seasoned, and fried.

- Bluesberry Café, Clarksdale
- The Hollywood Café, Robinsonville
- Crawdad's of Merigold, Merigold

JUKE JOINT

The juke (rhymes with *book*) joint—where the blues found its voice—was often housed in a wooden shack in the backwoods and along rural dirt roads. The word *juke* originated from the Gullah word *joog*, which means "rowdy." There aren't many authentic juke joints left, but they are still recognized as birthplaces of the blues.

MUST SEE

- The live cast of Po' Monkey at Cast of Blues, Delta State University
- Dockery Farms twenty-five-cent currency, most commonly used to pay blues players
- The only known photo of Charley Patton (In it, he's playing slide-style guitar in a way adopted from Hawaiian guitarists.)
- One of the few known photographs of Robert Johnson (Almost every blues museum has copies of two of the three on display. The third was discovered in 2020.)
- The Muddywood Guitar at the Delta Blues Museum in Clarksdale

MUST READ

- *The Most Southern Place on Earth: The Mississippi Delta and the Roots of Regional Identity*, James C. Cobb (1995)
- *The Devil's Music: A History of the Blues*, Giles Oakley (1997)
- *Worse Than Slavery: Parchman Farm and the Ordeal of Jim Crow Justice*, David Oshinsky (1996)

MUST LISTEN AND WATCH

- "Cross Road Blues," Robert Johnson
- "Preachin' the Blues," parts 1 and 2, Son House
- "Pea Vine Blues," Charley Patton
- "I'm Your Hoochie Coochie Man," Muddy Waters
- *The Blues, a Musical Journey*, Martin Scorsese, producer, seven parts

GUITAR NOTES

Charley Patton learned to play guitar at Dockery Farms when he was a teenager. Patton developed his slide guitar style, fretting it with a pocket knife or a brass tube or bottleneck. He popped the bass strings— anticipating funk bass techniques by several decades—and beat the guitar with the thumb of his right hand while stomping his feet to deepen the pulse or create syncopated counter-rhythms. He may have used altered tunings—a tone or a tone and a half higher or lower than standard—to create specific effects for his instrument. His highly visual performances included playing the guitar between his legs or behind the back of his head—all showbiz gimmicks later picked up and perfected by the likes of Jimi Hendrix and Chuck Berry, among others.

4

THE LOWER MISSISSIPPI DELTA

Whether entering the Delta from the south or the north (we've done it from both directions), it's like a switch is abruptly thrown to reveal a spectacle of dramatic and often punishing contrasts spread out as far as the eye can see (thank you to Paul Simon for the image of "shining like a National guitar").

Approaching from the south, the change in geography is that sudden. You don't so much arrive as have the Mississippi Delta presented to you in a tableau of unending acres stretched to the horizon. Rich and poor. Renovated and shuttered. Vintage and contemporary. The one thing it is, all over, is flat. Anvil flat. Billiard table flat. Chalkboard flat.

We drew an east-to-west line through Cleveland and, in our travels, thought of the stretch to the north as the upper Delta and the remainder to the south as the lower Delta. For practical travel purposes it just made sense to look at each section separately. The entire Delta is formed and heavily impacted by the flow and ravages of the Mississippi. The entire region has a long and heartbreaking struggle with the inequity and harshness of a plantation economy. The lower Delta was the site of the country's most devastating flood, forever changing the landscape, the economy, and the people. The power of the river is never forgotten here.

Most fans of the blues know about Clarksdale in the upper Delta. It's considered ground zero for every blues pilgrim. Across the wide expanse of the lower Delta, there is a wealth of blues history that may not have the press coverage and the cachet of Clarksdale, but it is notable as the birthplaces and street-corner busking sites of blues greats like Robert Johnson, Muddy Waters, B. B. King, and Jimmy "Duck" Holmes. It's also where "the Southern cross' the Dog" (read more about this in the section "Moorhead" in this chapter).

With time, the fullness of the blues was nurtured, grew, and flourished across the lower Delta. It's home to the haunting Bentonia sound at the historic Blue Front Café. The lower Delta is also where B. B. King (the "King of the Blues") was born and raised and never forgot his hometown roots. No exploration of the roots of the blues in Mississippi is complete without spending a day at the excellent B. B. King Museum and Delta Interpretive Center in Indianola. And, of course, the lower Delta is also home to Greenwood, an important site of civil rights history, and its small neighborhood of Baptist Town. Clarksdale may claim the Crossroads (and, yes, that is a highly contested claim), but there is no doubt that the Greenwood area owns the spot where Robert Johnson died and was buried.

The lower Delta may not have Clarksdale, but it has its own wild stories, birthplaces, burial sites, fantastic museums, and live blues music scene in almost every small town. Miss it, and you'll be missing half the story.

Exploring the landscape of the lower Delta took us along historic Highway 61, the river-hugging Mississippi portion of the Great River Road National Scenic Byway. By visiting small towns, walking the famous levees at Greenville, and admiring the blues murals at Rolling Fork, we found an experience that brought land, water, and communities together. (experiencemississippiriver.com)

The sections below on the geography and people are snapshots of the main points to appreciate when understanding how the blues began, flourished, and spread. Chapter 2 provides a deeper look at the land and the history of the Delta. It's the spot to turn to for a much more detailed exploration.

LAND AND WATER

The Establishment of Plantations

The first plantation businessmen came from France, Spain, and Britain, bringing captured and enslaved Africans and buying up cheap land to build a slave-based plantation economy that would create huge wealth for the privileged class. The first crops included rice, tobacco, and indigo but evolved rapidly toward more lucrative cotton as world-wide demand increased.

Clearing the Land

The large swaths of the crude and wild frontier lands had to be cleared of forest and drained of standing water, an arduous, backbreaking undertaking that often took years, complicated by recurring flooding of the mighty Mississippi River. Only after the felling of trees and burning of stumps could the soil be prepared for the spring planting season. Businessmen sought out the slaves from Africa, who they felt were easily acclimated to the oppressive heat, humidity, and agricultural demands of the Delta.

The Levee System

With such an investment sunk into creating massive plantations, the landowners turned to manmade levees to control annual floodwaters. There were still regular cycles of flooding, managed with varying success by a system of natural and rudimentary levees. The destruction caused by the river often found its way into the lyrics of early blues songs.

The Great Flood of 1927

In 1927, the springtime flood was a game changer. It was one of the most destructive natural disasters on U.S. soil, and understanding the historical importance of the Great Flood is crucial to appreciating Mississippi, the land, the people, and the music.

Across the lower Delta, main streets of towns were swept away, houses were submerged, and crops and livelihoods were destroyed. The loss of income and a surge of ugly racism only made recovery worse; many packed up and went north to drier land with hopes for a more promising and equitable future.

The impact and importance of the Great Flood of 1927 cannot be overstated. It's a story of torrential rains, a swollen river, and the levee breaches that were a turning point in the history of Mississippi and the South.

THE PEOPLE AND THE STRUGGLES

The Economics of King Cotton

With the 1794 invention of Eli Whitney's labor-saving cotton gin and the demand for short-staple cotton in the early 1800s, cotton became an even more lucrative crop. The global demand for the crop was unprecedented—and the demand deeply impacted the economy of the South. Across the world, cotton was king.

Racial Injustice and Violence

The southern planters' vast prosperity depended on their ability to secure the political future of slavery, their "peculiar institution." Immediately after the American Civil War, the White planter class attempted to force newly freed Blacks to work on plantations in near slave-like conditions. By the 1950s, a rapidly changing economy and the growing civil rights movement began to challenge the entrenched system of White supremacy and racial segregation.

Labor Changed after the American Civil War

The moment the American Civil War ended, another struggle began—on plantations, in courthouses, and in state capitals—to hammer out the terms of a new labor regime in the cotton-growing regions of the defeated Confederacy. On January 1, 1863, President Abraham Lincoln signed the Emancipation Proclamation, but it had little immediate effect on freeing any of the nation's slaves. Businessmen and plantation owners fought hard to restore a post-Emancipation world as close to the prewar model as possible but without giving away a dollar in profits.

Immediately after Emancipation, many Black slaves stayed in the South—farmwork was the work they knew—and sharecropped for the larger plantations. Tenant farmers (both poor Blacks and Whites) used the land to grow crops and in return paid the landowner with the majority of the harvest. It was an unfairly skewed system, one in which the plantation owners reaped the profits and the freed slaves of the Delta would find themselves working the same fields they had toiled in under captivity.

Mass Migration

Several factors created a prescription for mass migration from the sharecropper economy and into the more densely populated urban centers like Chicago, St. Louis, Detroit, and Kansas City.

American involvement in European conflicts fueled the need for workers in the large factories of the North, and millions of people migrated out of the rural South for jobs and opportunities elsewhere. Many musicians left the Delta to follow the money, taking their music to big cities and other regions of America—in essence, spreading the mojo of the blues outward from the Delta.

Like in the upper Delta, mechanization using large planters and harvesters slashed the work available to field hands and sharecroppers. Unemployment soared and, together with the massive 1927 flooding of the river and racial inequality, contributed to what has been known as the Great Migration.

ROAD-TRIPPING THE LOWER DELTA

Like much of the upper Delta, driving across the lower reaches brought home the heartbreaking story of abandonment. Countless homes and businesses were boarded up as their owners left in search of a sustainable income and lifestyle. To us, this was the reason why understanding all of the forces—historical, cultural, technological, and political—was so important because the stories of these small towns, deserted main streets, and tumbledown homes with plywood nailed over the windows were about much more than just present-day economics. They tell a history of the Great Flood of 1927, of technology wiping out jobs once done by hand, of racial strife and violence driving people to find safer and more accepting communities. Learning about and appreciating that history was key to our search for the roots of this American-born music that flowed from the Delta.

With the American Civil War and then Emancipation of the slaves, it was blues and gospel that impacted heavily on life across the Delta, eventually spreading across America. It became the foundation for many of the musical genres that are popular today: African spirituals touched the music of protest with stories of overcoming great adversity, and the joyful, uplifting sounds of gospel influenced rock and roll and rhythm and blues.

After being thoroughly churched in the power of the blues while crisscrossing the upper Delta (at shrines like Clarksdale and Dockery Farms), we weren't sure if the lower Delta could meet our expectations. But what we found was a treasure trove of history and blues sites that easily pulled their own weight. As in the upper Delta, many were part of the Mississippi Blues Trail system—look for the large blue signs. (msbluestrail.org)

We began our exploration in Greenville, the small city that was at the tragic center of the Great Flood. Greenville may not have much present-day blues activity, but it has an amazing story to tell, one can take calming strolls along the levee, and it is home to the small but excellent 1927 Flood Museum. We can't say it enough: understanding the flow of the Mississippi River and the history of seasonal flooding is key to appreciating how the blues birthed, grew, and spread. It is a perfect illustration of how geography spawned history.

From Greenville, we made our way east along Highway 82 stopping at Leland, tiny Holly Ridge (in search of the grave site of Charley Patton, the "Voice of the Delta"), Moorhead, Berclair, and Indianola. On its own, Indianola is enough reason to venture into the lower Delta: the hometown and final resting place of B. B. King, one of the greatest of the blues greats. The B. B. King Museum and Delta Interpretive Center is, hands down, one of the most impressive music museums we've ever visited. And the town shines with pride for its hometown son. Onward from Indianola, we spent time in Greenwood and its historic neighborhood of Baptist Town, a true magnet for fans of all things Robert Johnson.

Zigzagging along back roads, we pointed the van farther south and stopped at towns like Belzoni, Rolling Fork, Yazoo City, and Bentonia, all rich with the history of the roots of the blues. Along the way, we sampled barbecue, sat on front porches listening to stories, and drove along dusty country roads in search of those distinctive Mississippi Blues Trail markers.

GREENVILLE

For a landscape that's fundamentally flat, there were certain elevated spots in the Delta where we felt drawn to the clash between humanity and Mother Nature. Standing atop the levee at the end of Main Street in Greenville was such a place—a city destined to be drowned. And in April 1927, it was. The Great Flood of that spring was a natural cataclysmic event that transformed the Delta. (visitgreenville.org)

We aimed our camper van toward Greenville to see Ol' Man River up close, to walk along the streets and to gawk from atop those storied levees. There are few places where the river is as intimately intertwined with the history of the blues as it is in Greenville. Yet it's one of those many history-steeped towns in Mississippi that has been overlooked, seemingly tossed to the bottom of history's dustbin.

The water rose and fell in Greenville, causing disaster and inspiring the lyrics of many famous blues songs. Like too many other places across the Delta, the Greenville live blues scene today is a shadow of its early self. But with a growing interest in the music, visitors are coming to Greenville for local events like the Mississippi Delta Blues & Heritage Festival, the oldest continuously operating blues festival in the world. Organized by the Mississippi Action for Community Education, over the decades, the festival has brought a who's who of the blues to their stage, including B. B. King, John Lee Hooker, Muddy Waters, Stevie Ray Vaughan, and Bobby Rush. A primary mission is to keep the flame burning and to promote and teach about the cultural roots and historical importance of the blues. (deltabluesms.org)

There was one fact that riveted us, putting the riverfront city on our must-see list: history changed in Greenville when the water rose, disrupting lives and landscape forever. That made it a place where we had to stop. Greenville may not get the press coverage of Clarksdale or have the blues cred of Cleveland, but life-altering history happened there. To truly understand the music and the Delta, a visit to Greenville should be a part of every blues pilgrimage. On the city's wide streets, along the sweeping concrete levees, and at the muddy riverbanks, the story of Mississippi, the Delta, and the blues changed course forever.

Greenville did have its heyday. From the 1940s to the 1970s, downtown Greenville's Nelson Street was an energy-filled neighborhood crammed with African American businesses, pool halls, nightclubs, and juke joints, a place where music spilled onto sidewalks every night of the week. There was no shortage of talent playing those clubs and busking on those street corners. Musicians like Sonny Boy Williamson II, James "Little Milton" Campbell Jr., Eddie Shaw, and James "T-Model" Ford gigged along Nelson Street. The history of the street is laid out on a Mississippi Blues Trail marker: "When down-home southern blues was at its commercial peak in the American rhythm and blues industry in the early 1950s, record companies headed for Nelson Street in search of talent."

That shine has tarnished in Greenville. We were warned about walking along Nelson Street, day or night. The city's historic downtown struggles with a mix of boarded-up storefronts and faded shops caught in a 1970s merchandise time warp. The crime rate and unemployment are high; job prospects and confidence seem in short supply. These days, Greenville has taken a hard hit with globalization and agricultural mechanization, slipping a few pegs down the ladder of economic power now that people, goods, and cargo are shuttled around the country on gleaming airliners and transports barreling along the interstate system. Rewind to an era when plantation crops were driving the commodity markets of the South, and Greenville was a happening place, the busiest river port between Memphis and New Orleans.

In David Cohn's book *Where I Was Born and Raised*, the renowned Greenville native pointed to the tempestuous relationship between humans and the water lapping at the doorway of his hometown. "The people of the Delta fear God and the Mississippi River," he wrote, "for God and the river are immortal and immemorial." Nowhere in Mississippi is this more true than in the city of Greenville.

All across the Delta, small towns were economic engines surrounded by massive cotton plantations that were home to thousands of slaves, field hands, and sharecroppers. It was the enormous serpentine levees holding back the waters of the Mississippi that expanded the available acreage for farming. Virtually all were constructed in the harshest conditions on the backs of generations of Black slaves.

In Greenville—and all across Mississippi—they'll never forget that day in the spring of 1927 when the levees were obliterated by the waters of the swollen river. Greenville was the epicenter of the catastrophic levee breach that drowned the regional economy and people of the Delta, accelerating the out-migration of thousands to the north in search of higher ground and jobs (and, with them, their Delta-born music).

To understand the Great Flood of 1927—the most destructive flood in the history of the United States—is to open a window into the history of the Delta. It was why we came to Greenville—to make sense of how the water of the Mississippi helped shape the blues.

Mississippi River Levees

The fact that *Chevy* rhymed so neatly with *levee* was the extent of our knowledge of the extensive levee system used to regulate water levels. We live in a part of the world where snow accumulation is the weather obsession, not river dikes. Don McLean's 1971 song "American Pie" ("drove my Chevy to the levee but the levee was dry") rose to number five on the Recording Industry Association of America's

Songs of the Century, probably introducing the word *levee* to millions of unsuspecting listeners.

But not in Mississippi, where levees are a fact of life and death. And in a riverside city like Greenville, the modern-day levee system protects the fragile city streets from the ravages of the rising water. At least it does today, but it wasn't always the protective barrier it is now.

A levee—the word comes from the French for "to raise"—is an extended embankment designed to channel a body of water to prevent flooding. The Mississippi River is contained and constrained, guided, and directed by a system of embankments that make up the largest flood control project in the world. It's said that the contemporary Mississippi River levee system is one of the few manmade structures that astronauts can make out from space.

Europeans who settled the South built the first levees to protect the city of New Orleans, but their design has changed many times over the years. From Cape Girardeau, Missouri, to where the Mississippi River enters the Gulf of Mexico, levees have varied in height from a modest few feet to more than fifty feet in some places.

The thing about levees is that they are very expensive to build and maintain because Mother Nature is forever trying to wash them away. They increase the value of land where they are built and, as a conse-

The Mississippi River levee system is visible from space
JOSEPHINE MATYAS

quence, provoke economic and political skirmishes. So what starts out as an engineering problem to control the flow of a body of water rapidly becomes a political problem as interests on both sides of the river compete to protect their land and property values at the expense of those on the opposite side of the river upstream or downstream.

The Great Flood of 1927 catapulted politics to the forefront, including the continuing power and cultural struggle between North and South. In *The Flood Year 1927: A Cultural History*, author Susan Scott Parrish quotes entertainer and newspaper columnist Will Rogers when he wrote about the southern attitude, "The cry of the people down there is, 'We don't want relief and charity; we want protection.'"

In Greenville, the top of the levee was a perfect spot for our morning walks. From that vantage point, we had a great view over the power struggle between people and nature. The wide slope of reinforced concrete shaped like a massive speed bump is a breathtaking piece of construction. Locals told us stories about there being two streets of old Greenville buried under the levee. Apparently, when the U.S. Army Corps of Engineers took over the levee system, they measured back two streets, laid a wide grid, and started the rebuilding process to create a substantially larger barricade to contain the rise of the water. But Mississippians are storytellers extraordinaire, and they grinned and spun tales about old airplanes and people buried under that mammoth earthen and concrete speed bump.

After walking atop the massive levees, the next logical stop was the 1927 Flood Museum to get the history of flooding, the early levee system, and the structures in place today that were built after the Great Flood of 1927.

1927 Flood Museum

Mississippi is a spot where weather changed history. People across the Delta still talk about the Flood. Songs are sung, books have been written, and documentaries have been filmed about it. And on a side street, just spitting distance from the actual levees and the water, in a brick carriage house said to be Greenville's oldest structure, there's a museum dedicated to one of the most terrifying and devastating natural disasters on American soil.

Mike Bostic, the former museum coordinator at the 1927 Flood Museum, was our go-to guy on the history of flooding and the Delta. "There

The 1927 Flood Museum tells the story of an event that changed history
JOSEPHINE MATYAS

was a flood every year. For centuries, the river had been flooding and enriching all the soil," he explained.

The Mississippi River and its tributaries constitute the world's fourth-largest watershed (the area drained by a river and its tributaries), providing a drainage basin for more than 40 percent of the United States and creating one of the country's most important geological features. A lot of natural water flow finds its way into and down the storied river nicknamed "Big Muddy." The fall and spring before the 1927 flooding were times of record rainfall. So much water fell from the sky that tributaries like the Arkansas River began flowing backward due to the sheer volume of water in the Mississippi. A wall of water built up, moving south, heading directly for Greenville.

When the area levees finally gave way on Easter weekend in April 1927, water was washing over the top and rising at a rate of one inch per hour. Fire whistles sounded the alarm as the levee blew apart in thirteen major breaks, beginning in the morning at a rural settlement called Mounds Landing, just below the junction with the Arkansas River. The Mounds break still holds the record as the worst levee break anywhere in the United States. Within a few hours, that first break in the levee crumbled to three-quarters of a mile wide, discharging a torrent at twice the volume of Niagara Falls, laying waste to everything in its path. In the end, parts of seven surrounding states were underwater.

The floodwaters swept over the roofs of houses in Yazoo City, seventy-five miles away, submerging or damaging 137,000 buildings, killing 246 people, and displacing almost 700,000 others. Many homes of the era were built on stone foundations—the water filled the streets, and they just floated up and drifted off. In just a little more than a week, 1 million acres of land across the Delta were under at least ten feet of water. It took months for the Greenville-area floodwaters to recede—levels finally dropped by late summer. In addition to lives lost and ruined, the saturated ground wiped out any hope for the 1927 crop year. It was America's largest natural disaster, surpassed in cost only by Hurricane Katrina seventy-eight years later. For weeks, the Delta was in terror.

It was not just the physical landscape that suffered. The social and emotional costs were also staggering. Some Greenville residents found temporary safety on the roofs of buildings. The racial pecking order quickly came into play: White women and children were rescued and evacuated early on; Blacks were not so lucky—many were rounded up and left on a miles-long stretch of levee high ground. For weeks after the levee breaches, 10,000 Black refugees were stuck in makeshift Red Cross camps atop the narrow strip of dry land, with the swollen Mississippi on one side and flooded Delta farmland on the other. They watched as dead livestock floated by and fought with snakes looking for dry ground. It was a disaster like no other, made worse by some unscrupulous plantation owners who refused to rescue their stranded workers for fear they would lose their Black workforce in a mass exodus out of the Delta. African American labor was vital for the lucrative operation of the plantations, and landowners could not afford to lose their labor force, whatever the human cost.

"One thing they don't talk about is once the levee broke and all this water came in is that there was just one way for it to get back out, and that was for it to go back out the hole it came in," explained Bostic. "So the water sat around and got stagnant. The disease, the mosquitos, the dead animals, the dead fish just compounded the situation. And you've got these people stuck."

According to Bostic, a lack of construction standards along the entire lower Mississippi Valley magnified the crisis. "The problem with the levee system in 1927 was there was no regulation. There was no Corps of Engineers saying 'this is how the levee is going to be from here all the way to Natchez.' Everybody built what they thought was going to be a substantial enough levee, and there was no regulation saying this is how it's going to be."

The 1927 Flood Museum is open by appointment only, but when we called, the doors were opened mere minutes later. Inside the modest brick building, the sobering collection of period artifacts, photographs, and video document the flood's impact on life and death during the months that Greenville and much of the Mississippi Delta were underwater. It's well worth it to plan an extra hour to watch the museum's PBS American Experience film *Fatal Flood* based on the definitive book *Rising Tide*.

The impact and importance of the Great Flood of 1927 on the development and spread of the blues was substantial. Before the greatest flood of all, people would leave the fields at sunset, head home for dinner, and, in the evenings, sit on the front porch of their narrow shotgun homes and play music for entertainment. Much of it was improvised using household items like washboards or cans for drums. Stories of their lives became the songs that were played on those front porches; many were sad because that's how life was.

In the end, after the floodwaters had receded, scores of sharecroppers were already indebted for the lost season—they'd prepared the soil and invested in the seed, and planting had begun. Many packed up and left right away. Others stayed to work the following year's crops but by that point found their families so deeply in debt that they also bundled their few possessions and joined what became known as the Great Migration. They headed north to cities, carrying and transplanting the rich Delta blues tradition to their new hometowns. In Mississippi and in their new cities, the trauma of the flood provided inspiration for song in classics like "Broken Levee Blues" and "Flood Water Blues" by Lonnie Johnson, Charley Patton's "High Water Everywhere," and "When the Levee Breaks," first recorded by husband and wife Wilbur "Kansas Joe" McCoy and Lizzie "Memphis Minnie" Douglas and later covered by the British band Led Zeppelin.

Walnut Street

One of the few parts of downtown Greenville still offering live blues is along Walnut Street; with the widening of the levees, it became

The Walnut Street Blues Bar is a Greenville music destination on a street lined with commemorative stones
JOSEPHINE MATYAS

the roadway closest to the waterfront. It's a short stretch—just a few blocks long—but the Walnut Street Blues Walk Foundation has placed commemorative stones along Walnut Street for artists who contributed to the blues in the Delta, including Charley Patton, James "Little Milton" Campbell, and Tyrone Davis. At the center of it all sits the Walnut Street Blues Bar, a city juke joint in a building that was once a bait shop and is open on a bit of a hit-and-miss schedule (best bets are Thursday, Friday, and Saturday evenings).

LELAND

Just east of Cleveland, the small community of Leland is renowned for two things: as the home of Muppets creator Jim Henson (warning: frogs on billboards) and for its role in blues lore at the intersection of Highways 10 and 61. In the zenith of the blues, more than 150 bluesmen lived within a 100-mile radius of Leland. (lelandchamber.com)

Leland is famous in blues history for the intersection of Highways 10 and 61
JOSEPHINE MATYAS

The city's reputation has not always been Muppets sanitized. In June 1908, the national magazine *Collier's* slammed Leland as the "Hell-hole of the Yazoo Delta." At that time, the town was infamous for its flowing booze, crap shooting, and raucous nightlife—in other words, a perfect magnet for the blues. Bluesmen riffed on street corners for tips tossed into their collection jars by country plantation workers who hitched into town to kick out the jams on a Saturday night.

Downtown, a few of the brick walls have been livened up with colorful murals as part of the Leland Blues project to honor mid-Delta blues musicians like Pat Thomas, James "Son" Thomas, Little Milton, "T-Model" Ford, Johnny Winter, and B. B. King. Guitar icon Johnny Winter wrote and recorded "Leland, Mississippi Blues," which paid tribute to his family's Leland roots in the cotton business. In 1988, he became the first White musician elected to the Blues Hall of Fame. His link to the city is told on a Mississippi Blues Trail marker at the corner of Broad and Third streets in the heart of downtown.

On the main street, the Highway 61 Blues Museum pays tribute to these artists with a collection of posters, guitars, clothing, and records.

A few of the downtown Leland brick walls have been livened up with murals of blues players
JOSEPHINE MATYAS

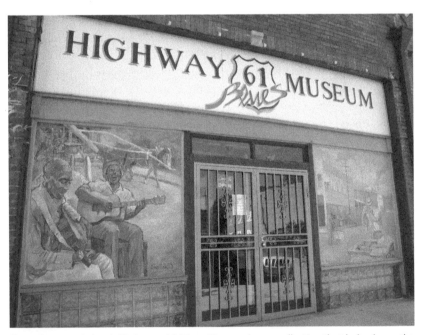

On main street Leland, Highway 61 Blues Museum has a collection that helps keep the blues flame alive
JOSEPHINE MATYAS

Live blues is often a part of the Highway 61 Blues Museum experience
JOSEPHINE MATYAS

There's not a lot inside dedicated to the *roots* of the blues, but there is a very organic collection that honors local musicians and their part in keeping the flame alive. (highway61blues.com)

HOLLY RIDGE

On a map, Holly Ridge looks like it's in the middle of nowhere (spoiler alert: it may not be in the middle of nowhere, but you can see it from there), but this speck on the map is the burial spot of one of the most important pioneers of the blues. Along our route, we normally weren't drawn to the burial sites of musicians and singers (with a few exceptions), but Holly Ridge is just a few minutes off Highway 82, which runs between Greenville and Indianola, and it's the final resting place of Charley Patton, the "Voice of the Delta," respected for his groundbreaking contributions at the turn of the twentieth century. Passing the side road to Holly Ridge without taking the detour would have been a mistake.

Charley Patton—the man called The Voice of the Delta—is buried in a lonely cemetery in Holly Ridge
JOSEPHINE MATYAS

Just a mile north of the highway, we bumped across the railway tracks and turned left at a dusty intersection in what passes for downtown Holly Ridge: large steel-sided structures on the left, a line of barns on the right, farm equipment and machinery parked everywhere, and a scruffy cemetery with one lonely tree sandwiched between Holly Ridge Road and the railway tracks. It took us about ten minutes of walking the rows and reading headstones to find the one for the man they also called the "Founder of the Delta Blues."

So significant were Charley Patton's contributions that the Mississippi Blues Trail chose to place its first historic marker at the grave site of the rambling bluesman they described as the "most important figure in the pioneering era of Delta blues." While Charley Patton is most identified with the blues at Dockery Farms near Cleveland, he spent his final years in Holly Ridge. Fellow blues musicians Willie James Foster and Asie Payton are buried in the same Holly Ridge cemetery.

MOORHEAD

Moorhead itself is another on the long list of Mississippi towns and hamlets beset by a pattern of abandonment, although during the early 1900s, it was a busy passenger and freight connection and a thriving frontier. In its heyday, eight passenger trains a day passed through Moorhead, and downtown sidewalks were packed on a Saturday night as plantation workers streamed into town to dance to the blues at local juke joints.

Moorhead is the spot where "the Southern Cross' the Dog" as immortalized in W. C. Handy's account of his first encounter with the blues
JOSEPHINE MATYAS

Blues players followed the money into town; Howlin' Wolf and Robert Johnson reportedly played together in Moorhead in the 1930s.

It was a must-see stop for us because it's the spot on the map with the perfectly perpendicular intersection of two railway lines, one north to south and the other east to west. Back in the day, the eastbound and westbound trains crossed the north-to-south lines several times a day, but today only the east-to-west Southern Railroad line is operational.

This is the spot where "the Southern cross' the Dog," as immortalized in W. C. Handy's account of his first encounter with the blues. At this very spot, the Southern Railroad crosses at right angles with the Yazoo Delta Railroad (the story is told in detail in chapter 3 in the section "Tutwiler"). The intersection of the rail tracks in Moorhead is commemorated with a Mississippi Blues Trail marker.

INDIANOLA

There are few towns anywhere that can boast a Delta blues pedigree like Indianola. (indianolams.gov)

To be precise, it's nearby Itta Bena, the small dot on the map eighteen miles down the road, where Riley B. King was born in 1925 and lived in a tenant shack for his first nine years until losing his mother to the complications of diabetes, then moving to stay with a grandmother. A year later, he was essentially orphaned again, and from age ten on, he fended for himself. Young Riley credited his mother with his own sense of kindness and fairness, goodness, and honesty. The life story of Riley (we came to know him as musical giant "B. B." King) is intertwined with the story of harsh times in the Delta and powerfully told at the B. B. King Museum and Delta Interpretive Center, one of the best blues museums in Mississippi.

B. B. King Museum and Delta Interpretive Center

At the core of this museum is the large, expansive heart of the man they came to call the unrivaled ambassador of the blues. And no one is a bigger fan than Robert Terrell, the museum's director of operations. "B. B. was very generous about everything—he was just that type of guy. He gave us so much. He would always sign guitars and give them away, or he would sign your Gibson guitar."

Indianola has blues cred as the home of the great B. B. King
JOSEPHINE MATYAS

Terrell comes from a Mississippi blues background himself. He picked in the cotton fields, and his father once ran the Harlem Club, a small juke joint in nearby Hollandale. "When you look at the history of the blues, I just want people to know that the blues has been here a long time—and it's here to stay. Don't just think about the music itself; think about the history of it, then you'll understand why it's important to support it. The blues is the truth no matter how you put it or where you put it. It's still the truth. The blues is a feeling—it's just a feeling—and that's why it's hard for some people to duplicate it. This is not something that you can learn. It's something that comes from the inside. Once you feel it, you know it's there. It's a music that everyone can relate to. It doesn't matter what your race or background is. Everyone has had the blues. So if I sing a song about not having any money, maybe you haven't had that problem, but you may have had a problem with your wife or one of your kids. It resonates with everyone. You know, growing up in the Delta and being a part of that hard labor, because I was one of those cotton pickers, people who worked in the cotton fields—thank god my father wasn't a sharecropper—a lot of that hard work, man, that'll bring a lot out of you."

The B. B. King Museum and Delta Interpretive Center is a world-class facility with exhibits on the blues and the Delta
JOSEPHINE MATYAS

As a young man in Indianola, B. B. King drove tractor at the brick cotton gin of the Johnson Barrett Plantation, now the site of the museum. He started playing guitar by watching a family member—a preacher—and it inspired him to want to learn and play. He began in church-steeped gospel with the Famous St. John's Gospel Singers but gravitated to the blues genre early in life, believing that singing the blues by Black people was to keep them from "sinking into nothingness." The blues was the sound track for an Indianola Saturday night, and it wasn't long before teenager B. B. was making a little extra coin playing the town's street corners. To B. B., the blues style conveyed an infinite range of emotions, both joys and sorrows, associated with the harsh times of his upbringing.

In his mid-20s, he broke out of Indianola, drawn north to the city lights of Memphis, where he put his stamp on the blues for all time. On raucous Beale Street the young musician studied, learned, and improved his craft, developing a distinctive vocal style and his trademark way of "bending" notes on his Gibson ES-355 guitar, nicknamed Lucille. On the streets of Memphis, he also found his stage name, first called the "Beale

Street Blues Boy," the "Blues Boy," and finally "B. B." "Memphis to me then was like the Eiffel Tower, or the Tower of Pisa or the Grand Canyon," he's quoted as saying. "God almighty, this was really something."

The gregarious entertainer once explained how the namesake of his guitar Lucille was a woman whose charms had set off a bar brawl at a rural juke joint in Twist, Arkansas. The fight was followed by a tipped can of kerosene, a fire, and B. B. running back into the inferno to save his guitar. To remind himself never to take such chances again, he named his instrument Lucille.

What's exceptional about this museum is that B. B. King donated so much from his personal archive long before he passed away, packing the rooms with artifacts from his life, his tours, and items he collected in his long career as a Memphis radio personality during his climb up the ladder of blues fame. His Big Red tour bus, musical instruments (including his 1960 Gibson ES-355), a custom-made concert jacket, a record collection, multiple Grammy Awards, and a re-creation of the early home recording studio that was his sanctuary are all lovingly

Displays at the B. B. King Museum show what life was like on the road for the touring musician

JOSEPHINE MATYAS

B. B. King's home studio is on display at the B. B. King Museum and Delta Interpretive Center
JOSEPHINE MATYAS

displayed. Over time, he amassed a collection of 30,000 blues record-ings, most of which he donated to the blues archives at the University of Mississippi in Oxford.

The galleries at the B. B. King Museum cover the Delta of the early twentieth century, a place of extremes where African Americans invented a new kind of music that radiated out from the South, revolu-tionizing popular music forever. Additional galleries focus on the life of young Riley, his fascination with and mastery of the blues, his years in Memphis and on the road touring, and his role as a blues icon in a chang-ing America. Each gallery intertwines the personal of Riley B. King with the politics, culture, and social conditions of the time. They show how the early blues were played in leisure but shaped by labor, the rebrand-ing of the "race records" of African American artists into the more palat-able rhythm and blues, and how the repressive and exploitive Jim Crow laws impacted the life of the touring musicians. Whenever a gas station owner refused service, claiming that his restrooms were out of order, B. B. would take Big Red to a more accommodating station. "The man said he don't have no restroom, and I ain't going let him put one-hundred-thirty-gallons of gas in here and can't use his restroom." With 300-plus touring dates a year, the highway became his home.

B. B. had a gift for performance and a genius for creating but was also known as a caring, community-minded person who was much bigger than just the blues. He was generous in nature, modest, and easygoing (all those qualities he admired in his mother). His grave site sits in the sunshine, just outside the century-old gin building where he once worked. The top stone is from Africa, the bottom one from India. (bbkingmuseum.org)

Club Ebony

A block away from the museum is Club Ebony, a high-class nightclub (quite distinct from a juke joint) that was established in 1947, bought by B. B. King in 2008, and then donated to the museum in 2012. In its early years of operation, the club was part of the Chitlin' Circuit, a loose network of performance stages, juke joints, and clubs that showcased African American performers during the restrictive and brutal Jim Crow era. Now undergoing restoration and renovation, the plan is for the space to open as a live music venue. Over the decades, the club's stage

Club Ebony in Indianola was once part of the Chitlin' Circuit
JOSEPHINE MATYAS

The intersection of Second and Church Streets in Indianola is the corner where young B. B. busked

JOSEPHINE MATYAS

B. B. King's handprints are set in cement at the corner of Second and Church Streets in Indianola

JOSEPHINE MATYAS

has been graced by some of the greatest talents of the blues, including Howlin' Wolf, Ray Charles, Little Milton, Willie Clayton, and, of course, B. B. King. Before his passing in 2015, King would travel back to Indianola to host and play his annual homecoming festival. It was tradition for him to end the event with a performance at Club Ebony.

Strolling downtown Indianola (it's compact), we admired the brick wall mural of the man who created a wider audience for the blues as well as a stop at the Mississippi Blues Trail marker at the intersection of Second and Church streets, the corner where young B. B. honed his chops gigging for spare change. His life story is told on screen in the 2012 documentary *B. B. King: The Life of Riley*.

Indianola was a full day, a good day steeped in the blues and the storied life of one of Mississippi's favorite sons. There was no better way to bring it to a close than blasting *B. B. King Live at the Regal* on the van stereo, driving west into a fire-red sunset.

BERCLAIR

Being on a bit of a purist streak after spending the day in Indianola—steeped in all things B. B. King—we decided it was worth the detour along the Mississippi back roads to look for the Mississippi Blues Trail marker at County Road 513 and County Road 305 outside Berclair (just past Itta Bena), where the "Ambassador of the Blues" was born in 1925 in a house on the shores of Bear Creek. There's no house left standing.

County Road 513 and County Road 305 outside Berclair mark where the "Ambassador of the Blues" was born in 1925
JOSEPHINE MATYAS

The road is dusty gravel. But if you're on a blues pilgrimage, this is one place you need to come and sit quietly for a while.

B. B.'s parents were sharecroppers, and for his first few years of life, he lived at the family cabin less than half a mile from the Mississippi Blues Trail marker at the intersection of these two country roads.

GREENWOOD

Just outside Greenwood, there's a large billboard splashed with the message announcing the "Cotton Capital of the World." That's quite a claim for a state known for a history and production of cotton stretching back centuries.

Greenwood sits at the far eastern reach of the Delta at the confluence of two rivers: the Yalobusha and the muddy Tallahatchie (yes, *that* Tallahatchie, the one made famous by Bobbie Gentry singing about the time Billie Joe McAllister took a leap off the nearby bridge in her sultry country ballad "Ode to Billie Joe"). They flow together to form the Yazoo River.

The town's main street is tidy and neat with a century of fine architecture, the upscale Viking cooking school, small bistros, and the beautiful Turnrow Books, a well-known and much-loved independent bookstore that carries dozens of titles on everything Mississippi. On Howard Street, a Mississippi Blues Trail marker recognizes the WGRM radio studio, where Riley King first played guitar in the 1940s on the air as part of a Sunday afternoon gospel group (several years before he took up his deejay role at WDIA in Memphis). Over the years, Greenwood spawned dozens of blues and rhythm and blues players and singers, including Dion Peyton, Fenton Robinson, and Hubert Sumlin, the last of whom played two decades alongside Howlin' Wolf and was ranked No. 43 in *Rolling Stone*'s 100 Greatest Guitarists of All Time.

While Greenwood is known for its historic downtown, cotton production, and the turbulent 1950s and 1960s civil rights era, when it comes to blues lore, it is best known for guitar legend Robert Johnson's date with fate and his three possible grave sites. The heart of the Robert Johnson story is in Baptist Town, but its tentacles reach to intersections, dusty roadways, and small church cemeteries surrounding Greenwood. It's a story that stretches the imagination but is one worth exploring. (visitgreenwood.com)

Baptist Town

At the end of Greenwood's main street, the railway tracks divide the people by race and class, just as they've done for generations. Up and over the tracks is Baptist Town, the oldest African American community in Greenwood and a melting pot of the Delta where people would pour in on a Saturday night for a break from the body and spirit-breaking grind of work on the sweltering cotton plantations and gins.

There's a clear creek that runs through the tough-scrabble neighborhood, and over the years, many people would come to the waters to get baptized (hence the name). In its heyday during the early 1900s (before mechanization forced a mass exodus to the cities of the North), Baptist Town was home to around 10,000 people. Today, that count sits at about 500.

The neighborhood has been compressed down to just a few streets, so it wasn't difficult to track down Sylvester Hoover, a tall, lanky man with a quick smile who has lived a large part of his life in Baptist Town. He knows cotton—having worked picking and chopping—and he knows this part of the Delta well. Besides running a small convenience store,

Baptist Town is the oldest African American community in Greenwood
JOSEPHINE MATYAS

Baptist Town near Greenwood is rich with Robert Johnson lore
JOSEPHINE MATYAS

he has become quite a local expert on all things Robert Johnson. Hoover runs three-hour tours through Delta Blues Legend Tours, taking visitors to the local blues and civil rights sites in and around Greenwood. He'll customize the route, but most visitors are interested in following in the final footsteps of blues performer and guitarist Robert Johnson. "I bought this store here, and people used to come here and say 'show me where Robert Johnson played his music.' And they asked me to show them where he's buried at, and I just kinda connected the dots together. (deltablueslegendtours.com)

"All the Blacks lived here in Baptist Town. It was all bundled up. Juke joints was everywhere—it was just a house where you sold whisky, played music, and gambled. 'Wrong side of the tracks' may have been coined in towns just like this one."

It's impossible to read about blues lore without coming across Robert Johnson's infamous stroke-of-midnight deal with Satan, where, at a (hotly debated) rural intersection known as the Crossroads, he allegedly made a pact to sell his soul in return for mastery of the guitar.

The man they called the "King of the Delta Blues" was born in 1911 in Hazlehurst, in the southern part of the state, and over his short twenty-seven years, he bounced around the Arkansas and Mississippi Delta, performing at juke joints and on street corners for spare change. He was known for his shuffling rhythms and slide guitar leads in songs like "Terraplane Blues" and "Cross Road Blues." (You'll find a much more detailed account of Robert Johnson's life in chapter 7.)

Sylvester Hoover has a tale to tell for every nook of Baptist Town. "There were a lot of musicians lived here in this neighborhood. [Legendary blues musician] Honeyboy Edwards said Robert Johnson would hide out in houses to keep from going to work 'cause Honeyboy said he could make more money playing his guitar than he could chopping cotton. He would make more money playing his music. When you pick cotton it would pluck your fingertips, and you couldn't play your music as well. Robert Johnson came to Greenwood to play on Johnson Street. Musicians go where they money is—and the women are going to follow them because they're making money every day."

According to Hoover, Robert Johnson may not have had much education, but he was something of a marketing genius. "He would market himself, you know, 'the devil's music' 'cause Honeyboy said he would have eight or ten songs on the wall and he'd ask 'what song you gonna play this Saturday night, Robert?' and Robert say 'Susan wrote that one and John wrote that one and I wrote that one and the devil wrote that—which one you think I'm going to play?' He always would choose the devil's music. The music he'd sing, you know, all he's doing is just telling a story about his life. He didn't *think* 'hellhounds on my trail,' he felt it in his heart. And a lot of other people felt the same way that he felt. So that's why his got across the way it did. All he's doing is just telling a story about his life, singing the way he feel."

Legend has it that Robert Johnson spent two or three years gigging, drinking and womanizing in and around the Baptist Town neighborhood en route to his early death by poisoning in the late summer of 1938. You have to be careful with some of this history; it has acquired the aura of mythology because so little of it was recorded in real time by legitimate observers. There's a sign at the corner of Pelican and Young streets—a stone's throw from Hoover's Grocery—proclaiming he died on that very spot. Locals will tell you it's outright confabulation (the actual location and situation of Johnson's passing is also fiercely contested). Another hand-painted sign across the street identifies the boarded-up building as "Robert Johnson bought his Prince Albert tobacco here."

But there is no doubt that Baptist Town and the whole Greenwood area played a major role in the final years of Johnson's life. There is much mystery surrounding his final days, his poisoning, death, and burial. Hoover suggests that it is actually in nearby Three Forks that Johnson visited the Crossroads, not hours away in Clarksdale. (It's important to keep in mind that this debate is contemplating a story about a story.)

Three Forks

Both Honeyboy Edwards and Robert Johnson performed regularly at what was once a popular juke joint in Three Forks, now an empty lot of tangled weeds at the intersection of Highways 82 and 49E. In the day, this would have been the Three Forks Plantation, surrounded by long lines of cotton plants stretching to the horizon.

"Everybody wants to claim the Crossroads," said Hoover. And, apparently, the Greenwood area is no different. Standing in that empty lot at Three Forks, we let Hoover lay out his case for us.

"This is where Three Forks juke joint would have been, right by this telephone pole. It would have been lined with sharecroppers' cabins along the riverfront. Honeyboy Edwards says it was here, and he was the last person to play with Robert Johnson. Honeyboy Edwards said Robert Johnson left here one Saturday night in a black pinstripe suit and red necktie—said he was going to meet the devil. And he say he come back maybe two-and-a-half, three hours later—he say he start hitting tunes like you never hear before—and that's where it started. Honeyboy said he don't know what he did at the Crossroads, but he never was the same. His hair stood up on his head when Robert Johnson start playing his music. He said you never seen nothing like it before. Whatever he did at the Crossroads, he never was the same again."

Robert Johnson, according to Hoover, was like a magnet after he went to the Crossroads. "He would just draw people to him. He would just start playing his music, and people would come from here and yonder to hear Robert Johnson play his music. He loved women and whisky and, you know, too much of either one of them ain't really good for you. And that was his downfall."

Hoover's theory about the actual location of the Crossroads is rooted in Honeyboy Edwards's account plus some simple geography. "Robert

Johnson couldn't have walked from Baptist Town to Clarksdale [almost sixty miles away] and back in three hours. That's impossible. But he could have done it here."

In our travels across Mississippi, we heard many versions of the Crossroads story. As Hoover reminded us, everyone is looking to claim the mythical intersection. At this point, we cautioned ourselves that we were debating a *story*—something that probably never happened. But it is interesting—and entertaining—to consider all the possibilities.

However, there is no debate that Robert Johnson spent his final days and hours in a saga that began at the Three Forks juke joint and ended with his premature death on a plantation outside Baptist Town. And stories abound about that final night. Was he poisoned with strychnine or rat poison by the husband of a woman he'd taken to fooling around with? Was he poisoned by a woman he jilted who was jealous of his new girlfriend of the hour? Take your pick. In any case, there were women involved.

Once the poison grabbed hold, Johnson took to bed in his room in Baptist Town and then to a tenant's home on the nearby Star of the West Plantation. Death soon followed, and at age twenty-seven—in death as in life—Johnson's passing set off another set of declarations and speculations, this time about his actual burial place. Three local cemeteries claim their gravestones mark the spot, and with Hoover as our guide, we drove from one small rural church to the next to check them out.

Three Cemeteries

Just down the road from Three Forks in Quito is Payne Chapel Missionary Baptist Church. In the cemetery is the first Robert Johnson memorial marker, placed by an Atlanta rock band that, according to Hoover, jumped the gun on the basis of some inaccurate information.

Just a mile down the road near Morgan City is the second (supposed) grave site at Mt. Zion Missionary Baptist Church, where an elaborate one-ton memorial obelisk was erected by Columbia Records. Visitors leave money, love letters, beer, and small bottles of whisky. Impressive as this marker is, it's still not the spot that's come to be accepted as Robert Johnson's final resting place.

The third church cemetery is generally thought to be the actual grave site. After his death on August 16, 1938, Johnson was buried in a simple pine box provided by the county at Little Zion Missionary Baptist Church on Money Road just north of Greenwood. This stretch of

Little Zion Missionary Baptist Church on Money Road is considered to be the actual burial spot of Robert Johnson

JOSEPHINE MATYAS

Music fans come to visit Robert Johnson's gravestone at Little Zion Missionary Baptist Church

JOSEPHINE MATYAS

country road is peppered with tumbledown, tar paper shacks and has been knocked around by several tornados, but each time the Little Zion community church has been spared.

According to Hoover, this small cemetery is the actual spot. "Lotta people come up here. I clean up here two or three times a week. This is my church. This church is 146 years old, built by field hands. This is the church I been to my whole life. Miss Rose told me where he was buried. At the Little Zion Church with the road in front and a river behind it."

According to Hoover, Rose Eskridge provided an eyewitness account, which he believes was the extra bit of evidence blues historians needed. "Miss Rose said they came to her house and told her husband Tom, 'Go to the barn and get a four-by-eight-foot box—go to the church and dig a hole and put 'im in it.' And that's what Tom Eskridge did. She walked up here to bring him some water. She just been married one week. She was twenty-one years old."

It was a hot summer afternoon, and Tom wanted a shady place to dig the grave, so they chose a spot under an old pecan tree. "She was an eyewitness. She was the last person to see Robert Johnson, on Earth, right here," said Hoover. He added that Rose told him they went down the road to get a 'bootleg' preacher—a preacher without a church—to commit Johnson's body to the ground. Rose, who was a longtime cook at the Star of the West Plantation, died in 2006 and is also buried at Little Zion.

The following Sunday, we accepted Hoover's kind invitation to join the morning service at Little Zion Church (his wife Mary is a choir director). We felt welcomed from the moment we hopped out of our camper van. It was a blazingly sunny spring morning, and we found seats in the hand-hewn wooden pews that "fit your bottom just right."

There was a barrelhouse-style pianist with huge baritone pipes, backed by half a dozen women in the ranks of the small but passionate choir. The songs of call-and-response gospel filled every nook and cranny of the modest wooden church (no shy singers in this group). We found ourselves sitting in witness of part two of the Saturday night/Sunday morning equation. Call-and-response is like a first cousin to the blues. It's an interactive musical dialogue that preachers and musicians use to reach out to and engage with the audience. The room was filled with shouts of "Amen" and "Hallelujah" back and forth between the choir and the congregation in the pews. While the subject matter may be different (hence the Saturday night/Sunday morning reference), they share emotion and intensity of song. As Sylvester Hoover explained, "On Saturday night they sing 'Baby' and 'Honey,' and on Sunday morning they take that out and sing 'Jesus' and 'God.' Identical, same music. Same people singing it."

It was a pleasure and an honor to be a part of their service and a perfect finish to our time in Greenwood.

BELZONI

There may be something in the water at Belzoni (self-proclaimed "Catfish Capital of the World") that produced the notable blues icons born in or around the small town: slide guitarist Elmore James, blues harp player Sonny Boy Williamson II, and blues piano master Pinetop Perkins (who often accompanied blues giant Muddy Waters, a gig that brought Perkins international recognition). The opening slide riff of James's "Dust My Broom" is probably one of the most iconic moments on the blues guitar.

On Jackson Street in Belzoni, a Mississippi Blues Trail marker recognizes the Easy Pay Store and Turner's Drug Store, sponsors of some of the first Mississippi radio programs to showcase the Delta blues. Turner's also produced Tallyho, a questionable alcohol-laced vitamin and mineral tonic. In the 1930s, 1940s, and 1950s, pioneer of the blues harp Sonny Boy Williamson II and Elmore James—"King of the Slide Guitar"—gigged on the sidewalk in front of Turner's and at various Belzoni juke joints and cafés.

ROLLING FORK

On Highway 61 (the Blues Highway), between Belzoni and Yazoo City, is the small town of Rolling Fork, the birthplace of McKinley "Muddy Waters" Morganfield, renowned as a pioneer of the electric blues. Muddy's mastery of the harmonica and the guitar went on to influence some of the modern day's best-known blues artists, including Bonnie Raitt and Eric Clapton, who described Waters in his autobiography as the "father figure I never really had."

Beside the downtown courthouse, the shotgun-style Muddy Waters Blues Cabin sits next to the Mississippi Blues Trail plaque honoring the self-taught guitarist and harp player. Murals throughout the town feature images of Muddy and other blues greats, and every spring, the city marks its musical blues heritage with the Deep Delta Blues & Heritage Festival. (lowerdelta.org/festivals)

YAZOO CITY

Coming from the north or from the south, the bridge at Yazoo City is a visual demarcation of the land that makes up the Delta. The very first time we drove into the Mississippi Delta, we made the trip from south to north through Yazoo City, and it was a take-your-breath-away moment. Below Yazoo City is an area of rolling countryside, much of it speckled with patches of thick forest. Just north of town on Highway 49 West, we slipped onto the long, low bridge, where the woodlots suddenly disappear and the panorama shifts to the fertile, broad bottomlands of the Delta. The terrain shimmers and shines.

The buoyant first verse of Paul Simon's "Graceland" provided the sound track for one of the more dramatic entrance points to the Mississippi Delta.

> The Mississippi Delta was shining
> Like a National guitar

With "Graceland," Simon captures that exact frame, crossing the bridge and looking down on the Delta's vast floodplains. Musicians may

Just north of Yazoo City on Highway 49W, the landscape shifts to the flat, broad bottomlands of the Delta
JOSEPHINE MATYAS

understand the reference, but most casual listeners will need a schooling on the National guitar. The National brand is a style known as a resonator guitar, an early technology designed to amplify the volume of the traditional steel-string acoustic guitar. The National's bulletproof, polished metal body—it literally shines—makes the instrument loud enough to compete with drums and horns but also produces a distinctive metallic and abrasive sound, iconic for its own sonority. Listen to the performance of "Aberdeen Mississippi Blues" by Bukka White for a surprisingly good recording of an early resonator guitar.

That beautiful introduction to the landscape of the Delta—from south to north—is so transfixing that any time we've traveled the opposite direction, we do a U-turn and head back over the bridge just to experience that take-your-breath-away moment once more.

Just off the highway outside of Yazoo City, Ubon's Restaurant promises the "best funeral a dead pig could have." Here, they "eat everything but the squeal" and waste nothing. The ribs and brisket are flavorful and moist, with meat that falls off the bone. The six hours of cooking or eighteen hours of smoking tease the senses. Leslie Roark Scott is the sixth generation of the family to own this roadhouse, which wins award after

At Ubon's Restaurant, the pitmaster promises "the best funeral a dead pig could have"
JOSEPHINE MATYAS

award for the quality of the barbecue. The family sauce recipe goes back generations, and bottles can be purchased for home cooking. Appetizers included fried dill pickles, deep-fried pork skins, and fried cheese sticks.

Out front of Ubon's, there is a Mississippi Blues Trail marker for Arnold Dwight "Gatemouth" Moore, a popular blues singer circa 1940s who migrated to gospel and preaching after he felt the calling (there's that Saturday night/Sunday morning theme again). Both B. B. King and Rufus Thomas cited Moore as a major musical influence. (ubonsbbq.com)

BENTONIA

This lonely whistle-stop on the rail line, surrounded by rolling cornfields and small patches of trees, is home to the distinctive Bentonia Sound and the Blue Front Café, a well-known and much-loved stop on the Mississippi Blues Trail. The inside of the café is worn, with concrete floors and an oil-barrel woodstove blazing away. As the oldest surviving juke joint in the state, it's a popular pilgrimage site for blues fans from around the world.

The historic Blue Front Café is home base to the distinctive Bentonia blues sound
JOSEPHINE MATYAS

The music that comes out of Bentonia stands apart from other styles of the blues, marked by open tunings and chords with a distinctly minor (sad) feel. Bentonia blues are lonesome and haunting, with a high-pitch moaning often sung at a falsetto. The guitar's minor chords are created by droning open strings, imparting an ominous or eerie feel. Guitarist Nehemiah "Skip" James is considered a pioneer of the Bentonia school; his distinct, complicated style created a busier sound, deviating from the typical blues of its time.

"It put me in a trance, the first time I heard Skip James do 'Cypress Grove Blues,'" said Ronnie Eldridge, an amateur blues historian and keeper of the flame who is fervent about and promotes the Blue Front Café. "I'd never heard nothing like that before."

A Mississippi Blues Trail marker out front of the café acknowledges the rich heritage of this out-of-the-way place, recognizing the ground-breaking generation of bluesmen like Jack Owens, Henry Stuckey, and Skip James. The late Owens, a local farmer, singer, and guitarist, held to the old ways: they say he was the last farmer in the area to plow with a mule, hang bottles in the trees, and bury money in the ground. Just a few miles outside Bentonia—off Rose Hill Road—there's another Mississippi Blues Trail marker to recognize Owens as a pioneer of that distinctive Bentonia sound.

Owens's singular contributions have been carried into the twenty-first century by Jimmy "Duck" Holmes, a retired educator born to sharecroppers and one of the oldest active players of the country blues tradition. Holmes is the operator of the Blue Front Café, which has been in his family since its inception in 1948, when Duck was an infant. During the long days of the cotton harvest, the café doors were open 24/7, serving the community as grocery store, barbershop, and juke joint, sometimes selling moonshine corn liquor out the back door. Duck has been called the "Last of the Bentonia Bluesmen," as he is the last direct musical descendant of Henry Stuckey, Skip James, and Jack Owens.

"A lot of these guys from Jackson, they come here and play, just to say they've played here," explained Eldridge. "There's an appeal to being associated with the Blue Front."

The sparse, rustic building is no longer a regular music or dance venue, but it still opens its doors for private parties and special events. Sitting inside, listening to Duck ease into the Bentonia-style blues gave us a feeling for how it must have been in its heyday. "There is something Duck does that is unique," Eldridge noted. "It goes all the way back to

Africa, a tradition, to just make up a song as he plays. Duck is a perfect example of it; he can just make it up."

Typical Bentonia blues guitar tunings include—from lowest to highest—an open E minor chord—E-B-E-G-B-E (note the minor third, G natural)—or D minor—D-A-D-F-A-D, where F natural is the minor third. Lots of other musicians went on to use open tunings in minor keys—Bukka White (cousin to B. B. King), Albert Collins, Arthur "Big Boy" Crudup, and Henry Townsend—but it's most consistently associated with the Bentonia sound.

FINDING FOOD AND DRINK

A Plate of Mississippi Barbecue

If your heart can take it, barbecue is mingling with the locals as well as a true taste of southern culture.

- Betty's Place, Indianola
- Ubon's Restaurant, Yazoo City
- Cajun Shotgun House & BBQ, Greenville

Southern Fried Chicken

Does it get any more southern than fried chicken? Soaked in a marinade or batter, coated, seasoned, and then tossed into a skillet or fryer of oil until crispy and golden. You'll find it everywhere, but nowhere is it as good as at the cook's mama's place.

- The Crystal Grill, Greenwood
- Lusco's Restaurant, Greenwood
- Sherman's, Greenville

Pond-Raised Catfish

Mississippi leads the country in pond-raised catfish. It's on every restaurant menu—fried, grilled, or blackened.

- The Crown, Indianola
- Lusco's Restaurant, Greenwood

- Belzoni's Catfish Café, Belzoni
- Fan & Johnny's, Greenwood
- Nola, Indianola

Comeback Sauce

The house sauce of Mississippi that's used for dipping and topping almost anything. A zesty, versatile mix of mayonnaise, ketchup, chili sauce, and seasonings.

- The Blue Biscuit, Indianola
- Fan & Johnny's, Greenwood

Fried Dill Pickles

Batter them and toss into the deep fryer for a tangy, crunchy snack.

- The Blue Biscuit, Indianola
- Sherman's, Greenville

The Blue Biscuit in Indianola is right across the street from the B. B. King Museum and Delta Interpretive Center

JOSEPHINE MATYAS

Hot Delta Tamales

Warm corn-shuck–wrapped bundles could be easily taken to the cotton fields during the fall picking season.

- Doe's Eat Place, Greenville
- The Crystal Grill, Greenwood

MUST SEE

- The blues murals on the brick walls in downtown Leland
- Watch *Fatal Flood*, the PBS American Experience documentary at the 1927 Flood Museum in Greenville
- Study the equipment and how it's set up at B. B. King's home recording studio inside the B. B. King Museum and Delta Interpretive Center in Indianola
- Find B. B. King's set of handprints in the concrete at the corner of Second and Church streets in Indianola
- Take the blues history/Robert Johnson tour with Sylvester Hoover in the Baptist Town neighborhood of Greenwood

MUST READ

- *Where I Was Born and Raised*, David Cohn (1967)
- *Blues All Around Me: The Autobiography of B. B. King*, B. B. King and David Ritz (1996)
- *Rising Tide: The Great Mississippi Flood of 1927 and How It Changed America*, John M. Barry (1997)

MUST LISTEN AND WATCH

- "Back-Water Blues," Bessie Smith
- "High Water Everywhere," Charley Patton
- "Dust My Broom," Elmore James
- "Cross Road Blues," Robert Johnson
- "Three O'Clock Blues," B. B. King

- "It Must Have Been the Devil," Jack Owens
- *Deep Blues: A Musical Pilgrimage to the Crossroads*, directed by Robert Mugge (1991)
- *B. B. King: The Life of Riley*, directed by Jon Brewer (2012)
- *When Weather Changed History*, The Weather Channel documentary series (2008-2009)

GUITAR NOTES

B. B. King's distinctive guitar style—bending single notes with a pronounced vibrato—is associated with his trademark 1950s-era Gibson ES-345 (the guitar he played most of his life). B. B. used very light gauge strings—10s or lighter—and played a one-note style, almost never playing chords of two or three notes. His trademark sound was a one-note riff. His left-hand vibrato—rapidly wiggling the string back and forth across the neck—created the bold, identifiable trembling sound. By bending notes—stretching the string across the neck of the guitar—the pitch was raised microtones, creating a crying or wailing effect. Another part of King's signature style was that he rarely played and sang at the same time.

5

MISSISSIPPI OUTSIDE THE DELTA

Across Mississippi—inside and outside the Delta—the shared history is a painful one for both Whites and Blacks, especially those who are descendants of enslaved Africans brought to America against their will. The slave-based, plantation economy was widespread; Black people worked to the bone to fatten the pockets of White merchants, plantation owners, and businessmen.

This was the economic and social reality across the blues-rich Delta; it was just as true in other parts of the state and, indeed, across much of the South. While the enormous cotton plantations were concentrated in the Delta (the soil there being enriched by the seasonal flooding of the Mississippi River and perfect for agriculture), the parts of the state to the south and east were also very dependent on the work done by enslaved individuals. These plantations produced tobacco, rice, and cotton or processed indigo, and all prospered at an extreme human cost.

The sections below on the geography and people are snapshots of the main points to appreciate when understanding how the blues began, flourished, and spread. Chapter 2 provides a deeper look at the land and the history of the Delta—it's the spot to turn to for a much more detailed explanation.

LAND AND WATER

The Unbreakable Bond between the Blues and the Land

In the South, the land was prime for large, expansive plantations of cotton and other crops that were lucrative for the owners. In the southwest part of the state, the loosely packed, brown loamy earth was especially well suited for the planting and cultivation of cotton on a massive scale.

The blues came partly from the call-and-response songs, the field hollers, and the work songs of the slaves and the sharecroppers whose back-breaking task it was to till the soil, plant, and harvest the crops. Many of these traditional work songs helped to coordinate movements and keep tempo during repetitive manual tasks.

Riverboats and Railways

Many large plantations were located along the banks of the rivers—the Mississippi and the Yazoo—and inland close to the network of rail lines that linked the state to other parts of the South. Early on, the traffic of riverboats and railcars made it easy for blues musicians to hop from one community to another in search of making enough money to just keep going. In this way, and together with their love of performance, the blues spread from the flat plantations of the Delta through the rolling hills and onto the prairies of the northeast.

Traveling the Natchez Trace

The historic Natchez Trace Parkway has a story stretching back 10,000 years, long before European settlers arrived in Mississippi. Now a tranquil recreational roadway and a part of the National Park Service, the natural travel corridor once bisected the traditional homelands of the Natchez, Chickasaw, and Choctaw tribes. In the plantation era, it was used as a land route for merchants from the North.

The landscape continuously changes from forest to meadows. It crosses through distinct ecosystems—bayous and swamps, limestone caves, deciduous woodlands—providing protection as a "habitat corridor" for the animal life. In the south, it's alligators and armadillos; in the north, fox and white-tailed deer. In all, the parkway is home to birds, mammals, amphibians, and reptiles.

THE PEOPLE AND THE STRUGGLES

The Concentration of Wealth

In towns like Natchez, incredible wealth was on display, and the divide between the living conditions of Blacks and Whites was as pronounced as ever. The city was one of the busiest slave trading centers in the nation, and the buying and selling of enslaved human beings was central to this explosion of plantation and cotton-fueled prosperity.

The Forced Migration

In the first half of the nineteenth century, the Forks of the Road slave market in Natchez resulted in one of the largest involuntary movements of labor from the northern slave states to the southern ones. More than 750,000 enslaved African Americans—considered "surplus" in the states of Maryland, Virginia, and Kentucky—were purchased by slave traders and then sent in groups to be put on the human auction block in the South. Families resisted being torn apart by the inhumane practice of being "sold south," and many individuals attempted escape or self-mutilation to make themselves damaged goods.

Growing Up Black and Poor in Jim Crow Mississippi

When President Abraham Lincoln signed the Emancipation Proclamation in 1863, it declared "that all persons held as slaves . . . shall be then, thenceforward, and forever free."

The reality for most newly "freed" Black persons was something different. Immediately after Emancipation, the White planter class attempted to enforce what were known as the Black Codes, a system of rules and regulations to force freed Blacks to work on plantations under conditions that closely mirrored slavery. In the Reconstruction era—the chaotic years following the American Civil War—many states across the South introduced what were known as Jim Crow laws with the intention of disenfranchising and segregating the African American population. These Jim Crow laws and the system of White supremacy stayed entrenched until the passage of the 1964 Civil Rights Act.

The Blues Radiated Out from the Delta

The blues may have begun on the cotton plantations and in the workhouses across the Delta, but it didn't take long for the infectious and soulful music to spread and flourish in communities across Mississippi and into neighboring states. The twentieth-century history of America has largely been the story of people moving from rural, agricultural areas into industrialized cities, often clustered along the coastlines and into the Midwest.

Musicians were often on the move—chasing gigs and sometimes running from bad luck—and the rivers and railways they rode played a major part in facilitating the spread of the blues to communities. Boats and railcars were loaded with bales of cotton headed to ports along the Gulf Coast. On board, musicians packed the blues with them, and in cities like New Orleans, it mixed and cross-fertilized with the beginning notes of jazz. At its core, the blues are rooted in the experiences of life, both bad and good. It spoke to people because, as a music, the blues could convey an infinite range of emotions.

ROAD-TRIPPING MISSISSIPPI OUTSIDE THE DELTA

We were sad to leave the Delta but knew that the tentacles of the blues reached south and east of its border and that our exploration to find the roots was not yet over. The regions that surround the Delta are varied—from forests of tall pines to the rolling hills of the northeast.

The Natchez Trace Parkway bisects the state from Natchez in the southwest corner to Tupelo near the northeast border with Alabama and Tennessee. The commercial-free, woodland-lined roadway is a National Scenic Byway that winds its way through the history of the South and was once a major travel corridor for traders and merchants. In full, it goes from Natchez, Mississippi, to Nashville, Tennessee. In the early 1800s, northern farmers floated crops and livestock on wooden flatboats down the Mississippi River to the ports of Natchez and New Orleans, sold their goods, and then traveled the land route homeward to the north. Driving even a short stretch of the Natchez Trace can be a peaceful and calm interval to reflect on the tumultuous history of the state.

Our first stop was the state capital, Jackson, then south into distinctly hillier country where we explored the land of Robert Johnson's youth at Crystal Springs (where his grandson runs the Robert Johnson Blues Museum) and to Hazlehurst, Johnson's birthplace and home to the small but very interesting Mississippi Music Hall of Fame.

We detoured west to where Highway 61 meets Vicksburg (birthplace of Willie Dixon) and then south to Natchez, a city that was once home to the wealthiest slaveholders in the nation. Then we turned east across the state to Meridian, a city established in the 1800s as a railway town. Meridian plays a part in Mississippi blues history as home to Jimmie Rodgers and Peavey Electronics, the makers of the Delta Blues amp used by blues and rock and roll artists everywhere.

Our final stretch exploring the roots of the blues inside Mississippi took us up the east side of the state, from Meridian north to West Point, birthplace of Howlin' Wolf, and finally to Tupelo, tucked along the Natchez Trace Parkway as it crosses the northeast tip of the state. Tupelo is in the heart of the Hills Region and is the birthplace of the "King of Rock and Roll," Elvis Presley. While Elvis was not a roots blues artist, he was certainly heavily schooled in both gospel and the blues, and his worldwide popularity helped to spread the influence of the blues around the globe.

Outside of the Delta, many cities and towns were part of the continuing evolution of the blues. Blues players unloaded their instruments at street corners and in juke joints and clubs, fiddled with the tuning (or not), and sometimes mixed with other existing styles of music. These slow-cooker communities—like Jackson, Vicksburg, Meridian, and Tupelo—were about the nurturing and growth of America's music.

JACKSON

Although it sits to the south of the expansive Delta farmlands, there are a dozen Mississippi Blues Trail markers in the Jackson area, recognizing a more urban-influenced blues. Jackson can boast a larger number of the historic blues plaques than any other city in Mississippi. Located in the central part of the state, right between the Delta and the Gulf Coast, the music that was cooked in this city took jazz and zydeco and mixed it with the blues to create an interesting rhythmic gumbo. Today, they call it the "City with Soul." (VisitJackson.com)

Like many other larger cities, the state capital is a place where people were in transit—catching buses or trains, many hightailing it out of the Delta. For some, it was a springboard to bigger and better opportunities in metropolitan centers. While people were in transition, leaving their rural lives behind and heading for larger cities, Jackson was a major urban hub for the African American community. It was also a popular stop for many Black musicians and groups who were traveling through on the Chitlin' Circuit, booking whatever gigs they could in Jackson's small clubs and juke joints. Nicknamed after the soul food dish chitterlings (stewed pig intestines), the Chitlin' Circuit included performance venues throughout the East, South, and upper Midwest areas, where it was safe and acceptable for African American musicians and entertainers to perform during the era of racial restrictions and conflict. Musicians were always on the move along the one-nighter venue, sometimes spending months touring the South with one gig in each club before moving on. In the Jackson area, Chitlin' Circuit clubs like Stevens Rose Room and the Rankin Auditorium hosted touring acts, including Elmore James ("King of the Slide Guitar") and Sonny Boy Williamson II.

Museum of Mississippi History

This immersive downtown museum is devoted to the stories of people who shaped the state of Mississippi. It's a good spot to become familiar with the pain and the beauty of the state's historic arc—from the arrival of iron-shackled slaves transported across the ocean to America to the inequitable plantation society of the Cotton Kingdom to how mechanization upended the agricultural economy across the South. It opened in 2017 to commemorate the Mississippi bicentennial as one of a duo of new museums dedicated to telling the state's complex history. (museumofmshistory.com)

Mississippi Civil Rights Museum

Unveiled in 2017, the galleries at the Mississippi Civil Rights Museum focus on the years from the end of the American Civil War to the mid-1970s, the height of the civil rights movement in America. The history shown in the photos, films, and interactive exhibits lays the groundwork for understanding the fight for equality and the long struggle for civil rights. Wound into this are the roles of church, family, and community, all parts of the bedrock that eventually birthed the blues. (mscivilrightsmuseum.com)

Farish Street Historic District

To understand the growth of the blues in a major Mississippi urban area, we stopped at the Farish Street Historic District, a part of the downtown recognized as a national historic place in 1980. Although it is now a row of boarded-up storefronts (albeit with a streetscape that has undergone some impressive renovations, showing the first part of a slowly ongoing restoration initiative), Farish Street was once home to many of the city's Black-owned businesses, juke joints, and a happening blues scene. According to the Southern Foodways Alliance, in the post–World War II boom, the neighborhood "served as a cultural and business hub for the African American population of central Mississippi.

The Farish Street Historic District was once the largest economically independent African American community in Mississippi

JOSEPHINE MATYAS

Born during Reconstruction, the Farish Street District was forged by Black Mississippians searching for spaces to call their own. In its mid-twentieth-century heyday, Farish Street was the largest economically independent African American community in Mississippi."

Besides being the center for civil rights pioneers—activist Medgar Evers had his office here—Farish Street housed the headquarters of Trumpet Records (there's a Mississippi Blues Trail marker at 309 North Farish Street), the "first record label in Mississippi to achieve national prominence." Originally a hardware store, the new owners acquired a stock of rhythm and blues 78-rpm records along with the nuts-and-bolts inventory when they bought the business lock, stock, and barrel in 1949. Proprietors Willard and Lillian McMurry opened the Record Mart on the site and launched the Trumpet Records label from the retail store, later adding a recording studio in the back room. It's notable for its place in Jackson's African American music scene and as the first recording releases of several Mississippi blues legends, including Sonny Boy Williamson II, Willie Love, and Elmore James. James's classic slide guitar adaptation of "Dust My Broom" (secretly recorded at the end of a Sonny Boy session at Trumpet), reached the national rhythm and blues charts, gaining him popular respect and celebrity. After just four years, Trumpet Records was gone, out of funds by 1955.

We walked a little farther up the street to the Alamo Theatre—its restored marquee dominates the streetscape—known for its association

F. Jones Corner on North Farish Street is listed on the National Register of Historic Places and has housed a juke joint since 2009

JOSEPHINE MATYAS

with blues and jazz acts, including Nat King Cole, Elmore James, and local talent and powerhouse Dorothy Moore. As a teenager, Moore was a consistent winner in the Alamo's Wednesday night talent contests, leading to a recording contract and a local association with Jackson's Malaco Records. She is best known for her megahit "Misty Blue" on the Malaco label.

The live music scene in the neighborhood has been revived at F. Jones Corner (on North Farish Street). Originally a filling station, the building—which is listed on the National Register of Historic Places—has housed a juke joint since 2009, hosting local and regional blues musicians on weekend nights. (fjonescorner.com)

Malaco Records

We went looking for the Mississippi Blues Trail marker at Malaco Records—still an operating record label also known as the "Last Soul Company"—placed there in recognition of its role in the nurturing of rhythm and blues, southern soul, blues, and gospel. Founded at this site in 1967, the family-owned studio was the first state-of-the-art recording facility in Mississippi. We were planning a brisk read and photo of the trail marker outside but were quickly welcomed in, the southern hospitality rolled out, and we found ourselves sitting in the office of Tommy Couch Jr. As son of the founder, he grew up in the recording business.

"Malaco started as a promotion company," explained Couch, "but soon it started recording its own acts. 'Mississippi Fred' McDowell was one of the first—'I Do Not Play No Rock 'N' Roll' was recorded here." *Rolling Stone* listed this album as one of the top blues recordings of the 1970s. The magazine's Michael Goodwin wrote, "McDowell plays the blues, plays them wide-open and full-out, plays them because he has to . . . a priceless, once-every-twenty-years wonder of a musician who towers above the electric garbage that floods from the studios and the radio stations. . . . The beat comes from somewhere deep inside, and it has an incredible power behind it—a power that comes close to tearing McDowell's songs to pieces."

According to Couch, musicians and singers were drawn to Malaco for the sound of the room. In addition to Mississippi Fred, it attracted artistic giants, including Dorothy Moore ("Misty Blue"), "Little" Milton, Bobby Rush, and Jean Knight, who recorded "Mister Big Stuff" in the Malaco Studios (later released by Stax Records out of Memphis and

Re-creation of the Malaco Recording Studio is on display at the
Delta Blues Museum in Clarksdale
DELTA BLUES MUSEUM

going on to become a national rhythm and blues hit, selling double plati-
num, and being nominated for a Grammy).

"The sound Stax had was brilliant. It was really good," said Couch.
"What was going on at Stax, and Muscle Shoals, and at Malaco, it was
such a natural interwoven fabric to make the music. No one ever considered color, so no one cared. It wasn't like 'we need a White guy or we
need a Black guy.' The best musicians just came together, and no one
cared about anything else except making great music." (malaco.com)

Hal & Mal's

We'd heard about the regular Blue Monday event, hosted by the
Central Mississippi Blues Society at Hal & Mal's, a landmark, family-
owned Jackson blues club. The walls of the club are an authentic blues
archive—plastered with signed photos of various blues players. Musicians are invited to come jam (on two different Monday nights, Craig
picked up his Fender Precision bass and took to the stage for a couple
of songs). About three decades ago, the rambling space—once a train
depot—was renovated by brothers Hal and Malcolm White into what
has become a stronghold of the Jackson music scene. The club is per-

fectly positioned to catch musicians on the road traveling between gigs in New Orleans and Memphis.

It was at Hal & Mal's that we had several up-close brushes with iconic Mississippi blues singers and players. We found ourselves seated next to Dorothy Moore and Craig jammed with Jackson blues legend "King Edward" Antoine, who has performed with legends such as Muddy Waters, Howlin' Wolf, Buddy Guy, Junior Wells, and Sam Myers. His experiences at clubs in the North were reflected in the blues that rolled off the stage—more soul inflected, more Chicago than Delta.

The octogenarian always seemed to have a smile, both onstage and when we sat down with him before he stepped into performance mode for Blue Monday.

"The blues came from the Delta. It moved to Jackson, then New Orleans, then on from there," King Edward said. "The blues is a feeling, man. The blues comes from gospel. In the church. Blues tells a story about all the life that you lived; you've got the blues around you all the time."

According to Edward's manager, Peggy Brown, "Jackson gets overlooked in the blues scene. But Jackson is where a lot of the music was recorded in the early days at places like Trumpet Records. Jackson is known because a lot of the guys from the Delta came here to record. The Delta blues came to Jackson and became urbanized with the addition of horns and a more rhythm and blues sound."

Brown claims that in a state known for its divisive and violent racial history, the music of the blues helped soothe the divide. "Back in the days, Black guys played down in the Subway Lounge [a popular basement club in Jackson with regular jazz and blues shows from the mid-1980s until the building's demolition in 2004]. People—Black and White—sat elbow to elbow. They both loved the music. The music is the common denominator. Everyone comes together around this music." (halandmals.com)

King Edward Hotel

On the western edge of downtown Jackson is the towering, twelve-story King Edward Hotel (originally opened in 1923 as the Edwards Hotel). The Beaux Arts–style hotel once held a temporary recording studio in the 1930s for OKeh Records and was used by singers of the blues, including

Bo Carter, Robert Wilkins, and Joe McCoy. Prior to World War II, most recording studios were located in the North, so musicians had to travel hundreds of miles to reach one. Record companies like OKeh sometimes opened temporary recording studios in hotels across the South.

Mississippi Music Experience

The Mississippi Musicians Hall of Fame is the umbrella organization overseeing the Mississippi Music Experience at the Iron Horse Grill. They also administer the excellent Mississippi Music Museum to the south in Hazlehurst, birthplace of Robert Johnson. Located at the eatery, in what was an early 1900s smokehouse, the Mississippi Music Experience is a time line of the history of Mississippi music from the 1800s to the current day, along with some interesting memorabilia and exhibits. (theironhorsegrill.com)

CRYSTAL SPRINGS

Leaving the Delta behind, south of Jackson the land begins to roll, green with pockets of forest lining the roadway. We were en route to Hazlehurst (birthplace of Robert Johnson and home to the small Mississippi Music Hall of Fame) but found we were passing right through Crystal Springs and the Robert Johnson Blues Museum, operated by the Robert Johnson Blues Foundation.

The museum is a modest, one-room venture operated in a storefront on the main street by Steve Johnson (grandson to the blues legend). Opening hours are by chance or appointment (we weren't so lucky, but a neighboring shopkeeper produced a key, opened up for us, and let us walk through). Robert Johnson fans will be interested in the photos, posters, and instruments, including an old piano that the museum claims Johnson played at one time. (robertjohnsonbluesfoundation.org)

In Crystal Springs, there's also a Mississippi Blues Trail marker to recognize Tommy Johnson, one of the most influential Mississippi blues artists in the early part of the twentieth century. Tommy Johnson is known for his distinctive falsetto moan that was adopted by many of his contemporaries and followers. His original songs include "Canned Heat Blues" and "Big Road Blues."

According to the Blues Trail marker, this Johnson has a story of a crossroads meeting that precedes Robert Johnson's: "Johnson learned to play guitar from his older brother LeDell and as a young teen ran away to the Delta. He returned two years later an accomplished performer, which, according to LeDell, Johnson attributed to a meeting with a mysterious figure at a crossroads. The story, which involved Johnson handing over his guitar to a large black man who tuned it for him, predates the similar and more famous tale of the (unrelated) bluesman Robert Johnson selling his soul to the devil at the crossroads."

Not to put too fine a point on it, but there's a lot of mythology in the blues.

HAZLEHURST

A little to the south—avoiding the interstate and sticking to rural Highway 51—we stopped at the Hazlehurst train station, home to the Mississippi Music Hall of Fame. Under the umbrella of the Mississippi Musicians Hall of Fame, it's home to a collection of donated items covering

The Hazlehurst train station is home to the Mississippi Music Hall of Fame, a small museum with a wide collection
JOSEPHINE MATYAS

blues greats like Robert Johnson, Charley Patton, and Muddy Waters as well as all other Mississippi-born music genres, including country, rock, classical, gospel, and jazz. We were drawn to this small museum as marking the birthplace of Robert Johnson and to the significance of the station—from here Robert Johnson hitched a ride in a boxcar north to the Delta. The circa-1858 train depot still services the Illinois Central, which blasts through twice a day, once in each direction.

There's a Mississippi Blues Trail marker just outside the railway station in recognition of Johnson's birthplace on the outskirts of town. The original homestead was razed when Interstate 55 was constructed, but early plans describe it as a common "saddlebag" design, with two large rooms on either side of the front door. On display, the home's fireplace surround is the only intact part of the home to survive the demolition. Johnson lived in Hazlehurst while he was a young child, before his stepfather and mother moved the family to Memphis, although he returned here many times.

Robert was an illegitimate child—his mother was Julia Ann Dobbs, and his birth father, Noah Johnson, was an itinerant field hand. At the time, the local economy was based on lumber and row crops. His stepfather was a very poor farmer.

According to Dr. Jim Brewer, founder of the museum, "There are so many stories about Robert Johnson that cannot be documented. Sometimes, it's all kind of a 'choose the story you like best.'"

Nine-year-old Robert played his first music on three nails and three strands of wire, a diddley bow. He nailed the wire to the side of his house and used a bottle to keep the strings from lying flat and to tune his homemade instrument. Seven years later, he got his first guitar, and three years after that, he approached Son House to ask him to teach him to play, but the older bluesman complained that Johnson was "just making a racket." "Honey Boy" Edwards was a little more precise: "chicken scratch."

Johnson was determined to make a living without picking cotton. Undeterred by the criticism of his playing, the young Johnson returned to his hometown to ask local blues guitarist Ike Zimmerman to become his mentor and teacher. Legend has it that he kept Zimmerman up late into the night with both men sitting on gravestones in a local cemetery. Johnson was determined to learn everything he could about the guitar and the blues. And every Saturday morning, he could be found practic-

Hazlehust is where Robert Johnson allegedly returned to learn his mastery of the guitar from Ike Zimmerman
JOSEPHINE MATYAS

ing on the front steps of the Hazlehurst courthouse, gigging at local juke joints every Saturday night.

After several years (stories report between one and two years), Johnson returned north to the heart of the Delta, an accomplished guitar player. "They say it sounded like two guitar musicians playing, and few blues artists have been able to replicate his sound," said Brewer.

Here again—outside the Delta itself—we bumped up against a hot debate about the true location of the infamous Crossroads. "There are three places in the Delta that claim to be the Crossroads," said Brewer. "But if you look at the lyrics, we think it is more about a state of mind."

In addition to the in-depth biography of Robert Johnson, the Mississippi Music Hall of Fame charts a time line of the blues, beginning with Charley Patton at Dockery Farms, through the early recordings by ethnomusicologist Alan Lomax for the Library of Congress, and right to the departure of Muddy Waters for Chicago, transforming the country blues of the Delta to the urban blues. (msmusic.org)

VICKSBURG

While Vicksburg is best known for its role in American Civil War history—the Vicksburg National Military Park is the area's number one tourist attraction—the city also played a rich role in blues history. Vicksburg is home to six Mississippi Blues Trail markers that pay homage to a music historian and the various blues artists who lived and played in the city. (VisitVicksburg.com)

Catfish Row

In 1948, when Greenville author David Cohn wrote, "The Mississippi Delta begins in the lobby of the Peabody Hotel in Memphis and ends on Catfish Row in Vicksburg," he was sketching out a wide definition of the Delta. Yes, the music of the blues did stretch that far south (and even further). Ironically, there was no actual place named Catfish Row in Vicksburg; Cohn was painting a scene of a community of Black-owned businesses, gambling houses, and music venues. Today, the term Catfish Row is more of a marketing construct.

The Catfish Row Museum (scheduled to open in 2021) is dedicated to telling the story of the people who lived beside the great river. It is under construction in the old Monte Carlo Club on Washington Street, a venue for nationally acclaimed blues and rhythm and blues acts throughout the 1970s and 1980s. When completed, the museum will include exhibits on the backstory of the blues as well as a live music venue. (catfishrowmuseum.org)

Vicksburg's Mississippi Blues Trail Markers

During the 1940s and 1950s, Vicksburg was home to the Blue Room, one of the hottest blues clubs in the South. The doors first opened as a modest, one-room bar but expanded into a multipurpose complex that saw blues greats like B. B. King and Antoine "Fats" Domino play the main ballroom. Following World War II, a popular band known as the Red Tops played their blend of blues, jazz, and pop at local clubs, including the Blue Room, which operated from the 1940s until it closed its doors in 1972.

A marker recognizes the significance of the storied Highway 61 (the Blues Highway), a long stretch of blacktop that connects riverside

Along the Vicksburg waterfront, markings on the levee show how high the river levels would have been if the levee had held
JOSEPHINE MATYAS

communities from New Orleans in the south to the Mississippi River's northern headwaters in Minnesota, generally following the flow of the waterway. Dozens of blues artists have recorded songs about the roadway, including Son Thomas, "Honeyboy" Edwards, and "Mississippi Fred" McDowell. Fast-forward to the mid-twentieth century, and Bob Dylan brought the famed roadway back into the mainstream with his blues-based *Highway 61 Revisited*.

In the early twentieth century, Vicksburg was a lively river port and the biggest city in the state with a large and active African American community, concentrated mainly in a neighborhood on the edge of the city known as Marcus Bottom. It was alive with music clubs where blues artists met, socialized, and played, such as the South Side Park Dance Hall, the Playboy Club, Big Will's, and the Red Dot Inn.

A small stretch of roadway in the center of Vicksburg has been named Willie Dixon Way in honor of the city's son who gained recognition as a bass player, producer, and songwriter (at Chess Records in Chicago). Willie Dixon's prolific blues compositions led to his being recognized as one of the genre's most influential artists, a songwriter for Chess Records, and a major contributor to what became the bedrock of the British blues movement. Dixon played on hundreds of tracks at Chess and, before his death, established the not-for-profit Blues Heaven Foundation to encourage a new generation of blues players, housed in the original Chess Studios on Chicago's South Michigan Avenue.

He has been venerated on one of the Vicksburg Riverfront Murals, showing the smiling musician with his double bass gigging at the iconic Blue Room.

NATCHEZ

There are few Mississippi—even southern—towns as architecturally pristine as 300-year-old Natchez. Sitting on a steep bluff overlooking the grand Mississippi River, at one time, Natchez was home to the wealthiest plantation owners in the nation (it's said that in the mid-1800s, half the nation's millionaires lived in tiny Natchez during the high point of the cotton plantation economy). With its position high above the waterway, Natchez held a military, strategic, and economic position of strength on the Mississippi River, and for many years, the river was a stopping point along a major trade route. Boatmen from the Ohio Valley would float

Natchez sits high above the Mississippi River
JOSEPHINE MATYAS

goods downstream; unload their flatboats, tugboats, and barges at the ports at Natchez or New Orleans; and then return north on foot or on horseback along the Natchez Trace. By 1825, steamboats that could do the return trip had made the Natchez Trace largely obsolete for commerce. (VisitNatchez.org)

This concentration of great wealth from the era of King Cotton is on display in the town's grand antebellum homes and gardens, but it came at a terrible human cost. As early as 1720, French plantation owners were importing Black slaves from Africa to clear the land and prepare the Natchez-area wilderness for massive plantings of tobacco and indigo. Around 1724, Jean-Baptiste Le Moyne, Sieur de Bienville (the three-time governor of Louisiana), instituted a *Code Noir* in the neighboring territory, a system of regulations meant to quell uprisings and undesirable behaviors. For example, no slaves could gather in crowds, drink liquor, or carry a weapon without the written permission of their owners. For those who broke the *Code Noir*, there could be floggings, lashings, brandings, mutilation, and other forms of torture. Undoubtedly, this had a moderating influence on the isolated Natchez settlement as well.

In the 1760s, the French withdrew from the area, giving the lands east of the Mississippi River to the British. Dozens of White settlers moved to the Natchez area along the great river, establishing large plantations on huge allotments of land, ranging in the tens of thousands of acres. With such acreage to maintain, these planter-minded settlers needed a large and docile workforce of slaves. For the next few decades, conflicts between the Spanish and the British created a time of extreme turmoil for enslaved persons, who were essentially chattel.

Natchez was a major terminus of the domestic slave trade, which continued in America for decades after the importation of slaves to the United States was officially abolished in 1808. Before an 1833 ban on trade inside the city limits—due to a local cholera outbreak, not the inhumanity of the practice—enslaved people were sold at the riverside landing and on downtown street corners. The ban barely made a dent, as the trading houses moved just outside city limits to Forks of the Road (now a historic site inside the current-day city boundary), creating the second-largest slave market in the Deep South, where individuals and families were sold until 1863. Professional slave traders used the land at the "fork" in the road to house, feed, and display enslaved persons for sale in inspection rooms where buyers could make purchase decisions.

As in much of the South, the local laws and conventions were stacked against the Black population. Slavery was a fact of life in Natchez. Planters feared slave uprisings and thus sometimes separated families; many African captives were forced to take Anglo names and adopt Christianity.

Immediately after the end of the American Civil War, White planters in Natchez tried to enforce the Black Codes, coercing free Blacks to work on plantations in near slave-like conditions. The political and social rights supposedly gained by the African Americans were short lived. The barbaric Jim Crow regime segregated Blacks, firmly relegating them to the status of second-class citizens. Their attempts to open businesses and become a part of the local political process were met with strong resistance from the White population. At the same time, the unfairly stacked system of sharecropping was introduced as a way for Black families to work a section of land, receiving a share of crops as wages or payment against the rent and debts they owed. Under the system, most sharecroppers were unable to repay their loans each year, falling farther and farther into debt. Sharecropping was an economic trap.

In the early 1900s, Natchez was hit with the one-two punch that shook most of the South. In 1907, the boll weevil pest devastated the cotton crops. In subsequent years, the mechanization that took away the jobs done by farmhands, the brutality of segregation and racial violence, and the economic bind of sharecropping accelerated the Great Migration, the mass movement of African Americans from towns like Natchez to northern cities, where jobs and opportunity beckoned. By the 1920s, that migration had become an exodus moving northward. Add to the momentum the Great Flood of 1927, and when the waters receded, rather than return to their money-losing farms, thousands of poor Black and White sharecroppers exited Mississippi in search of a better life.

Back in Natchez, the pull of tourism dollars took the picture-perfect antebellum homes and gardens and rolled it all up into what was a depiction of idealized life in the Old South. Make no mistake, the architecture and landscaping in the heart of town are breathtaking—it's one of our favorite stops in Mississippi—but this beauty obscures a horrific history. The African American Museum of History and Culture on Main Street traces the story of African Americans in Natchez. Exhibits cover the era of slavery, the Forks of the Road slave market, the Civil War, Reconstruction, the Rhythm Night Club Fire, and the civil rights era up to the present day. (mississippimuseums.org)

Rhythm Night Club Fire

Natchez has its place in blues history with the horrific Rhythm Night Club Fire, the fourth-deadliest nightclub fire in world history. On the night of April 23, 1940, Walter Barnes and His Royal Creolians from Chicago was onstage, the place was packed with young African Americans, and the windows and doors were boarded up to keep out gate crashers. The fatal blaze started when a cigarette ignited highly flammable Spanish moss hung from the ceiling for decoration. The locked doors and covered windows made escape from the flames impossible. The inferno spread quickly, killing 209 people. As the fire raged, the band continued to play in an effort to calm the crowd. Poems, films, and music, most notably Howlin' Wolf's recording of "The Natchez Burning," tell of this tragic evening.

The small Rhythm Night Club Memorial Museum is filled with newspaper clippings, photos, and memorabilia from the era. It was built by Natchez citizens Monroe and Betty Sago, who now own the property where the Rhythm Night Club once stood, to commemorate the victims of the fire, their families, and the community that was so affected by the tragedy. A Mississippi Blues Trail marker honors the site. (rnconsitemm.org)

THIS TABLET WAS ...
OF THOSE WHO LOST THEIR LIVE
RHYTHM CLUB FI
APRIL 23, 1940

KATIE ADAMS FREEMAN
HELEN GAULDEN
CARRIE WOODS GAYLOR
WILLIE GIBSON
JUANITA GILBERT
ANDREW GLASPER
JESSIE EDNA GREEN
ROSALIE GREY
JOHNNY H. GUY
HARRIETT HACKETT
JOS. HAGAN, JR.
MARIE HALL
RICHARD V. HALL
OLIVER HANDY
ALBERTA HAR...

BEN LEWIS
MARSHALL EDDIE L
THELMA LEWIS
CHARLEY LIGHT, J
GLADYS LIGHT
WILLIE LINDSLEY
BERNETTA LLOYD
FRANCES LLOYD
THELMA LLOYD
WILLIE LLOYD
JOHNNIE BOY LOG
MARY L. LOGAN
ETHEL LYONS

The Natchez Rhythm Night Club fire was the fourth deadliest in world history
JOSEPHINE MATYAS

Smoot's Grocery

There's a strong movement in Natchez to preserve the blues. In town, it is found at Smoot's Grocery—a one-minute walk from catching the sunset at the bluff overlooking the river. The building was originally a small grocery store by day and a juke joint by night. It has been painstakingly restored using repurposed materials to create a blues lounge and live music venue with an emphasis on Americana, world music, and the blues. Smoot's is part of the Americana Music Triangle, and on some nights, you'll find a mix of local groups as well as bands from New Orleans, Nashville, Memphis, and the Delta. (smootsnatchez.com)

Biscuits & Blues

For more than two decades, Biscuits & Blues on Main Street in downtown Natchez has been serving up traditional southern fare (cat-

Smoot's Grocery in Natchez has been restored as a live blues venue
JOSEPHINE MATYAS

fish, fried chicken, and barbecue) with a healthy dose of live blues. (biscuitblues.com)

MERIDIAN

Sitting in the foothills of the Appalachian chain, Meridian is a midsize city that was settled primarily around the timber and cotton trade and as a railroad junction. By the mid-1800s, there were eight different rail lines crossing through the city (only a few are operational now), making it easy for Meridian to secure entertainment acts traveling from the North to New Orleans. With the comings and goings of musicians and players, some of their influence must have rubbed off and stayed. Meridian is renowned for the musical creativity of Jimmie Rodgers, the "Father of Country Music," and as the manufacturing base of Peavey Electronics, whose amplifiers are found on bandstands everywhere. It's also the home of the new Mississippi Arts + Entertainment Experience, which was under construction when we visited Meridian, but information on the mission of the MAX and its exhibits is included here. (VisitMeridian.com)

Mississippi's Arts + Entertainment Experience: The MAX

Opened in 2018, the MAX is the state's newest museum dedicated to the creative legacy of Mississippians who have exceled in their contributions to arts and entertainment.

The immersive, interactive galleries include a look at the roles played by the land, family, church, and community and the ways they influenced the creative spark for musicians, writers, artists, and performers. Mississippi blues legends—including B. B. King, Howlin' Wolf, Robert Johnson, Elvis Presley, Muddy Waters, and John Lee Hooker—are part of the Hall of Fame, a soaring 360-degree multimedia exhibit that tells the personal stories of the artists who trace their roots to the Magnolia State. The MAX also recognizes and tells the stories behind the places steeped in musical history that sparked and nurtured the blues, including Dockery Farms, Malaco Records, Ace Records, and Ground Zero Blues Club. (msarts.org)

Jimmie Rodgers

He may be regaled as the "Father of Country Music," but Jimmie Rodgers was certainly influenced by the blues unfolding around him in the early part of the 1900s. A downtown Mississippi Blues Trail marker dedicated to the man with the distinctive yodel, also known as the "Singing Brakeman," recognizes his role as one of the founders who popularized country music.

With the versatility of his voice, Rodgers took to reinventing himself in settings from vaudeville and medicine shows to songs of the poor man's South. It was his distinctive yodel that influenced fellow Mississippian Howlin' Wolf to adopt his own trademark larger-than-life howl.

There is no dispute that Rodgers was heavily influenced by the southern blues and most likely crossed paths and even shared performance space with blues players like Robert Johnson and Arkansas slide guitarist Robert Nighthawk. More than one-third of his recording catalog was based in the blues, and when he took to the country music stage, he was fortuitously spreading the message and music of the blues to a wider audience.

Meridian celebrates its hometown musical legend at the Jimmie Rodgers Museum with displays of memorabilia, artifacts, and his famed guitar. (jimmierodgers.com)

Peavey Electronics

We went in search of a look at the Mississippi Blues Trail marker in front of Peavey Electronics and ended up sitting in the office of innovator Hartley Peavey, the founder of the Meridian-based company that ships the amplifiers known as the sound of the Mississippi juke joint.

Peavey's story is fascinating and one that is intertwined with the unfolding of the Mississippi blues and its transformation to rock and roll.

"My introduction to the blues was kind of a fluke," explained the man whose Peavey amplifiers have contributed to the sound of modern electric guitar. "I've always been somebody who would tinker with things. Back when I was in high school I used to fix radios and TVs. One of the local juke box operators put all of his nicer juke boxes in the White places and he put all of his older juke boxes in the Black places, many of which were called juke joints. This guy heard that I could repair electronics and thankfully for me because I didn't really know much, most of his old juke box amplifiers were basically just a rectifier and two output tubes and a couple of preamp tubes. What was wrong with them most of the time was the tubes—they ran all night long, filthy, really hot. And I would fix them, and he thought I was a genius. And I wasn't going to tell him any different."

Peavey soon found himself with stacks of old blues 78s discarded from the juke joints because they became scratchy from the wear and tear of being spun nightly. As a teenager, he was surrounded by equipment and instruments, much of it the products that moved through his father's Meridian music store. He recalls his father as being a businessman who remembered the lessons of the Great Depression: "He could squeeze a nickel until the buffalo screamed."

It was blues and rock and roll that captivated the mind of young Hartley. "In 1958 my dad sold pianos, and band instruments, and very few electric guitars. He had one electric guitar and it was known in our store as The Guitar. Someone would come in to look at The Guitar, and he would very ceremoniously take it down off the display shelf and put it on the glass countertop and open the lid. It was what they called a Les Paul Custom, The Fretless Wonder. I remember it had three humbucking pickups, black, a beautiful guitar, and he kept that guitar until just a short while before he sold his business in 1960."

In the fall of 1957, Peavey went to a Bo Diddley concert in Laurel, Mississippi, an evening that changed his life. Diddley was instrumental in the transition from blues to rock and roll. "He had a guitar. I think it was a Les Paul Standard, the one with the flat top, covered in rabbit fur. And he was jumpin' around on stage doing his do-chicka-chicka-chicka, so I went home and told my dad 'I want to be a guitar player.' He said, 'Oh son, you don't want to be a guitar player. Guitar players are sorry, they don't pay their bills.'"

Peavey cycled through guitar lessons, playing all the while on equipment that just wasn't up to the task. Enter the innovative streak in a young man desperate to be a part of the unfolding electric guitar culture.

When his "squeeze a nickel" dad refused to indulge in the guitar pickup Peavey wanted, the young electronics whiz decided to make his own. "I ordered six big old magnets out of the classified section of *Popular Science* magazine. I went down to the local supply house and got the smallest wire they had, it was number 38, and 38 is a fairly big wire. I sat at our dining room table and hand wound the pickup and guess what? It worked. Not that well, but it worked. So now I had a guitar, now I had a pickup, and now I needed an amplifier."

Back to the drawing board, where Peavey cobbled together his first amplifier, one he admitted to "sounding horrible." After improving the design, he added the Peavey logo—originally created as a doodle back in eleventh grade—and within years was manufacturing and shipping portable sound gear to grateful gigging musicians everywhere.

Peavey credits his growing love of music to the blues. "I had all these old blues records from the juke boxes and because I didn't have any money I started listening to them. I fell in love with B. B. King's playing on the Crown label, and I bought them all."

As it turns out, Hartley Peavey was far from the only White guy to fall in love with the blues. "A lot of these blues guys were able to cross over. So, the blues got respect. B. B. once told me, 'I was playing at the Fillmore West. I played my set and as the lights came up there wasn't a Black face out there.'"

Peavey Electronics has played a central role in preserving and propagating the blues. "The blues need to be protected as much as possible," insisted the visionary and innovator who now holds a place on the Walk of Fame at the MAX. "It's our heritage." (peavey.com)

WEST POINT

The fertile farmland of what's called the Black Prairie region of Mississippi drove the engine of the cotton mills of the early 1900s. Right on the rail lines, the traffic of railroad cars helped to energize the economy of West Point, a small city very close to the border with Alabama. (wpnet.org)

There was a whole lotta growing happening around West Point, and there must have been something in the water too because White Station—a dot on the map just outside West Point—was the birthplace of six-foot-six, 300-pound Chester Arthur Burnett, known to blues lovers as Howlin' Wolf.

Wolf was the real deal when it came to stoking the urban, electric-amplified blues in the cities of the North, most notably Chicago, where he moved to in the early 1950s and lived for the rest of his life. As a child (and as an adult), he had excess energy to burn—perhaps what led to the childhood nickname that stuck with him the rest of his life. It's said that his mother always despaired that he "played the devil's music."

He learned his guitar chops as a teenager by watching and listening to Charley Patton at juke joints and at Dockery Farms, and he learned

West Point honors its hometown son, Howlin' Wolf
JOSEPHINE MATYAS

his blues harmonica from Sonny Boy Williamson II. His third powerful instrument was definitely his brooding, growl of a voice, which lent his songs an earthiness and honesty. Influenced by the blues-country vocal style of Jimmie Rodgers, Wolf was quoted as saying, "I couldn't do no yodelin', so I turned to howlin'. And it's done me just fine." Indeed.

Before moving to Chicago when he was in his forties (by way of bands and gigging in Arkansas, where he caught the attention of Ike Turner, who was scouting for Memphis producer Sam Phillips), Wolf earned his living farming the land and playing the blues at every chance he got. Once in the big city, he took hold of the live blues scene and ran with it under the Chess Records label. Phillips—who deemed Howlin' Wolf his greatest discovery—was quoted as saying, "When I heard Howlin' Wolf, I said, This is for me. This is where the soul of a man never dies."

Known for his energetic gyrations when performing live, Wolf recorded several blues classics, like "Moanin' at Midnight," "Smokestack Lightning," and "Little Red Rooster." His performances filled every nook and corner of a space, and, as musician and music critic Michael "Cub" Koda wrote, "No one could match Howlin' Wolf for the singular ability to rock the house down to the foundation while simultaneously scaring its patrons out of its wits."

Through the 1960s, Wolf spread his influence as he built ties with rock, heavily inspiring British musicians like Eric Clapton and the Rolling Stones. Just a few years before his death, he released *The London Howlin' Wolf Sessions*, a super-session blues album recorded with guitar great Eric Clapton, Rolling Stones drummer Charlie Watts and bassist Bill Wyman, multi-instrumentalist Steve Winwood, and Beatles drummer Ringo Starr, among others.

In tiny West Point, the flame of Howlin' Wolf's over-the-top energy and influence still burns bright. To honor and tell the story of their hometown blues legend, the Howlin' Wolf Blues Society was formed in 1995, opening the downtown Howlin' Wolf Black Prairie Blues Museum, an artifact-stuffed, one-room homage to the man whose music bridged from the Delta blues to the more modern electric blues. Located as a part of the Friday House Museum (one of West Point's oldest buildings), when we visited, the walls and shelving were filled with cigar box guitars, concert posters, ticket stubs, artwork, and old 78-rpm singles, including "Who's Been Talking?" on the Chess Records label. There was a red modified Les Paul Deluxe guitar signed and gifted by Pete Townshend of the Who, a Squier Stratocaster signed by Elvis Costello, and a Gibson Les Paul signed by Wolf's longtime band member, guitarist Hubert Sumlin.

The displays inside the Howlin' Wolf Black Prairie Blues Museum honor the energetic blues musician

JOSEPHINE MATYAS

A red modified Les Paul Deluxe guitar signed by Pete Townshend is at the Howlin' Wolf Museum

JOSEPHINE MATYAS

Signed guitars and posters are part of the artifact-stuffed Howlin' Wolf Black Prairie Blues Museum in West Point

JOSEPHINE MATYAS

Downtown West Point honors Howlin' Wolf with a colorful block-long mural

JOSEPHINE MATYAS

As of early 2021, a new downtown museum is in the planning phase and will be opened under a new name, the Black Prairie Blues Museum. When renovations are completed, the displays from the existing museum will be moved into the new digs.

One of downtown's long brick walls has been transformed into a colorful mural of epic-size proportions (just like the man himself). A black granite statue of "The Wolf" along with a memorial bench and marker honoring Lillie Handley Burnett ("Mrs. Wolf") and a Mississippi Blues Trail marker are in West Point City Park in the center of town.

Every year, on Labor Day weekend, West Point kicks off its annual Black Prairie Blues Festival to celebrate the infusion of the blues with the Black Prairie spirit.

OXFORD

If for no other reason—Oxford holds its own as a pretty and historic university town—it's worth a stop to visit the Blues Archive project at the University of Mississippi. A Mississippi Blues Trail marker acknowledges the work done at the university in documenting African American blues culture. (VisitOxfordMS.com)

Curator Greg Johnson brought his background in music history and library and information science (plus a healthy passion for the blues) to the archive's mammoth undertaking and primary mission to acquire, preserve, and make accessible the various collections related to the blues.

"We are set up as a research archive," Johnson explained, "which means we're set up for folks to come in and request materials and we'll pull them out. If you're wanting to come and see case after case of pre-made things with signage telling you a good narrative of blues history, we do have some of that, but that's not the primary mission."

The project took off in 1982 and 1983 when B. B. King contributed his personal collection of sound recordings, 78s, albums, and even a few wax cylinder recordings, instantly establishing one of the largest blues music archives in the country. A year later, the Blues Archive officially opened its doors to the public.

Word spread, and people started sending in their own collections. "Sometimes it's folks downsizing and other times it's people who know their kids don't appreciate the music they're collecting and that when they die it's either going to be thrown away or sold off piece by piece. A lot of people want to keep their collections intact."

The Blues Archive at the University of Mississippi in Oxford has more than 70,000 sound recordings of the blues in its collection
JOSEPHINE MATYAS

Johnson has his fingers on where everything is located in the impressive stacks, which include material that has never been posted on YouTube or the internet, rare video and audio concert footage, tens-of-thousands of posters and photographs, books and magazines (many signed), home-shot movies, interview tapes, four original Robert Johnson 78s, and almost 70,000 sound recordings in formats from wax cylinders to DVD. The archive includes the first vocal blues recording by an African American female performer, a 1920 song called "Crazy Blues" by Mamie Smith.

For a blues purist (dare we say geek?), it's nirvana. "Anybody can go out and easily purchase the complete recorded works of Robert Johnson," he said, "but they can't go out and easily find a 78 and see the actual artifact. It's pretty cool.

"There are also a lot of blues fans who want to see some things they can't find on Amazon or on YouTube or iTunes or Pandora. People think everything has been digitized and that it's all out there and available on the Web. I can tell you clearly that is definitely not true."

In addition to the material contributed by B. B. King, the Blues Archive is home to the *Living Blues* magazine's collection of records, photos, subject files, and memorabilia as well as the Trumpet Records collection and the Sheldon Harris collection of sheet music (the latter was an author and educator of blues and jazz).

We wanted to know Johnson's thoughts about the roots of the blues and how the music developed.

"Even the definition of what is blues is murky and there's a lot of gray area," he explained. "You look at an artist like Jimmie Rodgers—according to record industry labels he's a country musician, but so many of his songs are harmonically a twelve-bar blues with an AAB rhyme scheme for the lyrics. He even has the word *blues* in the title and he learned to play from a blues musician. So, is that blues? Is it country? Does it matter? Ironically there's this reverse influence of a blues musician being influenced by country music which was influenced by blues, so it's all a big mash.

"The development of blues coming out of field hollers; people singing to themselves to pass the time, through the drudgery of doing the same task over and over again out in the fields, just alleviating the boredom. That is one of the paths that leads to the development of modern blues, but there are also a lot of influences of non-blues popular forms of music, even minstrel, Tin Pan Alley, and vaudeville."

At the same time, jazz was developing alongside the blues. It may seem that there is a linear progression to each genre of music, but Johnson sees it as something more complex. "We like to think of everything in linear paths: blues growing out of field holler, and work songs, and then that turning to jazz. Down in New Orleans there's one sound sort of forming and in the Delta these other sounds forming, but there's a cross influence. You've got the Mississippi River connecting the Delta and Memphis down to New Orleans, so people are hearing all these sounds that are starting to develop. There was an urban blues developing alongside a sort of country blues and all of those singers—the classic blues singers Bessie Smith and Claire Smith—they were as much influenced by vaudeville and minstrel singing as they were by country blues. It's a big mix that's complex to describe."

Johnson has a lot of insight into the ways blues were experienced across Mississippi.

"There were itinerant musicians traveling around from lumber camp to lumber camp making some money that way. When you're a performer, particularly if you're a good performer, it's the end of a long workweek, you're the center of attention, you're what's getting everybody up dancing and having a good time. You want to be that person that's getting all the attention, probably the women are interested, there are tips. There's evidence that in a work song situation, like in Parchman Mississippi Penitentiary, there was the person who could sing really well, in some cases they had a position of respect and authority among the other people. There are a lot of call-and-response in work songs, so sometimes the person who was really good as a song leader would sing the phrase and the group would respond. He got out of doing some of the manual labor because he was good at keeping a group together, so it actually benefited the plantation owner because this guy is helping keep everybody in line and keep their spirits and morale high. He would be rewarded with not having to sling as many axes or hammers or whatever. There's an incentive here—maybe in that case it's not economic. It's a form of less work."

Johnson pointed out that this style of music making is common throughout many cultures in Africa. "It's a very big distinction from the European forms of music making. In terms of art music in Europe, there's a performer onstage, and the audience out there, and there are very specific roles: as the audience you sit politely and listen, absorb. In a lot of African cultures there might be a core group of performers, but it's expected, it becomes a communal thing, it's working all together to make music."

The best way to experience the Blues Archive is to go to the website and look through the catalog and the various archival aids to try to determine what they have on a favorite artist or topic. The stacks are closed to the public ("partly for preservation and partly because we don't want our collection disappearing and being sold on eBay"), but the curators are happy to pull items and have them ready for viewing. Even if you haven't connected in advance, stop by to have a look at the materials on display. (libraries.olemiss.edu/archives)

TUPELO

As the blues spread out from the Delta and seeped into the surrounding countryside, it mixed in new ways with other music genres, like country and gospel. Nowhere was this interweaving brought home more clearly than in Tupelo, a small town in the northeast cotton belt of Mississippi, tight against the Alabama border. (Tupelo.net)

Tupelo is not the place that first comes to mind when thinking of the blues. But consider this: for many mainstream, white-bread listeners in the late 1950s, Elvis Presley was the conduit channeling the blues sounds of the Mississippi Delta through their radios and right into their living rooms. His mammoth contribution to the arc of American music history was in how he sanitized African American music for White people, blurring the lines between the roots music of blues, country, bluegrass, rockabilly, and gospel. And in the process, it was the blues that birthed rock and roll.

Roger Stolle, author of *Hidden History of Mississippi Blues* and a blues shop owner and promoter in Clarksdale, couldn't agree more. "When I was ten years old I was a Presley guy. August 17, 1977, was the first time I paid attention to music because he was everywhere. What I didn't realize is what I liked of his music wasn't the Hollywood years, wasn't the Las Vegas years, it was really the Mississippi-moving-to-Memphis years. So, it was the blues."

And in Tupelo, they have their finger on the pulse of that jump from blues to rock and roll by celebrating all things Elvis Presley. There is a tidy main street lined with brightly painted, six-foot guitars and an old-time hardware store anchoring the historic intersection at Main Street and Front Street, an Elvis-themed driving tour, a top-notch museum dedicated to the birthplace of the "King of Rock and Roll," and two Mississippi Blues Trail markers.

Tupelo Hardware

If there is a single location where the blues began its transition to rock and roll, it would be where the "X" is marked on the worn, wooden floorboards of the Tupelo Hardware. The shelving at the Main Street hardware store hasn't changed much in half a century—there are cast-iron skillets, cans of turpentine, glues, and a whirligig where shoppers scoop out nails sold by the pound. But the "X" has its own magnetic pull and a significant following.

There's a bit of showbiz razzmatazz happening at this spot. According to the store's Elvis specialist (likely this is the only hardware store in the world with an Elvis specialist on staff), Gladys Presley and her young son came to buy an eleventh-birthday present. Elvis wanted a .22-caliber

The Tupelo Hardware is nicknamed "the cradle of rock and roll"—it's where Elvis got his first guitar
JOSEPHINE MATYAS

The Tupelo Hardware—famous in Elvis lore—still operates as a family-owned hardware store
JOSEPHINE MATYAS

rifle (too expensive) but settled for a $7.75 guitar, probably the best eight bucks his cash-strapped mother ever spent. The store's third-generation proprietors like to joke that their establishment is the "cradle of rock and roll." With that guitar, Elvis Presley spent his early years growing a deep love of music and in the process changed music as it was known *forever*. (tupelohardware.com)

Elvis Presley Birthplace

Times were tough in the South during the Great Depression and especially tough for the young Presley family in 1935, the year Elvis was born (his twin brother Jessie was stillborn). Gladys and Vernon Presley lived in a two-room shotgun shack in East Tupelo (the wrong side of the tracks and home to poor Whites and African Americans), a small home that Vernon built after borrowing $180 for materials. Tupelo was surrounded by cotton fields and a community where church and gospel music held sway. The soulful strains of gospel have always been deeply intertwined with the blues of the Delta—both tell of joy and of sorrow.

By the end of the 1930s, the bottom had fallen out of the cotton market, jobs were scarce, and the small rural towns found themselves in

Elvis was born in this shotgun home on the grounds of what is now the Elvis Presley Birthplace
TUPELO CVB

the midst of a massive social and economic transformation. Vernon had worked as a sharecropper, and the family often faced setbacks (including Vernon's imprisonment at Parchman Farm, the Mississippi State Penitentiary, for forging a four-dollar check when Elvis was just a toddler).

At the same time, by the 1940s, 80 percent of the population owned radio sets, a new technology that changed forever the way music was experienced, making the world a much smaller place. For the first time in human history, people could listen to a voice or instrument that was not in the presence of the listener. Those on farms and in small communities like Tupelo were beginning to hear how others lived, through radio programming, the availability of Victrola phonographs, and 78-rpm records.

During the years Elvis lived in Tupelo (1935 through 1948), the Presley family radio would have been tuned to a diverse mix of musical styles, including Ella Fitzgerald, Billie Holiday, Jimmie Rodgers, Mahalia Jackson, and the Grand Ole Opry. The family would take the radio and hook it up to the car battery, listening to shows for about twenty minutes before the radio ran the battery down.

The story of Elvis's early years in Tupelo is told at the excellent Elvis Presley Birthplace, a state-of-the-art museum showcasing artifacts, photos, and audiovisual clips from his boyhood friends and Tupelo residents. In our opinion, the museum is more accessible and more authentic than the flashy Graceland in Memphis. The Elvis Presley Birthplace is designated a Mississippi historic landmark.

The museum's quiet grounds include the two-room, shotgun-style house—open the front and back doors, and you can shoot a shotgun straight through—on its original site, restored to circa 1935, the year Presley was born. The bedroom where he was born has undergone some sprucing up; where there is wallpaper now would have been newspaper covering the walls, and the family would have sold all their original furniture when they moved to Memphis, so the space is decorated with similar period pieces.

Once Presley reached stardom, he returned to Tupelo in the late 1950s for a large concert and donated the proceeds to the city to buy fifteen acres, the original home, and to begin the formation of the birthplace museum. He was insistent that the museum be located in East Tupelo, right at the original location of his boyhood home.

Also on the grounds is the humble wood-framed Pentecostal church that was at the center of the Presley family social world (moved to the museum from a few blocks away). This is where young Elvis learned to

Elvis acquired his love of gospel in this church, now part of the Elvis Birthplace
TUPELO CVB

sing and play guitar and acquired his passion for gospel music. His goal as a child was to be part of a gospel quartet. A short film pulls visitors into the typical evening service of a 1940s Assembly of God Pentecostal revival-style church. For a young boy who was fascinated with music of all styles, it is easy to see how the spirit-infused tunes of the church would be a driving force behind his career as a singer. Family and church would have formed the bedrock of the music he learned.

On the flip side of gospel sat the blues and the age-old battle between Saturday night and Sunday morning. The infectious rhythms and suggestive lyrics of the music of Blacks trapped in poverty and despair resonated in young Elvis's fertile mind. During his early years in Tupelo, he absorbed many musical styles—gospel, blues, country, and big band. These influences and cross-pollination of musical styles showed in his debut recording at Sun Records, with the jump blues single "That's All Right" on one side and a bluegrass number on the B-side. In the early 1950s, when *Village Voice* music critic Nat Hentoff first heard Elvis Presley singing "That's All Right" on the radio, he was convinced he was hearing Black Mississippi blues singer Arthur "Big Boy" Crudup. Two years later, his megahit "Heartbreak Hotel" reached number one on the country, pop, and rhythm and blues billboards, unleashing Elvis on the world.

The Mississippi Blues Trail marker at the site recognizes how Elvis incorporated the blues into recordings and performances throughout his career. His hits like "Hound Dog," "All Shook Up," and "Shake, Rattle and Roll" were all tunes rooted in the blues. His songs populated the rhythm and blues charts from 1956 to 1963 and were well liked in the Black community.

Inside the main museum building, the self-guided galleries are filled with photographs, old 78s, sheet music, his Graceland telephone, and even his calf-high black motorcycle boots. There are many pieces that bring home the hardship of growing up in rural Mississippi in the 1930s and 1940s. Around the walkways on the property are several statues—a bronze one of Elvis at age thirteen, dressed in overalls and walking with his guitar, and two statues together called "Becoming," symbolizing the transformation from Elvis the Boy to Elvis the Entertainer. (elvispresleybirthplace.com)

Elvis Presley Driving Tour

Download the self-guided driving tour app or pick up a paper guide at the visitor center to fourteen of the Tupelo spots that played a role

Shake Rag was the traditional Tupelo African American neighborhood where blues and gospel reigned
JOSEPHINE MATYAS

in Elvis's formative years. Markers at each stop give information on the significance of statues, schools, church, the hardware store, a local swimming hole, and Johnnie's Drive-In, a local restaurant that has designated a booth as Elvis Presley's favorite on his regular visits. Johnnie's serves up a menu that hasn't changed in decades, with service to the packed booths or outside to cars at the drive-in.

Tupelo's second Mississippi Blues Trail marker is in recognition of Shake Rag, the traditional African American neighborhood where the blues and gospel spilling out of the homes, cafés, and juke joints influenced young Elvis to develop his own unique sound. There are several interpretations of the name Shake Rag. People "shakin' their rags" feeling a fight, waiting passengers shaking a rag to get the train engineer's attention, and as a term used to describe African American music gatherings.

FINDING FOOD AND DRINK

A Plate of Mississippi Barbecue

The dishes will overload your calorie counter, but they've been cooking this way forever, and they don't intend to stop.

- JB's BBQ, Hazlehurst
- The Shed, Ocean Springs
- Leatha's Bar-B-Que Inn, Hattiesburg

Southern Fried Chicken

If they know how to do one thing in a southern kitchen, it's to prepare classic fried chicken.

- The Iron Horse Grill, Jackson
- LD's Kitchen, Vicksburg
- Biscuits & Blues, Natchez
- Stark's Family Restaurant, Hazlehurst

Pond-Raised Catfish

Catfish is a Mississippi staple. Farm-raised, it's on almost every restaurant menu in one form or another, from breaded and fried to stuffed into a po'boy sandwich.

- Taylor Grocery, Taylor
- Hal & Mal's, Jackson
- Ajax Diner, Oxford
- Weidmann's, Meridian

Comeback Sauce

Comeback sauce originated in Jackson, Mississippi, as the house dressing served at a Greek restaurant. Now it's found in almost every southern restaurant and used to spice up foods as a dip, sauce, or salad dressing.

- Mammy's Cupboard, Natchez
- Hal & Mal's, Jackson

Blue Plate Specials

A staple of the South: a low-priced main usually served with a choice of several sides.

- Walnut Hills Restaurant, Vicksburg
- Rooster's, Jackson
- Mama Jo's, Oxford
- Biscuits & Blues, Natchez

MUST SEE

- Gibson Les Paul signed by Hubert Sumlin at the Howlin' Wolf Black Prairie Blues Museum in West Point
- Sonny Boy Williamson II's original $10 recording contract, Blues Archive at the University of Mississippi
- Every January 8, the Elvis Presley Birthplace museum in Tupelo holds a daylong birthday celebration. In June, the town rolls out the red carpet at the annual Tupelo Elvis Festival

MUST READ

- *I Am the Blues: The Willie Dixon Story*, Willie Dixon (with Don Snowden) (1990)
- *Moanin' at Midnight: The Life and Times of Howlin' Wolf*, James Segrest and Mark Hoffman (2005)
- *Race, Rock, and Elvis*, M. T. Bertrand (2009)
- *Empire of Cotton: A Global History*, Sven Beckert (2015)

MUST LISTEN AND WATCH

- "The Natchez Burning," Howlin' Wolf
- "Highway 61 Revisited," Bob Dylan
- Highway 61 Radio, Mississippi Public Broadcasting, streamed online
- *Blue Suede Shoes in the Hood*, by filmmaker Charles Johnson (2004)
- *Sidemen: Long Road to Glory*, directed by Scott Rosenbaum (2016)
- *Last of the Mississippi Jukes*, directed by Robert Mugge (2003)

GUITAR NOTES

Willie Dixon from Vicksburg played upright bass and guitar but was much better known for his prodigious songwriting, arranging, and production at Chess Records in Chicago. He supplied the bottom-end bass pulse for hundreds of tracks by stars of the Chess studios, including Muddy Waters, Little Walter, Memphis Slim, Pete Seeger, Sugar Blue, Clifton James, Bo Diddley, Willie Mabon, Koko Taylor, Chuck Berry, Otis Rush, Little Milton, Howlin' Wolf, Eddie Boyd, and on and on. He wrote or cowrote some 500 songs, many of which were picked up and reproduced in various forms by English blues-based bands like Led Zeppelin, Cream, Fleetwood Mac, Ten Years After, and the Rolling Stones. Dixon's "I'm Your Hoochie Coochie Man" became the signature song for Muddy Waters.

6

THE BLUES BEYOND MISSISSIPPI

The Mississippi Delta—that part of the state we have focused on—did not have a monopoly on blues. What we have come to call the "blues" was germinating in every corner of the slave South before and after the American Civil War because it was a product of the Black experience under conditions of brutal oppression. As such, it reflected different elements in different environments. But what was common was the call-and-response form, the highly emotional telling of their shared experience, the borrowing from gospel and other popular forms, and the rhythmic structures around which the music was organized.

Singing was a form of group therapy, rooted in the African heritage of sociability, which was soul cleansing and provided a rhythm for every task. When transplanted to the New World, in cotton fields, lumber and turpentine camps, or building railways and levees, the habit of singing made the work slightly more bearable. At the very least—and it is not nothing—it kept the soul alive. It sustained hope for something better on the other side.

Music is a highly imitative form of human expression. When two musical forms or styles come into contact, they cannot but influence and borrow from each other. The people who gave birth to the blues—wherever in the Old South they lived—were hearing other popular styles of music too, including gospel (in church), ragtime and vaudeville (in traveling shows), marching band (on civic holidays), and jazz (in drinking establishments and other questionable venues).

After we left Mississippi, we were focused on the infiltration of the blues into two main cities: Memphis and the small group of towns that make up the Muscle Shoals area in Alabama. These two areas sit cheek by jowl with Mississippi and, within the parameters of this guide, are the closest to the roots of the blues. To us, exploring the blues across Mississippi without detouring through the Shoals and Memphis would be, well, unimaginable.

MUSCLE SHOALS

Muscle Shoals— the *New York Times* called it "a holy place in the evolution of rock 'n' roll"—is one of several small communities that loom large, bumping against each other in the northwest corner of Alabama. (visitflorenceal.com)

The area nicknamed the Shoals encompasses four merged towns: Florence, Tuscumbia, Sheffield, and Muscle Shoals itself, all of which sit astride the tranquil Tennessee River. There's lots of small-town feel, front porch swings, local shops, and chatter at the local diner. Heavyweight music cities like Nashville and Memphis are a few hours' drive, but this cluster of Alabama towns has produced some of the most important American music of the past six decades, drawing in the biggest names in early rock, soul, pop, gospel, and country music, all of which were heavily immersed in the blues. In the 1960s and early 1970s, many musicians and players were drawn to the region—home of the equally renowned Florence Alabama Music Enterprises (FAME) recording studios and the magnetic Muscle Shoals funky southern groove. They say the world came to Muscle Shoals, and it was definitively where music *history* was made.

A local collection of good old boys who came to be known as the "Swampers" drew stars and cranked out hits; they were a group of White session players from a small town who managed to channel Black rhythms and sensibilities, crafting a soulful sound capturing the particular quality that audiences craved.

"The blues had quite a bit of influence on the music we played," explained Swampers bassist David Hood as we sat down in Sheffield over bowls of chicken stew and sides of fried green tomatoes. "But I had to learn to play the blues. I started more in rock and roll, with rhythm and blues. I had to learn what was considered 'right' in the blues. Blues is very simple, and if you start doing a bunch of fancy things, it steps out of bounds." Hood obviously got it right because he went on to record with blues greats like Bobby Bland, Johnny Taylor, and B. B. King.

"We had one main radio station here," Hood recalled of his teenage years growing up in Sheffield, "and I didn't know the difference between rock and roll and rhythm and blues. But a lot of the artists that were my favorite were Black. I didn't know they were White or Black; that didn't matter, it was just the music I liked."

Paul Simon, Bob Dylan, Bob Seger, Rod Stewart, Aretha Franklin, Willie Nelson, Elton John, Cat Stevens, Boz Scaggs, the Rolling Stones, Otis Redding, Jerry Lee Lewis, and countless others lined up to record in a Muscle Shoals studio or to be backed by the Swampers.

Shoals native Ben Tanner, keyboardist with the Grammy-winning Alabama Shakes and once a studio engineer at FAME, knows about the magic transcending generations. "It's about the way the parts are interlocked. There's a feel to the way these guys played together that translated into hits. They were musicians who really put the song first, so people wanted to be a part of that experience. They just wanted to make their music here."

The Shoals is home to several recording studios, but there are two with the longest and deepest histories: FAME and Muscle Shoals Sound Studio. Both are still working studios open for public tours. A Mississippi Blues Trail marker placed outside the Alabama Music Hall of Fame is an official nod to the importance that surrounding states and communities played in the evolution of blues music.

FAME Recording Studios

In 1959, music producer Rick Hall founded FAME Studios in tiny Muscle Shoals, opening the door to what would become one of the most sought after recording locations in the world. Hall built FAME from the ground up and ran the studio until his passing in early 2018 (his story is chronicled in the 2013 documentary *Muscle Shoals*). The boxy, industrial-looking building was where the famous "Muscle Shoals sound" originally found its groove.

FAME Recording Studios is the home of the original Muscle Shoals sound
FAME RECORDING STUDIOS

Ben Tanner described the late Rick Hall as having "an ear for a song, for a feel. Rick would handpick his musicians and create a particular sound. After that, he could bring in any soloist and match the music."

It was Percy Sledge's 1966 hit "When a Man Loves a Woman" that went to the top of the charts and planted the Shoals on the musical map. In 1967, a recording session backed by the FAME rhythm section launched the mainstream career of a young Aretha Franklin with the blues ballad "I Never Loved a Man (The Way I Love You)." What followed was a bumper crop of hits, including songs like "I'd Rather Go Blind" by Etta James and "Mustang Sally" by Wilson Pickett. Over the decades, FAME has put its thumbprint on thousands of recordings.

These powerhouse singers were backed by the Swampers, FAME's house rhythm section, a talented group of studio musicians playing soul, funky rhythm and blues, rock and roll, and country: David Hood on bass, Jimmy Johnson on rhythm guitar, Roger Hawkins on drums, and Barry Beckett on keys. They were later immortalized in the blues-influenced southern rock band Lynyrd Skynyrd's song "Sweet Home Alabama": "Now Muscle Shoals has got the Swampers, and they've been known to pick a song or two." Word spread, and soon Rick Hall's phone was ringing off the hook from big-name producers and singers who wanted those same session players to make their tracks sparkle.

The tour at FAME includes the recording studios where many hits were created
FAME RECORDING STUDIOS

Entering the studios is a pleasant time warp experience—the front lobby has changed little since Hall opened the FAME recording studios; many of the furnishings are close to original era, and the wood-paneled walls are lined with photos of musical artists who rehearsed in Studio B and laid down their final tracks in Studio A.

FAME still operates as a working studio but is open at specific times each week for a forty-five-minute tour that goes through rehearsal hall Studio B and the venerable Studio A with its grand piano and control room that turned out hits by Etta James, Aretha Franklin, Wilson Pickett, Otis Redding, and many others. (famestudios.com)

Muscle Shoals Sound Studio (aka 3614 Jackson Highway)

After a business split from FAME in 1969, several of the FAME musicians left to set up their own recording studio, Muscle Shoals Sound Studio, in nearby Sheffield, nicknamed 3614 Jackson Highway and made famous by a Cher album cover of the same name. Muscle

Muscle Shoals Sound Studio is also known as 3614 Jackson Highway
MUSCLE SHOALS MUSIC FOUNDATION

Shoals was unique because it was owned and operated by its own funky-sounding session musicians.

Bassist David Hood explained how they taught themselves to be studio players. "We really didn't have anybody to follow. We listened to Booker T. & the M.G.'s at Stax, and we listened to the guys at Motown. It was hard to learn, and I didn't have anybody to copy or follow. It really is the interplay between the different players and how well they work together. But it was a great experience to be a young musician and have partners who were all into recording. And we kinda forged a new direction by being the band that owned the studio."

The songs rolled out from 3614, some with the Swampers and some with the artist's own band: Paul Simon, Bob Dylan, Bob Seger, Rod Stewart, Aretha Franklin, Willie Nelson, Elton John, Cat Stevens, Boz Scaggs, and the Rolling Stones all made record magic in the new digs. The Stones' "Brown Sugar," Bob Seger's "Night Moves," and Paul Simon's "Kodachrome" and "Loves Me Like a Rock" were laid down at the unassuming shotgun-style, cinder block building that had been a coffin warehouse and a gospel studio before being taken over as the Muscle Shoals recording studio. From 1969 until 1978, the Swampers rhythm section lent their mojo to more than 200 albums and thousands of memorable songs.

Musician Paul Simon has been often quoted for a call he made to Al Bell at Stax Records in Memphis, asking for the same Black players who played on the Staple Singers hit "I'll Take You There." Bell famously replied, "That can happen, but these guys are mighty pale." That group was the Swampers, which led Simon to Muscle Shoals.

When artists came to Muscle Shoals, it was in the middle of nowhere. Not New York and not Los Angeles. There wasn't even a bar to go to (the county was dry at the time), so they were able to stay completely focused on the music. Productivity soared. One good example is the famous Rolling Stones session when they were slated for three days to record one song (the band being known to eat up studio time). They cranked out one song in a single day and in the end used the leftover time to produce three additional songs—"Wild Horses," "Brown Sugar," and "You Gotta Move," showcasing Mick Taylor's bluesy electric slide guitar—all of which made it onto the *Sticky Fingers* album.

The control room at Muscle Shoals Sound Studio turned out hundreds of hits
JOSEPHINE MATYAS

The original baby grand piano is in the Muscle Shoals Sound Studio where Paul Simon recorded "Kodachrome"
JOSEPHINE MATYAS

In 1978, the Swampers moved to a larger facility, and by the late 1990s, the abandoned studio space at 3614 Jackson Highway had sat shuttered until it was restored by the not-for-profit Muscle Shoals Music Foundation and opened to the public in January 2017. The tour takes visitors through the studio and lobby space restored to its 1969 vintage. Walls are covered with framed gold records and awards, the Yamaha baby grand piano (in tune and ready to go) is the original used by Paul Simon to record "Kodachrome" and Lynyrd Skynyrd's "Free Bird," the vocal booths are the ones used by powerhouse singers like Linda Ronstadt, and the control room is up and running. The wall graffiti and original amp marking the spot where Swampers bassist Hood parked himself right outside the drum isolation booth has even been saved (look for the arrow and "David Hood was here from 1969–1978 playing bass" scrawled on the wall). Lore has it that Keith Richards wrote the last few verses of "Wild Horses" while taking a bathroom break (yes, the bathroom has also been preserved).

Photos and written material hang from the walls, including the invoice for the Stones' studio time to record "Wild Horses"—$877, which would

Swampers' bass player David Hood left graffiti on the wall inside
Muscle Shoals Sound Studio
JOSEPHINE MATYAS

have been divided by the four Swampers owners. Right outside the back
door is what became known as the Listening Porch. Musicians would cut
a bit of their tune, stand outside with the door open, and listen to the
playback coming from the control room.

Just visiting the space is akin to being dosed in musical history. While
few hard-core blues were recorded here, the studio was the recording
location for many blues-influenced songs, including the Staple Singers' "Respect Yourself" and "You Gotta Move" by the Rolling Stones.
(muscleshoalssoundstudio.org)

Alabama Music Hall of Fame

Tuscumbia is home to the Alabama Music Hall of Fame, a collection
of wide-ranging musical legacies that are rooted in the state, from the
blues of W. C. Handy and Dinah Washington to the country twang of
Hank Williams and the soul of Lionel Ritchie.

The trumpet belonging to W. C. Handy is on display at the Alabama Music Hall of Fame
JOSEPHINE MATYAS

The talent pool is wide and deep in this part of the nation: Martha Reeves, Wilson Pickett, Percy Sledge, Nat King Cole, Hank Williams, Lionel Richie, Emmylou Harris, and others turned out a lot of great twentieth-century music, including blues, rock, gospel, country, soul, funk, and pop. Hits like Percy Sledge's "When a Man Loves a Woman" were heavily influenced by gospel, blues, and rhythm and blues. They all share this incredibly powerful emotional expressiveness: the baring of the soul, which is characteristic of the blues.

In addition to the Hall of Fame portraits, there's an archive-stuffed exhibit, including instruments, posters, original sheet music, and a trumpet belonging to W. C. Handy, a working recording studio, and the Southern Star tour bus belonging to the supergroup Alabama.

The tour is self-guided, and you should plan at least an hour, and more if you can read music and appreciate the difference between soprano, alto, tenor, and bass. (alamhof.org)

W. C. Handy Museum and Library of African American Digital Music

Florence is the 1873 birthplace of William Christopher "W. C." Handy, the African American songwriter and self-anointed "Father of the Blues." The author, publicist, composer, bandleader, and musician was born in the simple, two-room log cabin, now restored as the centerpiece of the museum that celebrates his life and accomplishments.

As Handy told it, in 1903, while sitting on a rail station platform in Tutwiler, Mississippi, he was mesmerized when hearing a musical style that immediately caught his attention and imagination. There's more details of his experience in chapter 3 in the section "Tutwiler."

Although a skilled and trained musician himself, Handy did not invent the blues, but he certainly recognized a unique opportunity to introduce a new genre of music to the public by writing and marketing sheet music to spread the sounds. He founded Handy Brothers Music Co. and was the first to translate blues music to written form, building a catalog to create the foundation of what we know today as the blues. In so doing, Handy turned an oral tradition into a written language.

The W. C. Handy Museum in Florence, Alabama, is located in the cabin where the blues great was born
JOSEPHINE MATYAS

Bust of W. C. Handy, the "Father of the Blues"
JOSEPHINE MATYAS

Handy was a smart businessman who took the primitive strains of the blues, incorporated the style into his own compositions (most famously, "St. Louis Blues," "Beale Street Blues," and "Memphis Blues"), and published sheet music for songs that previously had been heard only on street corners, on front porches, and in rural juke joints. He popularized the blues, helped create a blues craze, and along the way took on his nickname.

Handy himself donated the seed money to set up the museum, which now includes several buildings and houses a large collection of objects relating to his musical career, trumpet, personal piano, and handwritten sheet music. The cabin is furnished as it might have been at the time of Handy's birth in the late 1800s. If you want to "go to the source," you'll find your way to this rustic, hand-hewn cabin in Florence. Handy's significance in the growth of the blues is recognized with a Mississippi Blues Trail marker at the birthplace. (wchandymuseum.org)

Each July, music lovers from around the world descend on Florence for the annual W. C. Handy Music Festival with performances by live bands and sessions that teach an appreciation of the blues. (wchandy musicfestival.com)

W. C. Handy's piano is on display at the W. C. Handy Museum in Florence, Alabama

The Shoals Gold Record Room is a celebration of the music of the Shoals in Alabama
JOSEPHINE MATYAS

The Shoals Gold Record Room

Located on the main floor of the SunTrust Bank in Florence, the Shoals Gold Record Room is a free, feel-good stop and a nod to the music legacy of the area. The expansive floor is tiled to resemble enormous guitar necks and strings, walls are lined with a hundred gold records produced or recorded in the Shoals, and a colorful music-themed mural depicts the musical landmarks and instruments of the Shoals.

Shoals Guitar Boutique

Musicians can get their guitar fix at the Shoals Guitar Boutique in Muscle Shoals, with a large selection of new and used guitars available for fondling. (shoalsguitarboutique.com)

Live Music

The Florence website and mobile app have an up-to-date listing of live music. Venues well worth a stop include Swampers Bar & Grille, the NuttHouse Recording Studio, and Cypress Moon Studios (the location of

A guitar signed by the Swampers is part of The Shoals Gold Record Room
JOSEPHINE MATYAS

the second Muscle Shoals Sound studios after they decamped from 3614 Jackson Highway). There's a good chance you'll hear top-notch players—some of them Shoals-area session players like original Swampers David Hood—but for certain, you'll leave with head and heart bursting with an appreciation for the music of this small corner of Alabama.

Established in 2019, the ShoalsFest music festival was an immediate sellout and a tribute to the musical legacy of the Shoals. (shoalsfest.net)

MEMPHIS

The one major city that embodies *all* styles of southern music—including the blues—would be Memphis, home of the legendary Stax Records, Graceland, and Sun Studio, where, according to popular legend, Bob Dylan fell to his knees and kissed the mark on the floor where Elvis launched the history of modern music with "That's All Right."

Memphis bumps up against the northern border of Mississippi and the blues-rich Delta, so it makes sense that the music would have trav-

eled up the Mississippi River and in the boxcars as the players hopped
from one gig to the next. The city was connected to the arteries that
carried culture, but it was also a major transportation hub. People came
and went, bringing all styles of music with them.

The blues came from the experience of hardship and was an instrument of survival, offering release and relief. Between 1935 and 1960,
millions of southerners left the land and moved to the cities. In the
South, that city was Memphis. In the 1960s, it was still a segregated city,
rife with racial and class tensions, but little of that mattered inside the
recording hubs like Stax and Sun Studio or in the bars on Beale Street,
where White and Black musicians socialized and cowrote music that
would sell in the millions and, in some cases, make them household
names as far away as Europe.

When it was too hot to work inside the studio space at Stax, musicians
and singers would unwind at the nearby Lorraine Motel, one of the only
places in Memphis where different races could share the swimming
pool, drink beer, hang out in the rooms, and write songs. The music
poured forth from recording studios like Stax, and artists traveled from
all parts to be part of that sound. Black and White collaborated in an
integrated organization existing within a city where segregation was the
rule. No one could have foreseen how all that would change with the assassination—on the balcony of that same Lorraine Motel—of Dr. Martin
Luther King Jr. in April 1968. Tragically, his death heightened a racial
sensitivity between the musicians—part of the story told at both the Stax
Museum and the National Civil Rights Museum on the grounds of the
former motel. (memphistravel.com)

Sun Studio

Sun Studio lays claim to being sacred ground: the birthplace of rock
and roll. Give him his due, record producer Sam Phillips had an ear for
music and knew talent when it walked through his door. As a result, the
magic that burst from Sun Studio was at the perfect intersection of talent
and entrepreneurship.

Among the names associated with this modest Memphis recording
studio are Ike Turner, Jerry Lee "The Killer" Lewis, Roy Orbison, Carl
"Blue Suede Shoes" Perkins, Johnny Cash, and Elvis Presley. The young
Presley was discovered when he sidled up to the microphone to record
a song for his mother's birthday. It was the moment blues fan Phillips

Sun Studio in Memphis was at the forefront of the birth of rock and roll
JOSEPHINE MATYAS

had been looking for: a White boy who could sing that music. In essence, Elvis "sanitized" the sexually charged African American music for White people, blurring the lines between the roots music of gospel, blues, country, bluegrass, and rockabilly (and, in the process, helping to birth rock and roll).

Phillips had a healthy passion for the blues. He aimed to capture the raw, untapped sound, laying the foundation for what eventually emerged as rock and roll. One of Phillips's favorite artists, Howlin' Wolf, recorded in the studio in 1951. Word spread down into the Delta and caught the ear of Ike Turner, whose band had "Rocket 88," a smokin' rhythm and blues tune about cruising the streets and chasing women. At the time, Phillips's studio was operating as the Memphis Recording Service, a recording hub for the larger Chess Records, and it was the successful recording of "Rocket 88" that propelled him to open Sun Studio a year later.

Sun had its first big hit with Rufus Thomas's "Bear Cat," a song that is considered the cornerstone of funk and soul. Blues artists Little Milton,

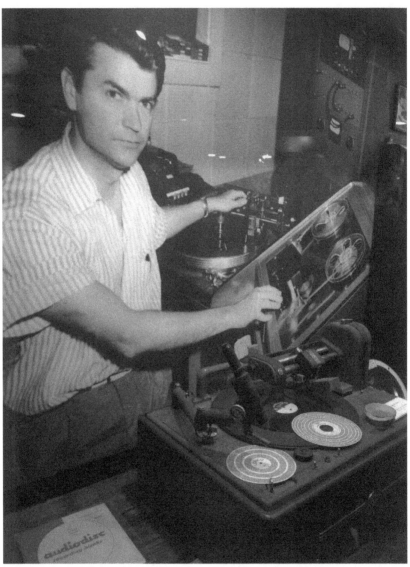

Record producer Sam Phillips was behind the hits that came from Sun Studio in Memphis
JOSEPHINE MATYAS

James Cotton, and Junior Parker all recorded at Sun Studio. But it was in 1954 when a young Elvis Presley walked through the door to record "That's All Right"—a mix of country and blues—that Sun found its niche. The switchboard at local station WHBQ lit up on the night "That's All Right" had its first radio airing. WHBQ host Dewey Phillips played it another fourteen times on that first evening. Rock and roll was a music driven by the insatiable appetite of White teenagers and the open hostility of their parents.

Included on the Sun Studio tour is the original, kitted-out sound studio (still used in evenings for professional recording sessions) with its enlarged black-and-white photo of the famous Million Dollar Quartet hanging on the wall. The photo captures an impromptu 1956 jam session between Elvis, Carl Perkins, Johnny Cash, and Jerry Lee Lewis, surreptitiously recorded by Phillips. Purists line up to take a photo with Elvis's original microphone or caress the guitar amplifier that fell off the roof of the truck—damaging the speaker cone—that became the sound of nineteen-year-old Ike Turner's "Rocket 88," the very first rock and roll song, depending on whom you talk with. (sunstudio.com)

Included on the Sun Studio tour is a kitted-out sound studio with the photo of the famous Million Dollar Quartet

JOSEPHINE MATYAS

"Blue Suede Shoes" was a hit that launched Sun Studio in Memphis
JOSEPHINE MATYAS

Stax Museum of American Soul Music

In the heart of the working-class neighborhood once known as Souls-ville USA, is Stax, now the only full-fledged soul music museum in the world. They say soul music was born in the church and alongside the hardship in the cotton fields. In the 1950s, it described a blend of hard bop, gospel, and the blues.

Musical giants like James Brown, Aretha Franklin, Sam Cooke, and Ray Charles were instrumental in bridging the worlds of gospel with rhythm and blues, setting the stage for the transition to the lightning-in-a-bottle sound of soul. By the 1960s, soul was named for a niche of gospel music with a heavy dose of secular lyrics, and the torch was picked up by singers like Otis Redding, who famously said, "If you listen to the song and your shoulders don't move, there's no groove to it." Groove was big. It stirred your insides and shook your outsides.

At the center of the hard-hitting, percussive Stax sound was house band Booker T. & the M.G.'s, whose tight but loose Hammond organ–infused groove was behind almost every one of the label's recordings

The Stax Museum is the world's only museum dedicated to soul music—a music style that combines hard bop, gospel, and the blues
JOSEPHINE MATYAS

through the 1960s. On a June afternoon in 1962, the M.G.'s killed some time and worked up a medium-tempo blues tune and within half an hour had the makings of "Green Onions" for the B-side of their project. According to *Atlantic* magazine, John Lennon reportedly showed his acrid sense of humor when expressing admiration in a Memphis interview for the group he called "Book a Table and the Maître-d's."

According to Al Bell, Stax Records president at the time, creativity just oozed out of the musical talents associated with the studio. It was an era dominated by A-list soul artists like Wilson Pickett, Sam & Dave, Aretha Franklin, the Staple Singers, Isaac Hayes (also one of the in-house writers), and numerous others. But without a doubt, the biggest star to emerge from Stax was Otis Redding. Although Macon, Georgia, was home base, Redding did most of his enduring work at Stax. Songs like Redding's "Respect" and Sam & Dave's "Soul Man" were widely interpreted as anthems of Black pride.

There's a circa-1906 Mississippi Delta church that was painstakingly moved from Duncan, Mississippi, and reassembled inside the museum.

At Stax is a wooden church moved from Mississippi, a nod to the connection between gospel, the blues, and soul music
RONNIE BOOZE

It's part of a nod to how blues is at the root of soul music, beginning far back in time with the influence of the rural churches. The highly passionate gospel style was characterized by improvisation and rhythmic syncopation, bringing together rhythm and the emotional power of the blues with sacred lyrics. Blues greats like Ray Charles and B. B. King were heavily influenced by the raw spirituality of the music that poured from the churches on Sunday mornings.

There are re-creations of the control room and a near-exact replica of Studio A, including Steve Cropper's Fender Telecaster, Duck Dunn's Fender Precision bass, Al Jackson's drum set, and Booker T. Jones's Hammond M-3 organ (the one used to record "Green Onions").

The museum is text and exhibit heavy and tells a fascinating history that combines tragedy and triumph. The experience is enhanced tenfold by taking the time to learn about the social and political climate of Memphis at the height of the Stax years, the period of time just before the 1968 assassination of Dr. Martin Luther King Jr. changed America. (staxmuseum.com)

The Stax Museum founder exhibit is a nod to the musical geniuses who came together to produce the unique Stax sound
RONNIE BOOZE

Memphis Rock 'n' Soul Museum

Plan on hours at the excellent Memphis Rock 'n' Soul Museum, a Smithsonian affiliate facility. Just outside, a plaque of the Mississippi Blues Trail marks the importance and history of the Mississippi-to-Memphis blues tradition.

A short introductory film gives a snapshot of the roots and emergence of blues music from field hollers and gospel to the city-bound movement as people decamped from the farms, looking to chase even glimmers of job opportunities. Then visitors don headsets and hop into the archive-stuffed galleries, reading, ogling, and appreciating, in some cases never wanting to leave.

The first galleries take an in-depth look into the roots of the music itself and how each generation added new instrumentation and tweaked the styles. They tell the stories of how workers and families would gather on front porches to relax, talk, and make music out of whatever was at hand—a guitar, spoons, a fiddle, a washboard, or even just tapping their feet. It wasn't until the late 1920s that radios and phonographs hit the market and brought music into rural households. Before that newfangled radio invention hit the streets, it was common for traveling musicians to carry their music to isolated communities and juke joints. They played on street corners, on one-night gigs, in brothels, and in roadhouses.

With time, the blues, country, and gospel mixed together, and the appeal of this music crossed the color line. W. C. Handy—who settled in Memphis for the most productive years of his career—popularized the blues through the arrangements he wrote for his own dance orchestras. By the mid-1950s, rock and roll emerged as a fusion of both Black and White traditions, spurred by Sam Phillips's willingness to provide talented but poor African Americans and Whites the chance to record. Blues greats like Mississippi's own B. B. King expanded the popularity of the blues, including his time as a deejay on WDIA radio in Memphis, the first all-Black radio station in the United States.

The archival items that grabbed our attention were the portable reel-to-reel recorder and mixing board used by Sam Phillips to capture the strains of the blues on his road trips, the original typed lyrics for "Heartbreak Hotel," the Gibson hollow-body "Lucille" guitar favored by B. B. King, and Ike Turner's first piano. (memphisrocknsoul.org)

Blues Hall of Fame Museum

Opened in 2015, the Blues Foundation's Blues Hall of Fame Museum on South Main Street was built to preserve the blues and to recognize the artists instrumental to the blues.

Ten immersive galleries, with multimedia video and audio displays, tell the stories of blues music from the early days of Son House and Robert Johnson, through the classic period of Lead Belly and Bessie Smith, and into the urban blues when artists like Muddy Waters and Howlin' Wolf moved north, touring the blues through cities and growing appreciative audiences.

Although the museum is small, there's an impressive collection of blues memorabilia, including Bonnie Raitt's brown bottle guitar slide, Howlin' Wolf's small travel suitcase, Muddy Waters's tour jacket and handwritten lyrics, and a bow tie belonging to Willie Dixon.

The museum is part of the Mississippi Blues Trail, in recognition of how the city of Memphis has long been connected to the Mississippi Delta, and is a center of the blues both for musicians and for blues fans worldwide. (blues.org)

The Blues Hall of Fame preserves the blues and recognizes artists instrumental to the blues
JOSEPHINE MATYAS

A Terraplane hubcap (circa 1934) at the Memphis Blues Hall of Fame was the inspiration for Robert Johnson's song "Terraplane Blues"
JOSEPHINE MATYAS

Memphis Music Hall of Fame

The fairly new Memphis Music Hall of Fame is worth a stop to visit the museum and exhibit hall (opened in 2015), featuring memorabilia, video, audio footage, and multimedia exhibits, spotlighting materials from all Hall of Fame inductees. The museum was unveiled as a tribute to Memphis's contribution to music, including gospel, blues, rhythm and blues, and rock and roll. (memphismusichalloffame.com)

Beale Street

If you had talent, downtown Beale Street was the place to be. B. B. King called his arrival on Beale Street in Memphis a "fantasy come true."

At its height in the early 1900s, the few blocks in the heart of the city were a center for African American commerce and business. It was known as *the* place for Blacks to go to get anything they needed. There was an especially dark period of unrest and business decline after the 1968 assassination of Dr. King, but later infusions of money and interest have seen its resurgence as an entertainment district with the opening

Beale Street in Memphis was the place to go to find anything you needed
JOSEPHINE MATYAS

Tucked away at the end of Beale Street is the small house W. C. Handy called home when he lived in Memphis
JOSEPHINE MATYAS

of clubs, bars, restaurants, and tourist-related businesses. The buildings fronting Beale Street's entertainment district have now been designated with historic status.

Mississippi-born blues singer, the late Rufus Thomas, said, "People came from miles away to come to Beale Street. I tell people if you were Black for one night on Beale Street, never would you want to be White again."

Tucked off the end of the busy street and surrounded by a white picket fence is a small blue and white shotgun-style house that was the Memphis home of W. C. Handy, the "Father of the Blues." Operated by the local Blues Foundation, it was in this modest dwelling that Handy composed some of his best-known works, including "Memphis Blues," "St. Louis Blues," and "Beale Street Blues." (bealestreet.com)

W. C. Handy lived much of his adult life in Memphis

Graceland

It's big, it's glitzy, and for two decades it was home to the "King of Rock and Roll," Elvis Presley. Visitors from around the world line up at the gates of Graceland (especially on August 16, the anniversary of his death), the fourteen-acre, 1939 southern-style colonial mansion that Elvis purchased in 1957 for $100,000.

Young Elvis was deeply influenced by both gospel and blues while growing up—poor and on the wrong side of the tracks—in small-town Mississippi. That story of his humble beginnings is told with grace and modesty at the excellent Elvis Presley Birthplace museum in Tupelo, Mississippi (see chapter 5 for a full description). Graceland, by contrast, focuses on the star power of the singer and performer after he found fame by breaking through the 1950s cultural barriers.

Now a National Historic Landmark, Graceland is inarguably one of the most famous rock and roll residences in the world. A self-guided tour winds through the rooms where "The King" spent time out of the limelight with family and friends. There's the "Grand Central" kitchen, which cranked out the southern-style meals that Elvis loved, and a basement TV room complete with mirrored ceiling, three televisions, a stereo, and an extensive record collection. The pool room is decorated with 350 yards of fabric, and the family room/"Jungle Room" is a time warp snapshot of green shag carpet and a custom waterfall.

It's all business at the newly enhanced Trophy Building, organized as an exhibit on Elvis's life and career with his Grammy Awards, gold records, and more on his TV appearances and thirty-one movies. The attire from Elvis and Priscilla Presley's 1967 celebrity wedding is also on display.

The final stop on the tour is Meditation Garden, where Elvis, both parents, and his grandmother have been laid to rest. There's also a marker for his stillborn twin brother Jesse, who is buried in Tupelo.

Immediately across the street, the new Elvis Presley's Memphis entertainment complex—ten state-of-the-art, immersive experiences—includes his collection of flashy hot rods and classic cars in the new Elvis Presley Automobile Museum.

And for those who can't resist, in addition to the usual T-shirts, mugs, and postcards, there is a gift shop overflowing with Elvis's likeness emblazoned on almost any item you can think of, including nail files, Mr. Potato Heads, and thermometers. (graceland.com)

CITIES OF THE NORTH

Long before the Delta migrants—Muddy Waters, Howlin' Wolf, John Lee Hooker, and others—took up residence in Chicago, the blues, or what would become known as the blues, was taking form all over the southern United States. These recordings were known as "race records" and were marketed specifically to Blacks on labels with names like OKeh Records, Emerson Records, Vocalion Records, and Paramount Records.

The Delta did not have a monopoly on the blues, nor did the Delta bluesmen and blueswomen migrate only to Chicago. They went primarily to where the jobs were—because they had to make a living—and to where the burden of racial oppression was slightly less onerous than Mississippi. Cities like St. Louis, Detroit, Cleveland, Kansas City, and New York were magnets for many thousands of migrants during the early decades of the twentieth century—they were the industrial engines of the American economy—and everywhere the Delta migrants relocated, they took their culture and music. Each of these metropolitan centers evolved a particular sound and style as they absorbed these new populations. Of course, each of these cities also had their own native sounds and music customs, and the Delta blues influenced—and was influenced by—the local sounds and styles, including ragtime and vaudeville.

So, we have come to know "blue-eyed soul"—a sound closely associated with the Righteous Brothers and other White artists who drank heavily from the rhythm and blues wellspring, which was itself influenced by the blues. Likewise, we know of the Philadelphia sound or soul—or Phillysound or TSOP (The Sound of Philadelphia)—which featured a more jazz-inflected genre with funk influences. Kansas City blues is associated with names like Gertrude "Ma" Rainey, Bessie Smith, Lucille Bogan, and Mamie Smith—women who blended gospel with blues with ragtime with rhythm and blues. Detroit became famous for the sound of Motown—a literal hit factory founded by Berry Gordy Jr.—which borrowed liberally from every musical genre in the American songbook but most heavily from rhythm and blues, soul, jazz, and even rock and roll. St. Louis enjoyed a rollicking nightlife as early as the 1860s, which translated into opportunities for musicians to play with and learn from each other. As early as the 1890s and 1900s, blues and ragtime were easy to find in St. Louis—and the cross-fertilization of these styles was a natural outcome. It has been suggested by at least one jazz historian that blues music to the west of St. Louis in the 1920s and 1930s influenced the development of swing. St. Louis is also the home of the National Blues Museum.

TEXAS AND LOUISIANA

Blues was everywhere across Texas and Louisiana too. Names like "Blind Lemon" Jefferson, "Blind Willie" Johnson, "Lightnin'" Hopkins, Melvin "Lil' Son" Jackson, Freddie King, Albert Collins, and "T-Bone" Walker—these men, mostly men, innovated with slide styles and fused gospel with their blues styles.

In the present tense, we associate Texas with blues artists like the late Stevie Ray Vaughan and ZZ Top. Freddie King's up-tempo shuffle instrumental "Hide Away" was picked up and recorded by Eric Clapton, with John Mayall on keyboards, and performed by thousands of other American and British-based blues artists and bands.

Like all major port cities, New Orleans is a mélange of cultures learning from, conflicting with, and influencing each other. Its geographic location on the Gulf of Mexico gives it easy access to the cultures and civilizations of the Caribbean and South America—and its proximity to the heartland of the United States, via the Mississippi River, means that the traffic in ideas, fashions, and styles flows in both directions. As one of the most culturally rich cities in the world, its music scene has been dominated by jazz, ragtime, rhythm and blues, and Cajun zydeco, but, of course, all of these are rubbing up against the blues. While New Orleans is renowned as one of America's greatest music cities, it is largely jazz that dominates. To this day, it is one of the most interesting cities in the United States. There is no other place like it in continental North America. (neworleans.com)

Everywhere people played music in this part of the world, they borrowed from what they heard around them—that is the nature of all popular art.

MUST SEE

- The original Yamaha baby grand piano used on Paul Simon's "Kodachrome" at Muscle Shoals Sound Studio
- A Terraplane hubcap (circa 1934) at the Memphis Blues Hall of Fame. The expensive Terraplane automobile was the inspiration for Robert Johnson's "Terraplane Blues"

- The guitar Jimmie Rodgers bartered for a set of spark plugs, a car battery, and a tune-up, on display at the Alabama Music Hall of Fame
- The four-page typed 1955 contract between Elvis Presley and RCA Records at Sun Studio
- Visit Alfred's on Beale, Rum Boogie Café, Wild Bill's Juke Joint, and B. B. King's Blues Club in Memphis for a taste of authentic blues

MUST READ

- *Race, Rock, and Elvis*, M. T. Bertrand (2009)
- *Beale Street Talks: A Walking Tour Down the Home of the Blues*, Richard Raichelson (1999)
- *Muscle Shoals Sound Studio*, Carla Jean Whitley (2014)

MUST LISTEN AND WATCH

- "I'd Rather Go Blind," Etta James
- "I Never Loved a Man (The Way I Love You)," Aretha Franklin
- "Loves Me Like a Rock," Paul Simon
- "Land of 1000 Dances," Wilson Pickett
- "Wild Horses," the Rolling Stones
- *Muscle Shoals*, an award-winning documentary film about FAME Studios and Muscle Shoals Sound Studio (2013)

GUITAR NOTES

There is something about the Fender Telecaster that eludes description as much as it draws adoration and praise. The first solid-body, mass-produced, electric guitar has adorned every style of music since its 1950 debut. Partisans, like Steve Cropper, are inclined to think that Leo Fender's original design struck the right balance between simplicity, elegance, tone, reliability, and comfort. It feels great in your hands and does everything you want it to. Even today, a Fender Telecaster and Fender Harvard amp can't be beat. Check out Cropper's Tele on "(Sittin' On) The Dock of the Bay," the Otis Redding Stax classic he cowrote with Cropper.

7

THE BLUES PIONEERS AND A GUIDE TO INSTRUMENTS

FOUNDING FATHERS OF THE DELTA BLUES

There is a general consensus among blues aficionados that a couple of names must be included in a short compendium of notable blues innovators not only for their contribution during their lives but also for their lasting influence on others. The important thing to know is that many of these men—and we're talking about mostly men in the early days—were constantly on the move around the Delta and outside of it. As such, they were sowing the seeds of what would become the Delta blues far and wide in their travels.

Charley Patton (Approximately 1881–1934)

Although the precise date of his birth is uncertain (sometime between 1881 and 1891), his importance in the origin of what became the Delta blues is not. He was unquestionably the most important of the early blues musicians and entertainers, and no less a figure than B. B. King calls him the "Father of the Delta blues." Patton's first name is spelled differently by different sources, but we'll go with "Charley" for our purposes. In any event, he refused to accept the name his parents gave him: Vivian.

For almost thirty years, Patton called Dockery Farms plantation—a short drive from Cleveland, Mississippi—home. He would, over the course of his life, alternate between playing music, working cotton, and preaching the gospel. By 1910, he was an established performer and prolific artist known for songs like "Pony Blues," only one of forty-two titles he recorded in a single year. One constant throughout his life, however, was his love of women—any woman, lots of women, available or not. Robert Palmer summarizes Patton's life in his book *Deep Blues*: "He went where he pleased, stayed as long as he pleased, stayed as intoxicated as he pleased, left when he wanted to, and had his pick of the women wherever he went."

Patton learned music at the knee of Henry Sloan—another itinerant musician associated with Dockery Farms and one of the earliest bluesmen anywhere—and no doubt numerous others who toured around the circuit on which Dockery Farms was a stop. Like many of his kind, Patton surely bore a burden of guilt for his love of the music he played—it being despised as the devil's music by appropriately churched elders, including Charley's father, who deplored the idea of his kid hanging out with whores, pimps, drunks, gamblers, and assorted ne'er-do-wells.

But Patton was not—as far as we can tell—drawn to the hard work of cotton, not when the allure of easy living with easy women was so readily at hand. Patton was a magnetic entertainer: a showman of the guitar, not content to simply play and sing songs but also to play behind his head and between his legs. Decades later, Jimi Hendrix would take Patton's antics to the next level. From time to time, Patton would swear off the blues lifestyle and take up preaching, but these conversions were not long resistant to the lure of loose women and plentiful moonshine—and soon enough, Patton was living on the edge again. He was known to be quick tempered and easily angered and found himself in more than a few fights, one of which left him with a nasty scar.

In 1929, he made the first of a number of recordings of his own songs celebrating his ribald lifestyle with liquor and women. "Tom Rushen Blues" tells the story of getting drunk and busted by Tom Rushing, the sheriff in Merigold, Mississippi. One of his most popular songs—"High Water Everywhere"—is about the catastrophic Mississippi Great Flood of 1927. By the peak of his powers, before his health began to decline, Patton was the most celebrated musician in the Dockery Farms region, which is saying something since that region—Cleveland, Drew, and Ruleville—was awash in music.

Patton's lifestyle of heavy smoking and excessive drinking took a toll, and he died between ages forty-three and fifty-three—depending on when he was actually born—in April 1934. His gravestone is in Holly Ridge, Mississippi, on the far side of the cemetery, just a short walk from the road.

Henry Stuckey (Approximately 1896–1966)

Henry Stuckey was probably fishing if he wasn't playing guitar. The singer/guitarist is deemed the creator of the Bentonia Blues style later exemplified by Skip James and Jack Owens. Stuckey never recorded anything, but the haunting E-minor guitar tuning is what makes the Bentonia style notable. Not that Stuckey set out to do that; he played music because he had six daughters and a wife to feed.

Regardless of whether he actually created the Bentonia sound, Stuckey seems to be the thread common to all Bentonia-associated musicians, including Cornelius Bright, Jacob and Dodd Stuckey, Adam and Bird Slater, and Jimmy "Duck" Holmes, the last of the Bentonia bluesmen. Stuckey claimed to have learned a new guitar tuning from some Bahamian soldiers during his service in and after World War I—an open D-minor (D-A-D-F-A-D) or open E-minor (E-G-E-G-B-E)—and brought it home to Bentonia, although open tunings are found elsewhere in Mississippi. Like many stories from this part of the world, the details are contested.

His postwar life consisted of family, fishing, playing the blues on a Stella guitar, gambling, and sharecropping. The family moved around a lot—Itta Bena, Morgan City, Greenwood, Bentonia, North Platte, Anding, and Satartia—and like all musicians to the present day, he played everywhere he went, influencing some and being influenced by others. But in the absence of actual recordings, we have no idea what he sounded like in performance.

"Sonny Boy" Williamson II, aka Aleck or Alex or "Rice" Miller (Approximately 1899–1965)

Little is known of Miller's youth with his sharecropper parents, including stepfather Jim Miller. But by the 1930s, he was playing juke joints, fish frys and picnic gatherings, baseball games, and other events as "Little Boy Blue" with the likes of Robert Johnson, Elmore James, Robert Nighthawk, and Robert Lockwood. With Lockwood, Miller launched the influential radio program *King Biscuit Time* in Helena, Arkansas, across a short bridge from Mississippi, passing himself off as the Chicago harmonica star John Lee "Sonny Boy" Williamson—*and he got away with it*. After John Lee's murder (at age thirty-four), Miller decided that he was "the original" Sonny Boy and kept that name for the rest of this life.

Their fifteen-year *King Biscuit Time* radio run was a huge success, but Miller had little desire to record until tracked down by the owner of Trumpet Records in Jackson in 1951. Although Trumpet didn't last, it set the ball rolling, and Miller recorded about seventy songs for Chess Records in Chicago—the company that picked up Miller's contract. His combination of singing and harmonica playing made a huge impression on the British blues fans, and he recorded with the Yardbirds and the Animals, making him one of the very few to have survived long enough to have started with Robert Johnson and finished with Eric Clapton, Jimmy Page, and Robbie Robertson. He died in his bed of a heart attack at age sixty-six. There's an excellent YouTube interview of Robbie Robertson talking about the Band's meeting with Sonny Boy called "Robbie Robertson Talks about Sonny Boy Williamson."

As a product of the juke joints across the South, Sonny Boy Williamson knew every trick of performance to get an audience up to cruising altitude and keep them there. He's best remembered for his great songwriting and performance and for very nearly taking up permanent residence in London, England, where the sting of Delta racism was considerably less intense.

Eddie James "Son" House Jr. (1902–1988)

Son House was born just north of Clarksdale, the son of a musician. He loved to sing from an early age but showed no interest in *playing* music; in fact, he seemed to fear even touching a guitar. The second of three boys, he was devoted to religion and churchgoing, and he hated the blues, at least for the first part of his life, on religious grounds. The family moved from plantation to plantation, and House was exposed to all kinds of influences in his youth.

The churchified young man began preaching at age fifteen, and by age nineteen, he was married and living in New Orleans. But he was allergic to manual labor—particularly farming—and there were just not enough paid preaching gigs for this handsome, intelligent, and sensitive man. Like his father, he acquired a taste for corn whisky and fell into drinking and womanizing, and before long he was unmarried and unmoored.

In his early twenties, he took up the guitar under the tutelage of James McCoy and became a competent but not outstanding player. Where he excelled was in his performance style, which was danceable, percussive, and kinetic. He applied the rhythmic intensity, vocal energy, and emotional drive of his youthful preaching—when he avoided the devil's music—to his blues performances. House soon discovered that playing juke joint and frolic parties put more coin in his pocket than preaching. So he followed the money.

His conversion to the blues was not without cost. In short order—sometime in 1927 or 1928—he shot and killed a man and was sentenced to fifteen years in the infamous Mississippi State Penitentiary (aka Parchman Farm), which was really a massive plantation run for profit by the state. Here, he would have come across a complex mix of people and music, something that could not but have left a deep impression on him, although he was released sometime in 1929 or 1930 (accounts differ) through the intervention of the White landowner for whom his family worked.

Following his release from Parchman, he came to know Charley Patton. They began to play together frequently, and House, always a keen observer of human nature, took a few pointers that served him the rest of his life. By this time, his bottleneck slide style and singing were good enough to warrant gigs with Patton and a nine-title recording session in 1930. Patton and House were a study in contrasts—House was guilt-ridden about his conversion to the blues; Patton was a noisy, passionate showman who loved everything about the music and lifestyle—but they converged on their love of alcohol.

Over the following years, he recorded with Charley Patton and on his own for Paramount Records in Grafton, Wisconsin, but they were commercial failures. It was Patton's influence that had brought House to the notice of Paramount Records. House's records did not sell well during the Great Depression—they are highly collectible today—although he worked steadily throughout Coahoma County with Willie Brown, a Patton associate. His recordings of "My Black Mama," "Preachin' the Blues," "Clarksdale Moan," "Mississippi County Farm Blues," and "Dry Spell Blues" have been described as popping "like a brick through a stained glass window"—so intense and demonic are the performances. Those recordings came to the attention of archivist Alan Lomax, and in 1941, Lomax dragged his 300-pound "portable" recording machine to House's door to immortalize him for the Library of Congress. House's personal influence on other players rather than the popularity of his recordings counts as his most important contribution to the blues.

For most of this time, House worked as a tractor driver on various plantations, but like all musicians of the era, House crossed paths with and influenced his share of peers, including Robert Johnson and Muddy Waters. In 1943, he relocated to Rochester, New York, then gave up music and worked as a railroad porter and chef.

And that should have been the end of it. But the blues was not finished with Son House. The folk blues revival of the early 1960s touched off a search for the originals from the Delta, and House was discovered in Rochester. The producer John Hammond asked a twenty-two-year-old Alan Wilson (later of Canned Heat) to reteach the old lion to play like his youthful self, and a whole new career opened up in front of him, including tours of Europe and the United States, commercially successful recordings, and festival appearances, including the Montreux Jazz Festival. House's career was reestablished as a folk/blues singer playing festivals and coffeehouses—even Carnegie Hall in 1965—during the folk music revival of that decade. He recorded several albums and informally taped concerts, some available on YouTube.

His later years were complicated by bad health—including dementia and Parkinson's disease—and he died in Detroit of cancer of the larynx in 1988 at age eighty-six (rather advanced for a bluesman). He'd been married five times over the course of his on-again, off-again blues career. Pictures of Son House show him cradling a National steel-bodied or resonator guitar with a chrome slide on the third finger of his left hand. His long, slender fingers suggest a hand perfectly suited to the guitar, and his vocal style evokes all the elements of a great singer of the blues.

Son House gave different accounts of his life and story to different interviewers at different times—a not uncommon trait among a certain class of entertainers—but it's clear that he converted to the blues with the same intensity he once held for his youthful Baptist preaching.

Chester Arthur (Howlin' Wolf) Burnett (1910–1976)

Charley Patton inspired a lot of bluesmen in his travels, and one of them was Howlin' Wolf, born in White Station in Clay County, just north of West Point, Mississippi. By the time the fully grown man walked into Sun Studio in Memphis, he was a strapping six feet six inches, wore a size sixteen shoe and looked more like a wrestler or construction worker than a harmonica-torturing blues singer.

But oh, what a performer! Sam Phillips recalled in a 1986 *Rolling Stone* interview, "Wolf had the most god-awful voice that could be classified as a set of vocal cords I ever heard in my life. And that I knew had to draw attention."

And Phillips was far from the only person to be so awestruck. In a 2004 interview in *Guitar World*, guitarist and singer Bonnie Raitt named Howlin' Wolf the one person who does everything she loves about the blues. He left quite an impression on the woman people call the "Queen of the Blues." "It would be the size of his voice—or just the size of him. When you're a little pre-teenage girl and you imagine what a naked man in full arousal is like, it's Howlin' Wolf. When I was a kid, I saw a horse in a field with an erection, and I went, Holy shit! That's how I feel when I hear Howlin' Wolf. And when I met him it was the same thing. He was the scariest, most deliciously frightening bit of male testosterone I've ever experienced in my life."

It was quite a climb for Wolf. Born into an impoverished background of soul-crushing Delta poverty, he lacked even the most basic schooling and would walk the railroad tracks—when not chopping cotton—looking for scraps of food. According to Ted Gioia in *Delta Blues*, his greatest aptitude was merely to *run*—to avoid the whippings and beatings that pervaded his young life. In an act of sheer overcompensation, and even at the height of his fame and late into life, he continued to take night courses to improve his meager education. Like most blues singers of his class and time, the church was his introduction to music. His mother was a prolific composer of her own gospel songs but was less than attentive to young Chester's youthful needs. The hardscrabble, dirt-poor child was as good as orphaned.

Around about 1926, Wolf moved to Dockery Farms and came under the influence of Charley Patton and rubbed shoulders with Robert Johnson and various other bluesmen on the circuit. On January 15, 1928—a date he remembered all his life—he acquired his first guitar at age eighteen. By this time, he was already an accomplished singer on homemade and handmade instruments, buckets, boxes (including a diddley bow), and the harmonica. And he could belt out a song with the best of them. To see him in YouTube videos—from his later years—is to watch a man-giant simply devour his blues with superhuman force.

The truth is that Wolf drank heavily from Charley Patton's well, taking Patton's performance style to the next level—anything to drive an audience to a frenzy. At the peak of his powers in 1950s and 1960s Chicago, Robert Palmer reports in *Deep Blues*, "He would dart around the stage, chanting a key phrase over and over, his face bathed in sweat, eyes rolling back in his head, while his band riffed one chord and the audience swayed as if in a trance . . . Muddy simply would not go to the lengths Wolf habitually went to. Muddy was a superstud, the Hoochie Coochie Man; Wolf was a feral beast."

Robert Leroy Johnson (Approximately 1911–1938)

The sensible way to approach the Robert Johnson story is to decide in advance that you're going to like one story more than the others and go with that. Johnson was born in Hazlehurst, south of Jackson, probably on May 8, 1911 (accounts differ, and pinning an exact date with accuracy is impossible). His father was Noah Johnson, and Robert's earliest years were spent in labor camps and in various plantations around Mississippi.

Like a lot of kids of that era, Robert bounced around among family members and residences—a confused and confusing experience for a child. In the course of this, he crossed paths with Charley Patton and Willie Brown and countless other musicians on the circuit. In 1929, he met and married sixteen-year-old Virginia Travis, but she and their baby died in childbirth the following year. For the eighteen-year-old Johnson—who was also known by the names Robert Dodds and Robert Spencer—this must have been a devastating blow. Robinsonville, however, where Johnson was living when Virginia died, was one of those places where Charley Patton, Son House, and Willie Brown would frequent, and Johnson got to know them.

Then Johnson vanishes. The best guess is that he returned to Hazlehurst, where he took up with and married an older woman. When he surfaced more than a year later, he was a much better player than anyone remembered him being when he left. And that's probably the origin of the devil-at-the-crossroads story.

Instruments come and instruments go through the hands of a musician. Johnson probably played a number of different guitars over the course of his short life. Montgomery Ward and Sears and Roebuck marketed guitars in their mail-order catalogs all over the United States, including the Delta. Johnson would have had access to guitars in stores

in Memphis and Clarksdale too as well as from other players in the circuit. Two likely candidates are Stella and Kalamazoo instruments—these
were common—and there is a chance he might have played a Gibson
L-1, although this would have been an expensive guitar in Johnson's
time. Kalamazoo was a down-market budget brand marketed by the
Gibson company during the Great Depression years—and some claim
that he used the KG-14 in his 1936 and 1937 recording sessions. It's
possible that he used archtops and flattops as well as a resonator guitar
at one time or another. If he was like other players of his place and time,
he would have been gambling (and losing) and hocking his guitars to pay
debts and buying them back and trading up when he had the coin. The
guitar in the iconic 1935 Memphis studio photograph could have been a
prop, or it could have been acquired for the photo itself. We can't see the
logo on the headstock or the tailpiece/bridge under his right hand. What
we can see—even clearer in the photo-booth portrait—is that Johnson
possessed fine, beautiful, long, tapered guitar-playing fingers.

Johnson traveled to San Antonio, Texas, in November 1936 for the
first of two sessions for the American Record Corporation, where he is
remembered to have set up facing into a corner—his back to the techni-
cians—and recorded sixteen songs over three days. Why face the corner?
Speculation is that he was trying to prevent anyone from seeing his
playing and stealing his licks, which seems unlikely since he was playing
in public all the time. Was he shy? Also unlikely. More likely is that he
learned on the street and in the juke joints that he could better hear his
instrument and voice if he projected both into the corner—a technique
called corner loading—so that the sound would bounce back to him. It's
the same reason people like singing in the shower: the tiles project the
sound back to you.

In June 1937, Johnson traveled to Dallas to record thirteen additional
tracks. Of the corpus, only "Terraplane Blues"—from the first session—
sold roughly 5,000 copies as a 78 rpm for the Vocalion label—a modest
regional hit that he never repeated. By one of those too-rare strokes of
luck, his recordings came to the attention of John Hammond Sr., who also
discovered or promoted Aretha Franklin, Pete Seeger, Bob Dylan, Leonard Cohen, and the future of rock and roll, Bruce Springsteen. Hammond
tracked down Johnson and booked him to appear at Carnegie Hall on
December 23, 1938, but Johnson died in late summer. So it was Hammond who really put Johnson on the map with his release in 1961 of *King
of the Delta Blues Singers*, a compilation of Johnson's recorded output.

Johnson died young, age twenty-seven, on August 16, 1938. Seems like he might have been poisoned, but it's not clear by whom or with what. Theories abound. The woman he scorned? The boyfriend or husband of the women he was hitting on at that particular gig? Truth is that Johnson was not averse to pulling from a bottle, and moonshine was everywhere in the Delta, and it would have been easy to add some rat poison to it. A little goes a long way, and it may not kill instantly—depends on the dose. Strychnine has a distinctive odor that even strong moonshine would not disguise. But what if Johnson was already three sheets to the wind and pulling on any bottle that happened by? That was not unknown in the juke joints and house parties that he played. Robert Johnson died three days later at the Star of the West Plantation near Greenwood. It was a painful death, according to witnesses. There's no evidence that he got medical attention.

Sadly, sometimes dying young is a good career move. At the time of his death, no one thought Johnson particularly notable. He was only one of hundreds of talented and charismatic young singer/guitarists gigging throughout the Delta. True, his songs and playing might have elevated him above his peers to some degree, and the thematic content of his lyrics was certainly memorable. His recorded output was a modest twenty-nine songs.

What elevated Johnson to his iconic status was his lucky discovery years later by acolytes like Eric Clapton and the Rolling Stones. Let's give the last word on Johnson to Giles Oakley in *Devil's Music*: "The legend of Robert Johnson has been created from the combination of tragic brevity of his life and the overwhelming sense of inner torment and foreboding in his blues. He only recorded some thirty odd songs but taken together they create visions of a restless, self-destructive interior world filled with secret fears and anxieties. At times he seems scarcely able to control the extremities of feeling which press in on him. As if on the edge of an abyss of complete psychic disintegration, his voice changes from high frenzy to little-boy vulnerability, while his slide guitar shifts from controlled affirmations to exaggerated effects. Even when his voice is quiet and softly lyrical and his guitar delicately deliberate, the haunted pain is always close to the surface."

McKinley "Muddy Waters" Morganfield (1913–1983)

Had he never moved north and defined the iconic Chicago sound, Muddy Waters would have been notorious around the Stovall Plantation area—hard by Clarksdale—as the maker of the best moonshine whisky in the area whose modest house doubled as a juke joint and who played guitar in a country band. Lucky for us the 22.5 cents per hour he made driving a tractor was not enough to keep him on the farm. Library of Congress archivist Alan Lomax recorded Muddy's country blues one Saturday afternoon, and on hearing the playback, Muddy was convinced that he was as good as any other musician whose records were increasingly available across the Delta.

By May 1943, age thirty, Muddy was a resident of Chicago, having sampled and rejected St. Louis and Memphis. By 1978, he'd won so many Grammy Awards that competitors wondered whether the ethnic or traditional recording categories had been invented just for him, and his Johnny Winter–produced records for Columbia were outselling the rest of his entire catalog. He was gigging as much as he wanted to—which was all the time—and hailed as the inspiration for an entire generation of British-born blues and rock and roll bands. Bassist Bill Wyman—in an interview posted to YouTube—is nearly rhapsodic about meeting Muddy for the first time in Chicago when he offered to help them move equipment for Bill's band, the Rolling Stones.

Although Muddy and his bandmates were not the first to *invent* electric blues, they can reasonably be credited with using amplification to make their blues tougher and rawer, more ferocious than just louder. Before Muddy, blues was a music for, by, and about Delta Blacks, but Muddy and his peers changed all that and launched it into the world. His recordings for Chicago's Chess Records—featuring a rotating cast of musicians like Little Walter, Willie Dixon, Jimmie Rodgers, and countless others—became the template for thousands of other Delta blues musicians. Through Muddy and his bandmates, an art form so disreputable that even its practitioners were inclined to disown it transformed popular music and spawned countless acolytes, including Eric Clapton, Jeff Beck, Jimmy Page, Keith Richards, Brian Jones, and Jimi Hendrix, to tag only the best known.

Look up Muddy's "Mannish Boy" performance from *The Last Waltz* on YouTube. To say that the music provoked a huge following is to understate the magnetic appeal of Muddy's style and stage presence, so it's appropriate to give the last word on Muddy to Leonard Chess, the son and nephew of the two founders of Chess Records, where Muddy did most of his recording. "It was sex. If you had ever seen Muddy then, the effect he had on women. Because blues, you know, has always been a woman's market. On Saturday night they'd be lined up ten deep." And where women gather to fawn over blues musicians, hard-drinking men won't be far behind. The combination of hard-drinking men and fawning women is every tavern owner's dream—and that means gigs for musicians.

William James "Willie" Dixon (1915–1992)

Willie Dixon was born in Vicksburg at the southern reaches of what some define as the Delta but really made his mark in Chicago as a bassist and songwriter at Chess Records. A big man—six feet six inches—he was one of fourteen children steeped in music from an early age. Dixon went to jail for the first time at age twelve for stealing fixtures from a torn-down house, and that, he says, is when and where he really learned the blues. Not long after, he was jailed again at the Harvey Allen County Farm—near the notorious Parchman Farm prison—where he witnessed prisoners being abused, mistreated, and sometimes beaten to death. Dixon himself lost his hearing for a few years after a blow to the head. Somehow, Dixon escaped and walked north to Memphis, where he hopped a train to Chicago.

By 1936, he was training to be a boxer and in 1937 won the Illinois Golden Gloves as a heavyweight novice but was subsequently suspended over a dispute about money. This whole time, Dixon was singing in Chicago gospel groups—even getting some radio time—before taking up the washtub bass (an oilcan, a stick, and a string). By 1946, Dixon had graduated to a real upright bass and gigged regularly with Muddy Waters, Little Walter, and other Chicago-based blues musicians. By the end of the decade, Dixon had formed a relationship with the Chess Brothers (Leonard and Phil), who were releasing blues records and becoming—as it turned out—the most important blues label in the world. Many of the blues classics recorded at Chess were written, arranged, and often produced by the city's first-call bassist, Willie Dixon.

Dixon's breakthrough as a songwriter was Muddy Waters's recording of "I'm Your Hoochie Coochie Man" in 1954. In 1955, Dixon charted his first number one with "My Babe" recorded by Little Walter. Dixon is considered one of the most important and influential record producers in the history of American popular music. He played bass or arranged on records for—or cowrote songs with—Chuck Berry, Bo Diddley, Fleetwood Mac, Otis Spann, Buddy Guy, Howlin' Wolf, Sam Lazar, Little Walter, Jimmy Rodgers, Johnny Shines, Muddy Waters, and Sonny Boy Williamson II. Dixon is credited as writer or cowriter on 500 songs, including blues standards like "Help Me," "I Can't Quit You Baby," "Little Red Rooster," "My Babe," "Spoonful," "I Just Want to Make Love to You," "The Seventh Son," "Wang Dang Doodle," and "You Can't Judge a Book by the Cover." As much as anyone, Dixon is credited with developing the Chicago Sound through his extensive association with Chess Records and output of classic blues tunes and collaborations with blues musicians.

Dixon established the Blues Heaven Foundation in the 1980s, a non-profit organization that provides scholarship awards and musical instruments to poorly funded schools. When he died at age seventy-six in 1992, the blues lost one of its great composers and performers. This son of the Delta made his mark on American and world music.

John Lee Hooker (Approximately 1917–2001)

Enigmatic barely suffices to capture the story of John Lee Hooker—but his boogie guitar style is distinctive, hypnotic, and irresistible. He was born sometime between 1915 and 1923—accounts differ—outside of Tutwiler, one of nine (or perhaps it was twelve) children. The numbers in accounts jump all over the place. His stepfather, guitarist Willie Moore, who played with Charley Patton, Blind Blake, and Blind Lemon Jefferson, among others, was a player whose influence John Lee credited all his years.

Like Muddy Waters, he was a regular churchgoer and absorbed the music and energy of that environment, even performing in choirs and gospel groups. Hooker's birth father—the Reverend William Hooker—took a dim view of Willie Moore's music but gave young John Lee a guitar on condition that it never be brought into the house. When his mother, Minnie, took up with Willie Moore, John Lee joined her, the only one of her children to do so and the only one of her children to show any interest in music.

When he surfaced in Memphis in the 1930s, music was still an avocation. It was not until 1948 in Detroit that Hooker was discovered at a house party, and his first hit, "Boogie Chillun," burned up the charts. Hooker quit his day job and never looked back.

By the end of his life, age eighty-eight or eighty-three, depending on when he was actually born, Hooker was in the Blues Hall of Fame (1980), Mississippi Musicians Hall of Fame, and the Rock & Roll Hall

of Fame (1991). He won the National Heritage Fellowship (1983)—
the U.S. government's highest honor in the folk and traditional arts—
and had his star planted on the Hollywood Walk of Fame. "Boogie
Chillun" and "Boom Boom" are on the Rock & Roll Hall of Fame's list
of the 500 Songs That Shaped Rock and Roll, and the former is also
on the Recording Industry Association of America's list of the Songs
of the Century.

Between 1990 and 2000, Hooker won Grammys for Best Traditional
Blues Recording (twice), Best Traditional Blues Album, and Best Collab-
oration with Vocals, capping it off with a Lifetime Achievement Award.

His musical style featured a throbbing, pulsing boogie groove—sometimes supplemented by his stomping foot—that he claimed to have
copied from his stepfather. Hooker called it "boogie," but it was not a
garden-variety boogie-woogie. Hooker's groove, according to author Ted
Gioia in *Delta Blues*, is "like a solution to a quasi-Newtonian puzzler:
How to pack the maximum amount of forward momentum into the few-
est number of notes."

Hooker was known for spontaneously creating new songs in the studio, and his idiosyncratic relationship to meter challenged everyone who
played—or tried to—with him. He worked or shared a stage with Eric
Clapton, Bonnie Raitt, Muddy Waters, Albert King, Peg Leg Sam, Ginger Baker, Chris Wood, the Rolling Stones, and the Animals.

In 1964, he told an interviewer for the British music magazine *Melody
Maker* that he knows why the best blues comes from Mississippi. "Be-
cause it's the worst state. You have the blues all right if you're down in
Mississippi."

John Lee Hooker—probably the most decorated man to ever come
out of the Mississippi Delta—died in his sleep on June 21, 2001, at his
California home.

Mathis James "Jimmy" Reed (1925–1976)

If some people didn't have bad luck, they'd have no luck at all—and
that might be true of Jimmy Reed. He sold more records than Muddy
Waters, Howlin' Wolf, Elmore James, or Little Walter, and his songs
were covered by no less than Elvis Presley, Charlie Rich, Lou Rawls,
Hank Williams Jr., and the Rolling Stones. But Reed could not control
his appetite for alcohol, and, combined with epilepsy, it cost him years of
life. His best-known songs—"Baby What You Want Me to Do," "Bright

Lights Big City," "Honest I Do," "You Don't Have to Go," "Going to New York," "Ain't That Loving You Baby," and "Big Boss Man"—are iconic tunes that one biographer celebrated as easily digestible, accessible, instantly recognizable, and easy to play and sing.

Reed was born in Dunleith, Mississippi, six miles from Leland, and settled in Gary, Indiana, not far from Chicago, where he recorded with Vee-Jay Records. At his peak, he put eleven songs on the Billboard Hot 100 charts and fourteen on the rhythm and blues charts, beating out B. B. King, among others. It was his not-in-your-face guitar sound coupled to his harmonica and vocal style that made Reed a welcome addition to so many record buyers in the 1950s and 1960s. His music was nothing special—he did not light up the guitar or harmonica—and his vocals paled by comparison with the emotional storm produced by Howlin' Wolf or Muddy Waters. But he produced hit after hit even while touring constantly and drinking himself out of a career and, ultimately, a life.

Diagnosed with epilepsy in 1957—it's possible that the condition afflicted him for many years previously—Reed also suffered numerous episodes of delirium tremens, the rapid onset of confusion, shaking, shivering, irregular heart rate, sweating, and seizures associated with withdrawal from alcohol. But the public couldn't get enough of Reed, even as he spiraled downward, because there's joy in his spare, simple blues. His legacy is his influence on the British blues bands, like the Rolling Stones, who drank deeply from the Delta wellspring from which Reed emerged.

Riley "B. B." King (1925–2015)

Fortune smiles on a few, and B. B. King would have been among the first to admit that a good dose of it came his way. In his autobiography, Eric Clapton wrote that King was "without a doubt the most important artist the blues has ever produced."

Born between Indianola and Greenwood, Mississippi—near a little hamlet called Itta Bena—on a plantation owned by Jim O'Reilly, the child who would become B. B. King would come to stand for almost everything and anything having to do with postwar blues. Many Delta guitarists learned music from listening to the early recordings of people like Blind Lemon Jefferson, Lonnie Johnson, Jimmie Rodgers, or Charley Patton—but few exceeded the tenacity of B. B. King, who collected some 30,000 recordings before donating them to the Blues Archive at the University of Mississippi in Oxford. Music ran in the family too: his mother's first cousin was Booker "Bukka" White, and he had a regional hit called "Shake 'Em On Down" which was one of the most emulated recordings in the Delta during B. B.'s impressionable years.

Tragedy struck early with the death—at age twenty-five—of Nora Ella King, B. B.'s mother. So nine-year-old Riley went to live with his grandmother, his parents having separated sometime before, where he made friends with a Victrola record player. A few years later, he was reunited with his father and his new family in their home in Lexington, Mississippi—a home that featured indoor plumbing and a family radio. King took to that radio like a duck to water. Shortly thereafter, however, B. B. got on his bicycle and rode it back to a humble dwelling in Kilmichael, where he essentially raised himself. Like a lot of people of his era, he migrated from plantation to plantation chasing the money and earned a reputation as a hard worker—once claiming to have picked 480 pounds of cotton in a single day. His first guitar cost him a whopping $20 but it got him into a gospel group modeled on the Golden Gate Quartet and the Dixie Hummingbirds and a gig on a Greenwood radio station. All the time, King was assiduously soaking up every note of music that came his way.

But luck followed him too: he soon found he could make more money playing on street corners than in churches, and over time he began hanging out in—or just outside of—night spots where he could peek through the cracks to watch the likes of Jay McShann (from Kansas City), Pete Johnson, Aleck "Rice" Miller, Robert Lockwood, Benny Goodman's band with a (gasp!) Black guitarist on an all-White bandstand, and Count Basie himself. These experiences he took back to his day job following a mule-drawn plow, sometimes for twelve hours a day, until 1946, when he got himself in a tractor accident and destroyed part of a barn. With that, he grabbed his guitar and his meager savings of $2.50 and beat it for Memphis.

It's said the blues came out of Mississippi, played around in Memphis, and then settled in Chicago, and B. B. King did much the same thing on his first visit, but then he returned to Indianola to pay off his debt to the farmer whose tractor he crashed. On his return to Memphis, however, King had a different experience. He got a regular gig with radio station WDIA and acquired the nickname "Blues Boy"—later shortened to B. B.—and began playing constantly. He was a regular entrant in the weekly amateur contest at Beale Street's Palace Theatre, but his career really took off after 1951's recording of "Three O'Clock Blues," which vaulted him onto the rhythm and blues charts and inaugurated one of the most successful show business careers in blues history.

The Memphis-acquired habit of playing all the time became the pattern for the rest of his life, even into his later years when he was touring the world. What kept King going? Probably the fact he was the real deal. As American music historian Ted Gioia, puts it, "His deep soulfulness, his full-of-soulness, his commitment to a music of emotion, played on the heartstrings as much as on the six strings kept his fans coming, kept his performances vital and his music alive."

King's guitar sound and style are immediately recognizable on the basis of a few bent or vibrato notes from that big left hand. He's that distinctive and, as adoring fan Keith Richards understates, a specialist. He very seldom plays more than one note at a time—Chords? Never!— but those one-note lines are infused with intensity and passion, love for the music, and love for his distinctive black Gibson ES-345 semi–hollow body guitars. The story has it that King named his guitars—he played hundreds over the years—after a woman who provoked a fight in a juke joint in Twist, Arkansas, where a barrel of kerosene was knocked over. King—a young man in 1949—ran back into the inferno to rescue his guitar. He named subsequent guitars "Lucille" in memory of that event, the name of the woman over whom the men were fighting.

King had one of the longest careers of any blues musician, touring well into his later years despite a lifetime history of high blood pressure and diabetes. The B. B. King Museum and Delta Interpretive Center in Indianola is a must-see for any fan of the blues. The center is jammed with memorabilia from the great man's life and career, including his home recording studio, one of his many touring buses, numerous stage costumes, and guitars he used over the decades. The center itself is built onto—that is, attached to—a large barn structure where young Riley rode a tractor on the then plantation to which he returned every summer for as many years as his health would permit to do a show for the locals.

INSTRUMENTS OF THE DELTA BLUES

In the Delta, like any areas with people coming and going, there were numerous musical instruments scattered across the communities at the turn of the century and well into the 1920s and 1930s. Most of them are probably lost by now to humidity, corrosion, and neglect, returned to the dust of the earth from which they emerged, forgotten under beds or stowed in attics or closets, or just vanished. We can say with some confidence that the instruments available to musicians of the Delta blues era left something to be desired in terms of quality. They were—with rare exception—mass-produced to be sold in mail-order catalogs like Sears and Roebuck and Montgomery Ward. Instruction would have been hard to come by even if the student could afford it, which most could not—especially among the lower working classes—and maintaining the quality of the instrument would have been a significant challenge given the humidity of the Delta. Corrosion-resistant guitar strings, for example, didn't exist until late in the twentieth century, and the guitar—because of its portability and range of expression—was the preferred instrument for many musicians and performers. One can only imagine how hard it would have been to replace a set of guitar strings once they had become so corroded by finger grease and atmospheric humidity that they actually hurt the player. Yet music always finds a way to make itself present in our lives—and people who love music have an irrepressible drive to create instruments and perfect and innovate them to feed the need to make music, solo and with others.

We start with the most primitive and conclude with the most sophisticated of instruments that would have been found in the Delta.

Diddley Bow

Find yourself a length of wire, perhaps baling wire or the wire off a broom handle, and stretch it out by securing its ends to a couple of nails—say, on the wall of your house. Now increase the tension of the wire by jamming something like a glass bottle or stick under one end. Vibrate the string and run a knife blade or a bottle up and down the length of the wire as it vibrates and voila!—you've got yourself a diddley bow or jitterbug. In the right hands—and with a little practice—it's evocative, powerful, and hours of fun. It can be removed from the side of one building and attached to another. It can inspire simple melodies. It can soothe or aggravate, depending on how it's approached. Anything that vibrates can be made to express a range of emotional states with sufficient creativity and persistence. It's hours of fun and a gateway drug to a more powerful experience (see below).

Even better, wire up two diddley bows on the same wall surface. Tune one to any pitch and vary the pitch of the other—using the first as a drone—and you're on your way to building a primitive guitar. You can view a short video of B. B. King talking about his childhood diddley bow on the website of the B. B. King Museum and Delta Interpretive Center. (bbkingmuseum.org/video)

Washtub or Gutbucket Bass

A short conceptual leap from the diddley bow is the gutbucket—or washtub—bass. For this, you need three things: a large galvanized wash bucket (bigger and boomier is better; the larger the tub the bigger the sound), a longish broomstick-like length of wood, and a cord or length of medium-weight rope (not too heavy, or it won't vibrate). Drill a hole in the middle of the bucket and run the rope through, securing it with a large knot on the *inside* so that it can't pull itself out—dead center if possible because that makes maximum use of the resonating surface. Secure the other end to the top of the broomstick and place the opposite end of the stick on the edge (or as close as possible to the edge) of the bucket. Put one foot on the edge of the upside-down bucket—but on the edge not on the bottom of the bucket itself. Now when you pull the rope tight by angling the stick back from the hole, the rope tightens and pulls the knot toward the hole. When that happens, the vibration from the cord or rope is transferred to the bottom of the bucket, vibrating it like the top of a guitar. Put one foot on the edge of the tub to prevent the tub from lifting as you pull back on the stick. It can be tricky to regulate the pitch of the bass, but it's easy to create a groove and pound that home relentlessly. And where the bass is concerned, groove is supreme. The instrument is reasonably portable and lots of fun to watch.

Upright Bass

The grown-up version of the gutbucket bass is the double bass—also called doghouse, upright bass, or bull fiddle—which looks like an over-sized four-string violin and works by transferring its fundamental note into the floor and turning every room into a resonating chamber. These were big, expensive, and less fun to transport because they were also fragile and took up a lot of space. But in the right hands—true of every instrument—they pounded out an unrelenting groove that supplied a solid pulsating foundation under every musician, ensemble, and song. The bass is as much felt as heard—often the instrument you hear outside on the street because it generates such long sound waves. Willie Dixon started on a gutbucket and graduated to a double bass, his primary instrument at Chess Records.

Guitar

And nothing goes better with a gutbucket or double bass than another, smaller stringed instrument to fill out the mid-range and high end.

No instrument is as reliably associated with the blues as the guitar—and for good reason. First, its portability meant that one could travel with it easily, which meant that musicians could move from gig to gig with their moneymaker slung over their shoulder or protected from the elements in a modest case of some kind. Second, the instrument is shaped—let's be honest—like a woman with all the right curves in all the right places, one end of which is a phallic-like neck, the holding and manipulation of which could easily be confused for masturbation. In fact, guitar wanking (aka musical masturbation)—the extended playing of surplus scales in a too-long solo that may impress nonplayers—is a source of irritation among other musicians. But the fact is that many a guitar player has been complimented on the beauty of his fingers, and no better example can be found than Robert Johnson himself, whose few photographs reveal a man with lovely, long, delicate, and shapely fingers. How many women could watch a man like Johnson play the guitar and not imagine those fingers caressing her?

Third, the guitar is held against the hips, from which it emits a variety of sensual—even sexual—sounds. Combine all of this with high-potency moonshine whisky—which was abundant—and the typical Delta bluesman could reap a rich and enjoyable sexual harvest, companioning lone or displaced women, as he traveled from gig to gig. Traveling guitar players regularly provoked undesirable hostility in the partners of women who took a shine to the visiting musician. Many a guitar player found himself having to flee for his life from jealous husbands and boyfriends.

Then too, these guys—for they were mostly men—knew how to show a woman a good time. They usually had a little coin to splash around from playing in jukes, on street corners, or at house parties, and they could afford to dress better, drink more, and gamble—maybe even give up farming altogether. The fact that they were compelled to move from gig to gig meant that—almost by definition—they were unattainable, at least for the long term, which added to their rakish charm. They affected a devil-may-care attitude about them, the classic bad boys, and if they were good enough, they could earn, with a single guitar, the fee for an entire orchestra.

Many players of the era adopted the use of chrome, brass, or glass tubes—aka bottlenecks—on the third or fourth finger of their fretting hand to enable use of microtones between the notes or frets. Slide guitar really took off when guitars became amplified because the power of the slide effect was suddenly much louder and tougher sounding. The slide— whether a tube, knife blade, beer bottle, or drinking glass—is a signature feature of the Delta blues. It replicates in smaller form the diddley bow and became a staple of the music as it took up residence in Chicago. Among the most recognizable sounds in all of Delta blues tradition is the slide guitar introduction to "Dust My Broom" by Elmore James. The introduction to the *Allman Brothers Band* version of "Statesboro Blues" offers another example of the slide on the ring finger of a guitar virtuoso.

So what's the big deal with the slide? It enables a much greater range of expression than fingers on a fretboard. The slide enables a player to evoke the notes between the notes on the standard piano keyboard; the bending and vibrato, the emotional impact unleashed by a good slide player, can sound like a distressed child, calling forth a range of powerful emotions, making the hair stand up on the arms, and bringing tears to the eyes. But this only touches the surface of why people love the blues.

By today's standards, the guitars of this era left much to be desired—the necks are unreliable, the strings too high—although some are highly valued as collector's items. They were mass-produced, and quality was highly variable—to play them today is to be reminded of just how far guitar technology has advanced. They went under names like Oscar Schmidt, Harmony, La Scala, Stella, Sovereign, and Kay. At the higher end of the market were names like Gibson, Martin, and Gibson's down-market brand called Kalamazoo, which Robert Johnson played. Silvertone was the brand name of guitars marketed through the Sears and Roebuck catalog. All things considered, they had the great virtue of being affordable and available.

The National Resonator Guitar or Dobro

The standard six-string guitar suffered from one major drawback: it was easily drowned out in a large or noisy setting, like the inside of a rollickin' juke joint on a Saturday night. There is a limit to how hard you can torture guitar strings before they break. So in order to get the sound of the guitar above the racket, the resonator guitar was invented. The

The National guitar was able to cut through noisy juke joints
JOSEPHINE MATYAS

design produces sound by carrying string vibration through the bridge to one or more spun metal cones (resonators) instead of to the soundboard (or top) like an ordinary guitar.

Originally, these were designed to be louder than normal guitars—to have their own nonelectrified amplifiers built into them—but they rapidly became prized for the distinctive metallic sound quality they created and found a home in many musical styles and as solo instruments. When played with a steel or glass slide, they could produce a range of nuances and effects. The best known of these guitars were produced by the National String Instrument Corporation and later by John Dopyera, who left National to establish the Dobro Manufacturing Company (the name coming from the first two letters of the designer's name plus brothers, hence DoBro).

The Harmonica, Mouth Organ, Mouth Harp, Mississippi Saxophone

Harmonicas—also called mouth organs, mouth harps, or just harps—are pocket-sized arrangements of slender metal reeds arrayed

The mouth harp is affordable and works in any style of music
JOSEPHINE MATYAS

along a piece of wood and sandwiched between two metal sheets that, when blown into or sucked on, vibrate the reeds and produce notes. In the right mouth, with the correct cupping of vibrating hands and manipulation of tongue and lips, it can howl like a hound, wail like a locomotive speeding downhill, soar like an arrow shot upward, or bleat like a trumpet.

Harps were easy to manufacture en masse, cheap to produce, even easier to transport—fits in a shirt pocket (it's believed that President Abraham Lincoln always carried one with him)—and can accompany any instrument in any song, employing a wide spectrum of nuance and emotion. Like any instrument, the harp is easy to play—just suck and blow and move your mouth back and forth—but hard to play well. Just do an online search for anything by Sonny Terry & Brownie McGhee, James Cotton, Howlin' Wolf, Big Walter Horton, Sonny Boy Williamson II, or Little Walter, all masters of the instrument. As you might expect, the reeds would not tolerate too much bending before they would deform and the instrument would slowly go permanently out of tune—and add to this the dust and humidity of the Delta plus the material ejected from the player's mouth in high performance—well, you get the idea. They were not made to survive too much torture, but they were comparatively cheap and easily replaceable.

Drums and Percussion

If you've a mind to make music, then you're beating on or pounding out time on something from a very early age—that is, when you're not doodling on a diddley bow or honking on a harp. Friends remembered young Howlin' Wolf—long before he could scrape together the cash to purchase a harp—hammering out time on an old pail and singing at the top of his already substantial lungs. The beauty of percussion instruments is that almost anything can be made to produce a sound (the quality of the sound being a decidedly secondary consideration). What matters are the spirit with which the sound is produced and the groove thereby created. Two pieces of hard wood cracked against each other in a consistent pattern is a groove—straight up!—and irresistible in the appropriate context. The human ear is compellingly drawn to repetition of sounds and rhythm, which is why we love poetry and music. It's also why we love the sound of the needle turning in the groove at the end of an

LP. In old film footage from the early 1920s, one can see the most amazing contraptions fashioned out of boxes, hinges, metal plates, springs, and almost anything that will make a sound when struck.

Where percussion is concerned, few things are as compelling as the washboard (technically a scraped or struck idiophone), which is played with the tips of the fingers—preferably covered by metal thimbles—or with pieces of bent metal with wooden handles. The thimbles do two things: they increase the sound the washboard produces, enabling it to cut through the competition, and they protect the player's fingernails from the abrasion of scraping across the surface of the washboard. The fully loaded tricked-out washboard is a magnificent thing to behold. Strapped up high so that it covers the chest and stomach, it can weigh several pounds once supplemented by cymbals, cowbells, horns, duck calls, klaxons, desk bells, and almost anything one can imagine that makes a sound and can be struck with one of the two hands momentarily diverted from the washboard itself. To watch a washboard player in full fury is to witness a thing of beauty and grace. Arms and fingers fly about with extraordinary skill and finesse, honking, scraping, tapping, and pounding out a rhythm that is too compelling to look away from.

A set of drums—a snare, hi-hat, bass drum, and at least one tom-tom and cymbal—is starting to cost real money. The skins are stretched across the shells, but the skins don't last forever, and the whole contraption has to be transported and cared for because there's a limit to how much abuse even so basic an instrument as a drum can tolerate. One can use a lot of things as a stick, even the hands, but there are limits here too—particularly once one aspires to more than just keeping time. A basic Ludwig drum kit would have been a good outlay of money for most musicians of the Delta blues era.

Banjo

Imported to the New World from West Africa, the banjo is, from its earliest design, essentially a percussive instrument. Four or five strings are stretched tight across a membrane or gourd, and the vibration is transferred to the membrane, which produces a note, varying by pitch across the stick or neck. It is, for all intents and purposes, a more portable version of the diddley bow with multiple strings (sometimes a drone), and the membrane takes the place of the house to which the diddley bow is attached. The banjo is not traditionally associated with the blues but is worth mentioning because it was so prevalent across the Delta during the birth of the blues, holding, with the violin, pride of place at plantation entertainments. A banjo could be purchased from the catalog for $1.75, or about half a week's wages. Where the banjo really found a home was in the medicine shows that circulated through the South selling, you guessed it, snake oil concoctions of every type and variety, often heavily laden with alcohol, cannabis, or opium. The bands that traveled with these medicine shows played every kind of music, including the popular music of Tin Pan Alley, ragtime, blues, jazz, and anything that would draw and hold a crowd. The banjo cut through the racket, turned heads, and captivated ears.

Piano

One has to include the piano in any reference to the instruments associated with the blues even though these were not as widely available as the guitar, the banjo, or the harmonica because they were expensive and heavy and required regular maintenance in the heat and humidity of the Delta. Where available, however, and in the right hands, they were powerful devices for the proliferation of the blues, as attested to by the wonderful pianists who eventually made their way north and played with the likes of Muddy Waters and Willie Dixon. Of these, among the best known was Joe Willie "Pinetop" Perkins, who played with Muddy Waters, B. B. King, Earl Hooker, and Robert Nighthawk. Interestingly, Perkins started on the guitar but migrated to the piano after an injury ended his guitar career. The beauty of the piano, of course, was its perfect combination of bass, treble, and percussion. The instrument functions through the pounding of felt hammers against strings, making it essentially a percussive instrument. The strings are tuned to various frequencies of the scale, enabling it to produce both melody and harmony simultaneously. The soundboard required to accommodate all these strings, however, and the harp to hold them all in place means that the instrument is heavy and fragile. And there are thousands of moving parts inside a piano, susceptible to shock and difficult to tune and maintain. So they would have made rare appearances on the front porches or in the juke joints that populated the Delta.

MUST READ

- *The Bluesmen: The Story and the Music of the Men Who Made the Blues*, Samuel Barclay Charters (1967)
- *Delta Blues: The Life and Times of the Mississippi Masters Who Revolutionized American Music*, Ted Gioia (2008)
- *Legends of the Blues: 100 Portraits and Bios*, William Stout (2013)

HOW BRITAIN THREW A LIFELINE TO THE BLUES

THE UNLIKELY LOVE AFFAIR

Post–World War II Britain was a grim place. Much of the best part of its cities had been bombed to rubble in the Blitz of the 1940s, and the country was still in the grip of economic austerity and rationing of everything as late as the 1950s. Demobilization and reintegration of the country's vast military service was a huge and complex challenge. Reconstruction of its once world-leading industrial centers was a protracted, expensive, and difficult ordeal. The treasury was bankrupt, and decolonization—the winding down of the empire—would, by 1965, collapse the global extent of British rule from 700 million to 3 million subjects. Young men were still subject to mandatory military—called "national"—service until New Year's Eve 1960.

"It was gray," recalled Keith Richards, who would go on to cofound the Rolling Stones. "When the hell we gonna get outta here? I thought we won! And you couldn't get any sweets either."

The recovery effort concentrated—quite naturally—on restoring Britain's economic fundamentals to position it to confront the next major challenge in the form of the Soviet Union, which had emerged from World War II with its industrial infrastructure running at full capacity and its ideology ascendant. The British "establishment" sought to restore the pre–World War I status quo as quickly as possible, seemingly oblivious to the fact that *everything* had changed around them. For the generation born during the 1940s—now coming of age in the 1950s and 1960s—it was a bleak and unpromising time, especially for working-class and disadvantaged kids on the lower rungs of Britain's shattered economic ladder.

In his memoir, *Life*, Keith Richards recounts a particularly harrowing youthful ordeal of having to visit an ex-army dentist twice per year—torture sessions that left him with a lifelong fear of dentists and only a plastic toy as compensation. "They were very depressing days," recalled Chris Dreja, who would go on to cofound the influential Yardbirds, "especially for young people."

Musically, things were not a lot better. The two world wars had nurtured a large contingent of well-trained musicians—military bandsmen—who could play anything you put in front of them, but most of what was available in the late 1940s and 1950s was dance band or "traditional" jazz from New Orleans, which had swept the United Kingdom in the late 1950s. But an appetite for an alternative was making itself felt too, at least among a certain class of restless music lovers not enthralled with the "Stranger on the Shore" pablum served up by songwriter and performer Acker Bilk.

The "King of Skiffle" Lonnie Donegan's "Rock Island Line," which utilized a skiffle groove and spawned its own craze, had already rooted itself in 1955, taking up residence in the mind of John Lennon, who fronted a combo called the Quarrymen in Liverpool and was on the verge of meeting Paul McCartney in July 1957. Skiffle combined elements of American music, including jug band, jazz, blues, and folk. Its high-energy delivery set the table for the arrival of rock and roll through, for many youthful Brits, movies such as *Blackboard Jungle* and *Rock Around the Clock* (both 1955). Elvis Presley exploded into British consciousness in 1956 with "Heartbreak Hotel" and then again with "All Shook Up" in 1957.

Then, so it seems, the rock and roll rage stalled. Elvis entered the U.S. Army. Jerry Lee Lewis disgraced himself by marrying his considerably younger first cousin. Chuck Berry transported a young woman across state lines for lewd purposes—a federal offense in the United States—and Little Richard found God. Rock and roll seemed to have lost its mojo, at least to a good many music lovers in the United Kingdom. The void was filled to some extent by the song factories of Tin Pan Alley in the United States and their imitators in the United Kingdom, but the initial rush of novelty had run its course.

What had also been going on this whole time—actually dating back to the worst years of World War II—was the slow infiltration of American 78-rpm records into the hands and collections of select British youth living in close proximity to Black American soldiers, airmen, and sailors in places like Liverpool and anywhere else the United States maintained military installations on British soil. This infiltration consisted of jazz, rhythm and blues (like Ray Charles), Delta blues, and other blues and jazz artists from Texas and New Orleans. These 78s included those produced by Chicago-based labels like Chess Records but also material from Trumpet Records in Jackson, Mississippi, and lesser-known labels across the American South.

The sound quality of these records, especially after repeated playings, left much to be desired, and the records themselves were brittle and easily broken. What lyrics could be deciphered were eccentric, foreign, and often incomprehensible to the English ear. But what emerged between the noise and crackles resonated deeply within a small society of music lovers, particularly in the southern quadrant of England. There was an intensity and directness in these sounds that spoke straight to the emotional core of its British listeners. It was dark and deep in a rather un-English manner. It was humorous, poetic, authentic, and laden with sexual innuendo—a long way from "English Country Garden." You could visualize the stories these songs told. Bill Wyman, bassist and cofounder of the Rolling Stones, recalls watching John Lee Hooker sing about a massive fire in a nightclub in Natchez, Mississippi, in 1940 in which Hooker's girlfriend—and 208 others—died. Real life-and-death stuff. It was an all-purpose musical experience, as good to dance or drink to as to make love to. These were blues records, known in the United States as "race records" and marketed primarily to Black Americans by musicians who barely registered in the consciousness of their American compatriots but would soon command a place of significance in British popular culture.

"When it's well performed, it's infectious. You don't need to know what it is. That's how people get hooked," mused Mick Fleetwood, who would lend his name to one of the more noteworthy British blues bands. And once it got into you, once your ear figured it out, it was hard to shake. And you didn't want to.

But if demand for this music was growing, there was a problem of supply. The records were not widely available except in specialty shops off the beaten track. The music's comparative rarity, at least initially, only enhanced its appeal, as did its association with slavery, the darkest chapter of the American story.

Names like Muddy Waters, Howlin' Wolf, Lightnin' Slim, and Lead Belly seemed exotic, genuine, and even dangerous compared with Bill Haley and the first generation of rock and rollers, even though the latter drank from the same inspirational wellspring as the Delta bluesmen. British fans went to unusual (sometimes illegal) lengths to seek out new recordings, even visiting total strangers on the basis of rumors that someone, somehow, had acquired a new record by Muddy Waters.

"Such a strange bunch of people," Keith Richards recalled in his memoirs. "Blues aficionados in the early sixties were a sight to behold. They met in little gatherings like early Christians but in the front rooms in southeast London." There was no way to duplicate these 78s, so you literally had to walk or take public transit to the home address where the record was rumored to reside and beg the owner to let you listen to it. "There was nothing else necessarily in common amongst them at all; they were all different ages and occupations," Richards wrote. "It was funny to walk into a room where nothing else mattered except he's playing the new Slim Harpo, and that was enough to bond you all together." And these encounters went on all the time, especially among musicians who simply could not get an adequate fix.

So it fell to visionaries—like the bandleader and trombonist Chris Barber—to take the bull by the horns and arrange British tours for the likes of gospel-rock singer Sister Rosetta Tharpe in 1957, Muddy Waters and Sonny Terry & Brownie McGhee in 1958, Memphis Slim, Big Bill Broonzy, Jimmy Rushing, Champion Jack Dupree, and so on in years following. Barber fronted a successful traditional jazz band. He was well connected and, equally important, financially able to assume the risk. Barber was also driven by a desire to see the "real thing" and to host them on his own bandstand—a guileless musician-oriented motivation to experience the genuine article up close. Years later, Barber would explain to British Broadcasting Corporation producers that his British peers owed an enormous debt to these foreigners.

Percolating right along with this infusion of the real thing was a growing realization that—perhaps, maybe—pasty-faced English, Welsh, and Scots lads could play this stuff too or at least give it a good try. After all, some had learned to play American-inspired rock and roll—the Beatles had gotten pretty good at it—why not learn to play the blues too? "You think of some dopey, spotty, seventeen-year-old from Dartford who wants to be Muddy Waters. In a way, very pathetic," Keith Richards reflected in a YouTube interview, "but in a way, very heartwarming."

The problem is that all music is easy to play but hard to play well—the same is true of musical instruments. Anyone can purchase a Fender Telecaster, turn it up, and run a slide up and down the neck. But that's not even the entry fee to the blues. Mastery takes years and even decades. Like all great art, the blues did not give up its secrets so readily just because a handful of obsessed British kids wanted to play it. Blues is more than a twelve-bar progression and lyrics about "losing your woman and waiting for the train and the train is late and you're drunk again and so on." Once you start to play it, it begins to slowly disclose itself to you, and you find yourself realizing that, after all, you don't know how to get those sounds, that energy, that passion. It's more than bending a string and punching out a groove with the right hand. It's ineffable. It takes 10,000 hours of dedication to figure out that you've only scratched the surface. You need to consign yourself to the "woodshed" for as long as it takes, especially if your lived experience in postwar England is so different from the creators of this art form. It might be only three or four chords, but there's a tremendous emotional dynamic and conviction behind its delivery, and it takes time to perfect.

And it takes people to play with who are as committed to learning it as you are. And in London in the early 1960s, that group of people clustered around a former bandmate of Chris Barber's jazz band named Alexis Korner and his rotating cast of musicians and friends known as Blues Incorporated. With Cyril Davies, Korner opened an establishment called the London Blues and Barrelhouse Club and was a tireless promoter of British blues and rhythm and blues musicians and bands. Korner's house band included—among others at one time or another—Jack Bruce (Cream), Charlie Watts (the Rolling Stones), Ginger Baker (Cream), Long John Baldry, Graham Bond (the Graham Bond Organisation), Malcolm Cecil, Jimmy Page (the Yardbirds, then Led Zeppelin), John Mayall (Blues Breakers), Eric Clapton (the Yardbirds, then Cream) Brian Jones (the Rolling Stones), Rod Stewart (Faces, then the Jeff Beck Group), and Dick Heckstall-Smith (the Graham Bond Organisation).

In bringing together all these blues lovers under one roof—and providing a place for them to play with each other—Alexis Korner entered

Lots and lots of players started on the more affordable Harmony guitars
JOSEPHINE MATYAS

the history books as one of the most important people in the development of British blues. If Chris Barber was the grandfather of the British
blues, Alexis was its father. On any given Saturday night, you could rub
shoulders at the London Blues and Barrelhouse Club with those who
would become the founding generation of British-based, American-
inspired blues bands.

These musicians and singers—and hundreds of others unnamed who
circulated through the early blues scene in different English cities—
would go on to create a distinctly British blues sound that, when they
took it back to the United States on tours, would provoke American
audiences and music journalists to ask "Where did this come from?" For
the truth is that Delta and even Chicago-based blues—which derived its
mojo from the Delta—was a minority taste and could very possibly have
died a premature death were it not for the fascination it engendered in
the first generation of British blues lovers. It's in this respect—in the
prominence that these British bands brought to American blues—that
Britain threw a lifeline to the blues.

NOTABLE BRITISH BLUES PERFORMERS

The Rolling Stones (1962 to Present)

Among the most fateful encounters in all show business has to be the meeting of Keith Richards and Michael Philip (Mick) Jagger on a train platform in Dartford Station, England, in 1962. Richards was enthralled with Chuck Berry's guitar playing and with all the Chess Records/Chicago bluesmen, and Mick was already a powerful singer in possession of (gasp!) an impressive record collection. It was the start, as they say, of a "beautiful friendship."

The "Glimmer Twins"—as they would come to be known—have been the core songwriting and performing team of the longest-surviving blues-infused rock and roll organization in history. The original lineup—which spearheaded, with the Beatles, the British Invasion of America—included singer-songwriter and guitarist Brian Jones (deceased in 1969 at age twenty-seven), drummer Charlie Watts, pianist Ian Stewart, and bassist Bill Wyman. Stewart was removed from the lineup in 1963 but remained as road manager for the next two decades.

Keith Richards remembered—in his memoir, *Life*—about the early days of the Stones that "every waking hour of every day was just sitting in front of the speakers, trying to figure out how these blues were made. You collapsed on the floor with your guitar in your hand. That was it. You never stop learning an instrument, but at that time it was still very much searching about. Chicago blues hit us right between the eyes. We were unpaid promoters for Chicago blues."

Indeed, in their earliest press conferences, on American soil, they extolled the Chess Records artists in the most generous terms. It's them—and Elvis, of course—they most wanted to meet and pay homage to. Years later, that dream came true—they even make a pilgrimage to Chess Records to record "It's All Over Now" and "Time Is On My Side"—and you can view YouTube videos of Mick Jagger sharing a stage with Muddy Waters. Keith Richards recalled that meeting Howlin' Wolf in 1965 was "awesome, actually, kinda like meeting an elephant." Wolf paid the Stones the ultimate compliment when he told them he "loves the stuff you been doing with my stuff"—big moment, for Keith, he said, "passed the test."

Decades later, reflecting on his life and mentors, Richards recalled his youthful devotion to the blues: "Me?" he told an interviewer. "I just want to be Muddy Waters. Even though I'll never be that good or that Black."

John Mayall & the Blues Breakers (1963 to Present, with Interruptions)

Also essential to any list—not for his hits, necessarily, but for his role as an incubator of the British blues—is John Mayall & the Blues Breakers. Arguably the "Godfather of British Blues," Mayall was not chasing commercial hits like the Yardbirds. Like Eric Clapton, Mayall was more purist in his intentions, but his long career launched the careers of countless other blues musicians the full catalog of which is too long to list. A sample will suffice: Eric "Slowhand" Clapton, Mick Fleetwood, John McVie, Peter Green, Aynsley Dunbar, Mick Taylor, Jack Bruce, Keef Hartley, Jessie Ed Davis, Patti Smith, Henry "Coco" Montoya, and on and on.

Mayall was a skilled showman, singer, guitarist, harmonica player, keyboardist, and front man, practiced at making an evening work and driving a band through their set. He was good friends with Alexis Korner, and there was a lot of cross-fertilization between their two communities as they circulated through venues like the Flamingo Club in London and other live music rhythm and blues venues (of which there were many at the time). The *Beano* album—featuring Mayall, Clapton, John McVie, and Hughie Flint on drums—became one of the most important of the early British blues records and set the table for Mayall to take his American-inspired, British-inflected blues to the United States, thereby returning it to its home and native land.

Although Mayall and Clapton eventually fell out—over a woman no less—this is the era when it was common to see "Clapton is God" spray painted around London. Clapton's immediate replacement was Peter Green—a player and singer with tremendous inner soul though less mature and seasoned than Clapton. And Green quickly recruited drummer Mick Fleetwood, who turned out to be a natural fit with Mayall's blues style. Soon thereafter, bassist John McVie, drummer Mick Fleetwood, and Green would spin off on their own.

Fleetwood Mac (1967 to Present, with Interruptions)

Another spin-off from the Alexis Korner/John Mayall community formed around guitarist, singer-songwriter, and regular Flamingo Club attendee the late Peter Green, drummer Mick Fleetwood, and, shortly thereafter, bassist John McVie. These three had already played and toured with John Mayall. When Green left the Blues Breakers and formed his own unit, he called it Peter Green's Fleetwood Mac. Their first record—of the same name—put them immediately on the map, reaching No. 4 on the U.K. charts and staying there for thirty-seven weeks without a hit single. By the time of their second record, *Mr. Wonderful*, the band was beginning to rotate members at a manic pace—a pattern that persists to the present—with the notable exception of Fleetwood and McVie themselves, making them the longest-serving rhythm section in contemporary music, having played together continuously since 1968 with a brief time out between 1995 and 1998 when the whole enterprise imploded in a sex-and-drugs debacle.

The first two records established the band as earnest journeymen of the blues, but their double album *Fleetwood Mac in Chicago* stands out for its mixture of longtime Chess veterans with their adoring young White English devotees. Recorded at Chess Records, the collection consists of live off-the-floor jams with Otis Spann (piano and vocals), Willie Dixon (double bass), Walter "Shakey" Horton (harmonica and vocals), Buddy Guy (guitar), David Honeyboy Edwards (guitar and vocals), and S.P. Leary (drums), playing along with Peter Green, Jeremy Spencer, Danny Kirwan (guitars and vocals), John McVie, and Mick Fleetwood.

Peter Green appears near the top of any list of important British-based blues guitarists and songwriters. His "Oh Well"—featuring a stop-time vocal—is one of the most innovative songs of the era. It now appears, with hindsight, that Green was a late-onset schizophrenic, no doubt accelerated by heavy LSD use. He endured a long and difficult psychiatric history before reemerging, uneventfully, in the late 1970s. He died in 2020 at the age of seventy-three. Danny Kirwan, who played guitar alongside Green from 1968 to 1972, though brilliantly talented, was also emotionally fragile, troubled, and a loner—his insecurity exacerbated by a traumatic family upbringing worsened by alcohol and drugs. He died in 2018 at age sixty-eight.

Jeremy Spencer, also from the early blues era of Fleetwood Mac, was as well emotionally fragile in nature and a drug user. Deeply insecure, Spencer would spend long hours in his hotel room reading the Bible. On a U.S. tour in 1971, hours before the band was scheduled to play the Whisky a Go Go in Los Angeles, Spencer walked out of his hotel room and joined the Children of God cult. It was days before the band discovered what had happened to him.

Cream (1966–1968)

Even before he had formally broken with Mayall, Eric Clapton began rehearsing with transplanted Glasgow-native singer and bassist Jack Bruce and jazz drummer Peter Edward "Ginger" Baker, both from the Blues Incorporated community that Alexis Korner cultivated at the London Blues and Barrelhouse Club. In two short years, Cream produced some of the best blues-inspired rock and roll ever recorded across four records: *Fresh Cream, Disraeli Gears, Wheels of Fire,* and their farewell record, *Goodbye.*

Baker and Bruce (drums and bass) were not—how to say this—the best fit of personalities given the grueling tour and recording schedule to which the band subjected itself. Baker alternated between a Jekyll and Hyde persona and a notoriously bad temper, even in old age. He maintained a long history with heroin and quit only to relapse several times. The ongoing personality friction between his two bandmates put Clapton in the role of perpetual peacemaker, but he had his own demons to contend with as he details in his autobiography, *Clapton: The Autobiography,* and the resulting implosion was expected by all three members. Still, for a short time, it was a great band that produced enduring rock and roll, gratefully employing American blues tropes, melodies, and even songs. Their version of "Crossroads" is the ultimate testament to Robert Johnson (whom Clapton came to idolize). When they reunited for four nights in May 2005 at the Royal Albert Hall in London, they put on a great show, immortalized on DVD. The audience consisted of a who's who of rock royalty. Sadly, Bruce and Baker were in failing health, and by the time they moved the reunion concerts to Madison Square Garden in New York, some of the old animosities had resurfaced.

Everywhere that Cream went when they toured America, they celebrated their admiration of the American bluesmen from whom they had learned so much. Clapton himself came to worship Robert Johnson, the tragic Delta bluesman, and has carried the torch for Johnson ever since. Cream's live version of "Crossroads" is a singular moment in the return to America of the Delta blues by these three Brits.

The Yardbirds (1963–1968)

Any list of influential British blues bands has to include the one band that—at least for a time—included on the bandstand no less than Eric

Clapton, Jeff Beck, and Jimmy Page, one after the other. The band formed around vocalist and harmonica player Keith Relf, drummer Jim McCarty, guitarist Chris Dreja, and bassist/producer Paul Samwell-Smith. They enjoyed a string of hits during their five years, including "For Your Love" (their breakthrough), "Heart Full of Soul," "Shapes of Things," and "Over Under Sideways Down."

Their early song lists drew extensively from the Chicago catalogs of Bo Diddley, Sonny Boy Williamson II, Elmore James, Howlin' Wolf, and Muddy Waters. Eric Clapton joined in 1963, and the band toured the United Kingdom and recorded with Sonny Boy Williamson II. They covered songs like "Smokestack Lightning," "Good Morning Little School Girl," "Boom Boom," "I Wish You Would," "Rollin' and Tumblin'," "Got Love If You Want It," and "I'm a Man"—all classic Chess Records blues tracks.

Music critics credit the Yardbirds with introducing many guitar and performance innovations and with anticipating punk, progressive rock, and heavy metal. The story goes that Clapton could not tolerate the Yardbirds' pursuit of hit records if those songs did not align with his own idea of the blues as he understood it. On March 5, 1965, *For Your Love* was released in the United Kingdom. Days later, Clapton quit the band, suggesting his friend Jimmy Page on his way out the door. But Page already had a good gig—a first-call session player in the London studio scene—and was cautious about getting into the politics of a post-Clapton Yardbirds. So he talked the band into hiring Jeff Beck. Beck filled Clapton's place two days later. The Beck years pushed the Yardbirds into wide-ranging experimentation and anticipated many elements that would emerge in rock and roll years after the band dissolved.

One night, as he tells the story, Page hit the metaphorical wall on his studio career after a full day of recording Muzak. He went out to see the Yardbirds. Page and Beck had been friends since age twelve, and on that evening—at the Oxford Union—Page learned that Beck's band would soon need a bass player to replace Paul Samwell-Smith. Page took the gig. Before long, Page found himself touring what Page refers to as the "underground scene" in the United States, where the band was doing well. One evening, while on tour in America, Beck had a meltdown, freaked out, and went mad, and Page took over the guitar duties.

And that was the end of Beck's time with the Yardbirds. In short order, that was the end of the Yardbirds too. Beck went on to form the Jeff

Beck Group—featuring Rod Stewart on vocals—and has since enjoyed a long and distinguished career as the world's premier Stratocaster mae-stro. Jimmy Page took over the name Yardbirds and returned to London. There's little doubt that Clapton, Beck, or Page would not have gone on to greater things if they had never played for the Yardbirds, but there's no doubt that the Yardbirds put them on the map of important British blues bands that would, before long, fire the blues back across the Atlan-tic to the attention of Americans.

The Animals (1962–1968)

Eric Victor Burdon, born in Newcastle upon Tyne, England, was one of the most distinctive singers of the British blues era. His voice and style (he claimed to have been enthralled by Louis Armstrong) combined American blues with British rock and roll, and the band that formed around him—the Animals—produced some of the most iconic Ameri-can-inspired blues songs, mostly notably "The House of the Rising Sun," "Baby Let Me Take You Home," "I'm Crying," "Boom Boom," "Don't Let Me Be Misunderstood," "Bring It On Home to Me," "We Gotta Get Out of This Place," and "It's My Life."

The original band consisted of Alan Price on keyboards, Chas Chan-dler on bass, Hilton Valentine on guitar, and John Steel on drums. Then, like Fleetwood Mac, the band started rotating members at a furious pace, uniting and blowing apart, reuniting, and melting down with a fury. Burdon, himself, went on to have a long career, carrying his powerful bass voice from project to band and concert stage to theater. His best-known contribution to the education of Americans on the Delta blues has to be "The House of the Rising Sun," which is one of those songs that seems to have been authored by no one but performed by everyone. Burdon's voice delivers the song, a story about growing up in a house of ill repute, with authority and passion. Even if they had never produced another song, this version would have put them on the map.

Bassist Chas Chandler, from the original Animals lineup, went on to play an important part in the future of rock and roll when he took an early interest in a young American named Jimi Hendrix. Chandler is also credited with the suggestion that Hendrix appear onstage with Cream, thereby bringing him into Eric Clapton's orbit.

Eric Clapton (b. 1945)

If there is one Englishman who deserves credit for bringing the blues back to its homeland, it's Eric Clapton. We have already met him in the Yardbirds, with John Mayall & the Blues Breakers, and in Cream. His long and storied career has been a personal mission to spread the Delta blues, as its spirit was taken up and evolved by the likes of Muddy Waters, the man Clapton idolized. He has shared the stage with almost every blues artist in the pantheon with the exception of Robert Johnson, whom Clapton raised to iconic status through his interpretation of, among other songs, "Crossroads," even going so far as to establish the Crossroads Centre drug and alcohol treatment program on the island of Antigua to assist musicians and artists, like himself, recover from addictions.

In 1999, Clapton inaugurated the Crossroads Guitar Festival, a series of concerts across the United States, to raise money for and spread the message of recovery from addiction. Like Jimmy Page and Keith Richards, he is an elder statesman of the world music scene and, all over YouTube and other media, only too willing to talk about his life, music, and recovery from drugs and alcohol. He has been seen playing every kind of guitar at one time or another but is most reliably associated, in his later years anyway, with the Fender Stratocaster—one of which, "Blackie," was auctioned off for a cool $959,500 in 2004, the proceeds going to his treatment center. More recently, Clapton has drifted toward jazz, making appearances with Wynton Marsalis and even reinterpreting some of his hits, like "Layla," in a jazz idiom.

Led Zeppelin (1968–1980)

Guitarist Jimmy Page was already, by his early twenties, a well-established London studio musician, including credits with the Kinks, Donovan, Cliff Richard, the Who, the Rolling Stones, David Bowie, and Joe Cocker—before he took up with the Yardbirds. John Paul Jones (keyboards and bass) was another studio musician from a family of performing musicians. Both were young in years but "old school" readers of music charts, which you had to be able to do to play the studios.

John Paul Jones claims he was moping around the house when his missus suggested he ring up Page—they'd known each other from their studio days—to make it known that he was available if Page needed a bassist. Page did. He had some contractual obligations to fulfill from his time in the Yardbirds. So, with the addition of Robert Plant and his friend John "Bonzo" Bonham, it was a very short passage from the end of the Yardbirds to the formation and first gig of the New Yardbirds and the rebranding of that band into Led Zeppelin.

The album *Led Zeppelin I* exploded into the consciousness of the music industry. It featured one song by Willie Dixon, a Chess Records icon, and a second by Dixon and J. B. Lenoir, another Chicago bluesman. The whole record paid homage to the blues in sound, spirit, energy, and song choice. Willie Dixon and Howlin' Wolf infuse the second Led Zeppelin record too. Even when—on later albums—Zeppelin moved explicitly into heavy rock, they never disclaimed their Delta and Chicago blues roots, endlessly recycling classic blues lyrics and themes in their music.

While other bands cycled through members regularly and routinely, Led Zeppelin had four members only. When John Bonham died in September 1980, Jones says, "we knew immediately that that was the end of the band. Bonham was not 'the drummer'—he was one-quarter of Led Zeppelin." His untimely death—of pulmonary aspiration at age thirty-two—was the end of the Zeppelin era.

John William "Long John" Baldry (1941–2005)

Among the finest British vocalists to sing the blues was Long John Baldry. Over this long career, he shared the stage with everyone from the Rolling Stones to the Beatles to Rod Stewart. At six feet seven inches, he was known as "Long John" from an early age. He did his time with Alexis Korner's Blues Incorporated and maintained a long relationship with the Rolling Stones, Paul McCartney (during his Cavern Club days), Nicky Hopkins, and numerous other blues musicians from the early 1960s until his death in 2004. One of his bands, Bluesology, featured pianist Reg Dwight, who took his stage name from saxophonist Elton Dean and John Baldry, becoming Elton John. Baldry ended his life as a Canadian citizen, dying in Vancouver in 2005.

AND SO, BRITAIN THREW A LIFELINE TO THE BLUES

What all these bands and artists had in common was that they had all fallen in love—indeed were obsessed—with the sounds, stories, poetry, rhythms, drive, darkness, sexual energy, and spirit of the Delta blues as it had been captured by Chess Records in Chicago and found its way, one 78 rpm at a time, into the hands of postwar English blues lovers. So when they arrived in America—as part of the extended British Invasion—all these guys wanted to talk about or pay homage to with the American press was the people they worshiped and whose songs they were performing on their U.S. tour dates: Muddy Waters, Howlin' Wolf, Elmore James, Chuck Berry, Bo Diddley, Little Walter, Lead Belly, Sonny Boy Williamson II, and on and on.

These were the artists and songs that had schooled these young Englishmen on the blues, and now they were bringing it home to White, middle-class American audiences who were hearing it—sanitized of its racial origins to be sure—for the first time. Many of the Delta and Chess Records bluesmen were as good as unknown to the American media that greeted and interviewed these young British musicians with their exotic English accents and long hair.

Without intending to, these British blues bands became evangelists for the Delta blues and its urban spin-offs. In a very real sense, they brought American blues—a minority taste within the United States—to the attention of a mass American audience.

MUST READ

- *Strange Brew: Eric Clapton and the British Blues Boom, 1965–1970*, Christopher Hjort (2010)
- *How Britain Got the Blues*, Roberta Freund Schwartz (2007)
- *Blues: The British Connection*, Bob Brunning (1986)

MUST SEE AND LISTEN

- *How Britain Got the Blues*, BBC Four documentary on YouTube
- *Blues Britannia: Can Blue Men Sing the Whites?*, BBC Four documentary (2010)
- *The Song Remains the Same*, Led Zeppelin concert video (1976)
- *Led Zeppelin*, Charlie Rose interview (2012)
- "Crossroads," Cream
- "Oh Well," Fleetwood Mac
- "I Just Want to Make Love to You," Rolling Stones
- "Hideaway," Eric Clapton

BIBLIOGRAPHY AND SUGGESTED READINGS

Abbott, Lynn, and Doug Seroff. "'They Cert'ly Sound Good to Me': Sheet Music, Southern Vaudeville, and the Commercial Ascendancy of the Blues." *American Music* 14, no. 4 (1996): 402–54.

Barry, John M. *Rising Tide: The Great Mississippi Flood of 1927 and How It Changed America*. New York: Simon & Schuster, 1997.

Beckert, Sven. *Empire of Cotton: A Global History*. New York: Knopf, 2015.

Bertrand, M. T. *Race, Rock, and Elvis*. Champaign: University of Illinois Press, 2009.

Booth, Stanley. *The True Adventures of the Rolling Stones*. New York: Vintage Books, 1985.

Brewer, Jon. *B. B. King: The Life of Riley: Survival Is a Word . . . This Is Its Story*. London: Global Book Sales, 2015.

Brunning, Bob. *Blues: The British Connection*. London: Helter Skelter Publishing, 2002.

Charters, Samuel Barclay. *The Bluesmen: The Story and the Music of the Men Who Made the Blues*. New York: Music Sales Corporation, 1967.

Cheseborough, Steve. *Blues Traveling: The Holy Sites of Delta Blues*. Jackson: University Press of Mississippi, 2018.

Chess, Leonard. Quoted in Mitsutoshi Inaba, *Willie Dixon: Preacher of the Blues*. Lanham, MD: Rowman & Littlefield, 2014.

Clapton, Eric. *The Autobiography*. New York: Crown, 2008.

Clayson, Adam. *The Yardbirds: The Band That Launched Eric Clapton, Jeff Beck, Jimmy Page*. San Francisco: Backbeat Books, 2002.

Cobb, James C., ed. *The Mississippi Delta and the World: The Memoirs of David L. Cohn.* Baton Rouge: Louisiana State University Press, 1995.

———. *The Most Southern Place on Earth: The Mississippi Delta and the Roots of Regional Identity.* New York: Oxford University Press, 1992.

Cohn, David. *Where I Was Born and Raised.* Notre Dame, IN: University of Notre Dame Press, 1967.

Cooper, Margo. "Joshua 'Razorblade' Stewart: I Sing from the Heart." *Living Blues,* no. 241 (January/February 2016).

Cooper, Mark, executive producer. *How Britain Got the Blues.* BBC Four documentary on YouTube, May 2009.

———, executive producer. *Blues Britannia: Can Blue Men Sing the Whites?* BBC Four documentary, 2010.

Davis, Stephen. *Hammer of the Gods: The Led Zeppelin Saga.* New York: William Morrow & Co., 2008.

Dixon, Willie (with Don Snowden). *I Am the Blues: The Willie Dixon Story.* New York: Da Capo Press, 1990.

Epstein, Brian. *A Cellarful of Noise.* New York: Doubleday, 1964.

Fleetwood, Mick (with Anthony Bozza). *Play On: Now, Then, and Fleetwood Mac.* Boston: Little, Brown, 2014.

Gioia, Ted. *Delta Blues: The Life and Times of the Mississippi Masters Who Revolutionized American Music.* New York: Norton, 2008.

Goodwin, Michael. "Mississippi Fred McDowell, 'I Do Not Play No Rock 'n' Roll.'" *Rolling Stone,* June 25, 1970.

Guralnick, Peter. *Searching for Robert Johnson: The Life and Legend of the "King of the Delta Blues Singers."* New York: Penguin, 1992.

Handy, William Christopher. *Blues: An Anthology.* Carlisle, MA: Applewood Books, 1926.

Harris, Sheldon. *Blues Who's Who: A Biographical Dictionary of Blues Singers.* New York: Da Capo Press, 1979.

Hjort, Christopher. *Strange Brew: Eric Clapton and the British Blues Boom.* London: Jawbone Press, 2007.

Jones, John Paul. Quoted in Eric Schaal, "Why John Paul Jones Was Key to Led Zeppelin." *Showbiz Cheatsheet.* Swedish TV interview, 2003.

King, B. B. *The Life of Riley.* Documentary, May 2014.

——— (with David Ritz). *Blues All around Me: The Autobiography of B. B. King.* New York: HarperCollins, 1996.

Koda, Michael "Cub." "Howlin' Wolf Biography." AllMusic.com.

Logoz, Dinu. *John Mayall: The Blues Crusader.* London: Edition Olms, 2015.

Lomax, Alan. *The Land Where the Blues Began.* New York: New Press, 1993.

Lomax, John. *Jail House Bound: John Lomax's First Southern Prison Recordings.* Morgantown: West Virginia University Press, 1933.

Myers, Paul. *It Ain't Easy: Long John Baldry and the Birth of the British Blues.* Vancouver: Greystone Books, 2007.

Oakley, Giles. *The Devil's Music: A History of the Blues*. 2nd ed. New York: Da Capo Press, 1997.

Oshinsky, David M. *Worse Than Slavery: Parchman Farm and the Ordeal of Jim Crow Justice*. New York: Simon & Schuster, 1996.

Palmer, Robert. *Deep Blues: A Musical and Cultural History from the Mississippi Delta to Chicago's South Side to the World*. New York: Penguin, 1982.

Parrish, Susan Scott. *The Flood Year 1927: A Cultural History*. Princeton, NJ: Princeton University Press, 2017.

Phillips, Sam. Quoted in Elizabeth Kaye, "Sam Phillips: The Rolling Stone Interview." *Rolling Stone*, February 13, 1986.

Raichelson, Richard. *Beale Street Talks: A Walking Tour Down the Home of the Blues*. New York: Da Capo Press, 1999.

Raitt, Bonnie. Quoted in "The Hour of Music That Rocks My World," *Guitar World*, February 1999.

Richards, Keith (with James Fox). *Life*. Boston: Little, Brown, 2010.

———. Quoted in David Remnick, "Groovin' High: The Life and Lures of Keith Richards." *The New Yorker*, October 25, 2010.

Schwartz, Roberta Freund. *How Britain Got the Blues: The Transmission and Reception of American Blues Style in the United Kingdom*. London: Routledge, 2007.

Segrest, James, and Mark Hoffman. *Moanin' at Midnight: The Life and Times of Howlin' Wolf*. New York: Thunder's Mouth Press, 2005.

Sidey, Hugh. Book jacket review of James C. Cobb, *The Most Southern Place on Earth: The Mississippi Delta and the Roots of Regional Identity*. New York: Oxford University Press, 1992.

Springer, Robert, ed. *Nobody Knows Where the Blues Come From: Lyrics and History*. Jackson: University Press of Mississippi, 2007.

Stolle, Roger. *Hidden History of Mississippi Blues*. Charleston, SC: The History Press, 2011.

Stout, William. *Legends of the Blues: 100 Portraits and Bios*. New York: Abrams ComicArts, 2013.

Thomas, Rufus. Quoted in Tim Cahill, "Walking Down Beale Street." *Slate.com*, November 20, 2002.

Thompson, Dave. *Cream: The World's First Supergroup*. London: Virgin Books, 2010.

Wald, Elijah. *Escaping the Delta: Robert Johnson and the Invention of the Blues*. New York: HarperCollins, 2004.

Whitley, Carla Jean. *Muscle Shoals Sound Studio: How the Swampers Changed American Music*. Charleston, SC: The History Press, 2014.

Willis, John C. *Forgotten Time: The Yazoo-Mississippi Delta after the Civil War*. Charlottesville: University of Virginia Press, 2000.

INDEX

Page numbers for figures are italicized.